PLAS

PITT
LATIN
AMERICAN
SERIES

My Missions for Revolutionary Bolivia, 1944–1962

VICTOR ANDRADE

My Missions
for Revolutionary Bolivia,
1944–1962

by

VICTOR ANDRADE

Former Bolivian Foreign Minister
and Ambassador to the United States

Edited and with an Introduction by
Cole Blasier

University of Pittsburgh Press

Library of Congress Cataloging in Publication Data

Andrade, Víctor, 1905–
 My missions for revolutionary Bolivia, 1944–1962.

 (Pitt Latin American series)
 Includes index.
 1. Andrade, Víctor, 1905– 2. Diplomats—
Bolivia—Correspondence, reminiscences, etc. 3. United
States—Foreign relations—Bolivia. 4. Bolivia—Foreign
relations—United States. I. Title.
F3326.A67   327'.2'0924 [B]   76-6656
ISBN 0-8229-3320-9

I wish to express appreciation to Professor Cole Blasier for translating
and editing my memoirs which have benefited from his profound knowledge of Latin America. I also acknowledge the work of Alice Poust, Rose-
anne Mendoza, and Santiago Mendoza, who assisted him in the translation.

Dedicated to the memory of
GUALBERTO VILLARROEL
whose heroic leadership and sacrifice
made possible the liberation of the Bolivian peasant
and opened a new era in the history of my country

Contents

Introduction

Cole Blasier

Victor Andrade's memoirs are about the sometimes conflicting and sometimes harmonious relations between Bolivia, one of South America's most colorful and violence-ridden republics, and the United States. Bolivia is among the few Latin American countries, like Mexico and Cuba, that have experienced a genuine social revolution. As a young army officer during the Chaco War and as a public figure, Andrade was intimately involved in the origins of that revolution and with the leaders of the Movimiento Nacionalista Revolucionario (MNR) whose governments revolutionalized Bolivia.

My Missions for Revolutionary Bolivia is noteworthy partly because few Latin American statesmen or diplomats write memoirs, and only a handful of them have ever been translated into English. Andrade does not confine this account to his official duties but gives a candid, many-sided account of his life in and out of government, including inside glimpses of revolutionary politics in Bolivia. Above all, Andrade's life experience presents a unique perspective on U.S. foreign policies. He combines a sharply critical treatment of U.S. official behavior with understanding and sympathy for life in the United States. Some of his experiences in this country may shock and embarrass U.S. readers; others may make them proud.

The United States was initially the Bolivian revolutionaries' worst enemy; later it became their most generous friend. As the Bolivian ambassador to the United States in the 1940s, 1950s, and early 1960s, Andrade was the revolution's most influential spokesman abroad. He was in large measure responsible for the huge outpouring of U.S. economic assistance to Bolivia that was for many years greater on a per capita basis than that to almost any other country.

Andrade is an authentic son of Bolivia with experience in the army, the mining industry, the administration of social welfare, and in politics. His reputation, however, was made in diplomacy, as ambassador and as foreign minister. Few Latin American diplomats had such an intimate

acquaintance with the United States, gained through long years of residence, travel, and sensitive insight. Although the representative of a small
and poor country, Andrade established himself with the leading figures
of his day. He knew every president from Roosevelt to Kennedy and was
a personal friend of Dwight Eisenhower. He was on good terms with
leading journalists, cabinet members, politicians, and most particularly
U.S. senators. He was remarkably effective in shaping public opinion
favorable to his cause and, in unorthodox ways, in manipulating executive agencies and Congress to achieve the purposes of his diplomatic
missions. As one of the most active and influential spokesmen at the San
Francisco Conference in 1945, he also has a fair claim to being one of the
fathers of the United Nations.

I first met Ambassador Andrade on a visit to La Paz in June, 1969.
I sought him out as the man who probably knew more than any other
person about the relations between the MNR and the United States.
He was then living in a European-style stucco house a few minutes from
the main plaza down the mountainside on which La Paz is perched. My
curiosity about him mounted as my taxi bumped along the cobblestone
streets. I stepped out of the cab, opened the gate, walked a few steps
through the walled patio, and sounded the entrance bell. Andrade met
me at the door himself, unattended by the bodyguards that sometimes
accompany Bolivian political leaders. He stood over six feet tall, of me-
dium build, his straight black hair and broad, open features revealing
his Spanish and Indian ancestry. He led me through a spacious and
austere hall to his spare study. Gracious and self-assured, he spoke fluent
and idiomatic English.

What struck me then about Andrade's career was that he achieved
so much with so little. Coming from modest origins, he represented a
small, poor, and often badly divided country. The Bolivian public service
is so precarious and sometimes physically dangerous as to be beyond the
comprehension of most Americans; Bolivia's history of political violence
and instability is scarcely surpassed elsewhere on a turbulent continent.
With a divided government at home and bitterly hostile compatriots
abroad, Andrade moved from one threatening and ambiguous crisis to
another.

The behavioral precepts of the Methodist missionaries who sponsored the school he attended as a boy in La Paz did not prepare him for
the cynicism, intrigue, deception, and ruthlessness he faced in Washington and La Paz—nor did he allow those precepts to hamper him. In dealing with his adversaries, Andrade displayed flexibility, resourcefulness,
and political cunning. His was a colorful personality in which was combined, on the one hand, sincere and openhanded friendliness and, on the

other, flamboyance and bluff. Although he had little money and was representing a country of no great status, Andrade managed to establish an influential personal position in Washington. His talents as a golfer, fisherman, guitar player, amateur chef, and raconteur helped him to promote his country's interests.

What is perhaps most remarkable about Andrade is his ability to analyze the American scene and turn its institutions to his purposes. Urbane and debonaire, the ambassador was not intimidated by protocol or diplomatic conventions. He cultivated acquaintances in many federal offices besides the Department of State, and in congressional, press, business, and academic circles. When faced with an impasse, he took the risk of setting one American institution against another or against his Bolivian adversaries. The high level of economic and later military assistance which his government received while he was ambassador demonstrates his capacity for understanding and manipulating Washington's massive political and governmental bureaucracies.

Bolivia, which straddles some of the highest peaks of the Andes, has a population of five million people. About two-thirds of these are Indians, a quarter *mestizo*, and most of the remainder white. The country has many natural resources, particularly tin, oil, and natural gas, but only tin has been heavily exploited. Bolivia gained her independence from Spain in 1825. Defeated in the War of the Pacific (1879–83), Bolivia lost her access to the ocean. Since then the Bolivians have made persistent efforts to acquire a port on the Pacific from Chile or Peru, a national cause to which Andrade has long been deeply committed.

Andrade did not come from the rich, landed Bolivian elite, closely linked to the tin mines. Neither were his origins peasant or proletarian. He attended an American missionary school and later the university, both in La Paz. As a boy he often traveled into the country to visit relatives during his vacations, and there he developed a personal attachment to the indigenous population and to the cause of the Bolivian peasants, who, at that time, were virtually serfs.

Bolivia entered a tragic war with Paraguay over the Chaco in 1933 and lost land in the west to the victorious but badly bloodied Paraguayans. During this war the traditional political leaders showed their inability to rule and the military leadership its inability to defend the nation. Andrade was one of the young army officers who later led the opposition to the old regime; the revolutionary movement was born, so to speak, on the battlefields of the Chaco War.

Following the war, Andrade worked for the tin-mining companies, Bolivia's most important industry. In the early 1940s, as minister of health, labor, and social security, he became closely identified with the cause of the miners in opposition to those companies. His study of the working conditions in the mines and the living conditions of the miners convinced him that Bolivia must obtain higher prices for its tin and use the increase to raise the living standards of the Bolivian worker.

During these years, Andrade helped to organize the veterans of the Chaco War, providing a link between the young professional army officers and the civilian political figures who conceived and carried forward the revolution. It was, for example, in the Gran Chaco that Andrade first met a senior officer, Germán Busch, who became the military "socialist" president of Bolivia in the late 1930s. In 1943, Andrade was responsible for introducing Major Gualberto Villarroel, a leader of progressive career elements in the army, to Víctor Paz Estenssoro, the leading political figure of the MNR, producing the military-political alliance which overthrew the old regime in December 1943. At that time the United States refused to recognize the new Villarroel government on the grounds that it was pro-Nazi, but later, through the efforts of Andrade and others, U.S. recognition was obtained. Andrade served in a number of posts in that government, including foreign minister, and was appointed ambassador to Washington in the fall of 1944. In the spring of the next year he worked closely with U.S. Secretary of State Edward R. Stettinius and Assistant Secretary Nelson A. Rockefeller in the negotiations that led to compromises which assured the support of the Latin American governments for the United Nations. His contribution to that conference was crucial when later he sought the collaboration of leading American officials and politicians in his efforts to promote Bolivia's causes.

The principal antagonists of the Villarroel government, and of Andrade in Washington, were the owners of Bolivia's large tin mines. Villarroel made the most effective effort up to that time to regulate the management and foreign exchange receipts of the mining companies. Opposed to all such reforms, the owners of the tin mines helped to overthrow Villarroel in 1946. Readers may have noticed that these memoirs are dedicated to the memory of Villarroel who was murdered during the 1946 coup. After 1946 Andrade went into exile, working first as a visiting professor at the New School for Social Research in New York and later for the International Basic Economy Corporation (IBEC) in Ecuador.

In 1952 the MNR returned to power in a series of urban insurrections that followed the refusal of the Bolivian military to honor presidential elections in which Víctor Paz Estenssoro had received a plurality of the vote. It was in this year that rapid social changes began in Bolivia. Most of the traditional political parties were swept aside. The three largest tin-mining companies were nationalized. Most of the large haciendas were broken up, including some belonging to Andrade's family, and re-distributed to Indian peasant smallholders. Andrade returned to Washington as ambassador, and the formerly hostile U.S. attitudes toward the MNR were reversed. In 1953, the U.S. government began first an economic assistance and later a military assistance program which together totaled $400 million. Aid from the United States reached a peak during the Kennedy administration when assistance to the Bolivian revolution served as a model for the Alliance for Progress. Meanwhile, however, divisions within the government were growing. Andrade resigned as ambassador in 1962 and returned to La Paz, ending his diplomatic career.

If there is a central theme to this volume, it is the struggle between the Bolivian revolutionaries, on the one hand, and the owners of the large Bolivian tin mines on the other. That battle was joined in La Paz and Washington under the Villarroel government of the 1940s and was continued in the 1950s. The "tin barons" used their money, influence, and every conceivable strategy to discredit the Bolivian revolution in Washington, to block the mineral sales and economic assistance that the MNR needed to survive. In that struggle the MNR and the ambassador emerged victorious: despite nationalization of the large tin mines, the U.S. government continued to refine and stockpile tin even when demand was low and, moreover, provided high levels of economic assistance to the MNR government. The two men who served as presidents of the MNR governments have publicly acknowledged that the Bolivian revolution could not have survived without U.S. official assistance, the assistance which Ambassador Andrade was instrumental in obtaining.

A hardy survivor of political battles in both capitals, Víctor Andrade is a colorful interpreter of a major theme of our times: the confrontation of the Third World with the Great Powers of the North. *My Missions for Revolutionary Bolivia* now takes its place as one of the few existing personal and candid Third World treatments of that fateful theme.

My Missions for Revolutionary Bolivia, 1944–1962

1

Schooling in War
and Politics

My early contact with Americans and their customs served me well on the dramatic occasion of my first visit to the United States in the spring of 1944. I came as a cabinet member of a revolutionary government which the United States not only had refused to recognize but had urged other American governments not to recognize. Much interest was aroused by my visit, and the most important newspapers and news services had sent reporters to await my arrival in Miami. I began the press conference in Spanish, but when the interpretation proved unsatisfactory, I switched to English. Afterward, a reporter, noting my American accent and questioning my assertion that this was my first visit, insisted that I confirm the fact that I had studied or lived a long time in the United States. My explanation touched the early years of my life.

I began my education in 1911 as a boarding student in the kindergarten of the American Institute in La Paz, a school founded by the American Methodist Church. All my primary and secondary education took place there. Because of my age and extra contributions from my family, I lived for some time with a married couple who were Methodist teachers. They had a son approximately of my own age, with whom I used to play and fight in English and Spanish.

My fluent English combined with my marked creole features, tanned skin, dark eyes, and straight hair, attracted much attention. Frequently I was called to the office, a little afraid at first, thinking that I had done something wrong. The motive for these summons was usually to ask me routine questions in English in the presence of a father who had come to investigate the instruction offered at the school. My appearance, as an obviously local child conversing fluently in English, was a conclusive argument to convince prospective parents to enroll their children.

3

I was born in Chulumani, capital of the Province of Sud Yungas where my father and his father owned agricultural property. They were descended from Hilarión Andrade, one of the fifty citizens who participated in the valiant rebellion which led to the proclamation of the independence of Alto Peru, now Bolivia, on July 16, 1809. My great uncle on my father's side was Crispín Andrade y Portugal, an illustrious member of the national convention which reorganized civil government in Bolivia after the tragic War of the Pacific (1879–83). And my mother's father was the eminent but poor lawyer Federico Usquiano to whom the government gave authority to register deeds to property in the Province of Cercado and in La Paz.

A few months after my birth I was taken to La Paz where my parents had settled. During my adolescence I spent vacations at our estate in Yungas. I made the trip on muleback over paths which had connected this region with the city of La Paz since precolonial times. From eleven thousand feet, the altitude of the city, we climbed to sixteen thousand feet in order to cross a mountain pass near the summit of the Andes. We braved the high winds, descending along sharp precipices to the subtropical zones of the Yungas at altitudes varying between three thousand and five thousand feet. I made this annual journey as a child, accompanied by an Aymara Indian guide with whom I chatted in his native tongue. Our time together on the way, at rest stops, and at night under the stars, forged my strong ties to my native people. In those days I decided to serve them if destiny ever gave me the opportunity.

Many of the other leaders of the revolution that began in 1943 received their primary and secondary education at the American Institute. In La Paz, the democratic ideas of American teachers had great influence on the intellectuals who conceived the revolution which overturned the oligarchical social order. Their ideas were not colored by the leftist phrases of the old world, nor limited to the dogmas of the so-called social revolution. They simply put the Bolivian first—his problems, his needs, and his aspirations. They tried to lift him up and incorporate him into contemporary civilized life without his losing his personality or his culture.

My father and I had planned that, after finishing my secondary education and my obligatory military service, I would go to the United States to study physics and advanced mathematics. Unfortunately these plans could not be carried out, as my father died unexpectedly a few weeks before I finished high school. I had to assume family responsibilities and accommodate the rest of my life to this hard reality. Between 1924 and 1930 I continued my advanced studies in mathematics and political and social science, while teaching arithmetic and algebra at the American Institute. I published a book on applied arithmetic which was for several years the official text in Bolivian high schools. I was also director of the weekly magazine *Variedades*, and contributed to *La Razón*, the daily newspaper of La Paz.

In 1930 I participated actively in the university movement which opposed the reelection of the then president of the republic, Hernando Siles, on the grounds that reelection was unconstitutional. This movement generated a two-day insurrection which, with the aid of cadets from the Military School, caused the fall of the Siles regime. As a result of my participation, I was suddenly thrown into public life and appointed deputy minister of public education. I remained in this post until the Chaco War (1932–35) in which I served as a junior officer in the army.

Depression and War

The Bolivian revolution was the fruit of two national tragedies, the economic collapse caused by the Great Depression and the Chaco War. Between 1929 and 1932, the price of Bolivian tin fell from forty-five to twenty-two cents per pound. The owners of the tin mines let the major burden of their losses fall on the working class, dismissing workers and reemploying them at lower salaries. The economic collapse was so far-reaching that the tin barons who controlled most of Bolivian tin production—Patiño, Aramayo, and Hochschild—viewed their interests as being seriously threatened. As a result, they reversed their traditional opposition to war, formerly viewed as signifying extraordinary tax burdens and as a threat to their sources of manpower. They now thought that a war with Paraguay and the accompanying mobilization would be the means of their salvation.

The Chaco War presented violent, Dantesque contrasts between the most holy examples of self-renunciation and the most abominable acts of cowardice. The anonymous populace—peasants, workers, youths from well-known families—silently suffered the tragedy and burdens of incompetence in the direction of the war. Hunger, thirst, and other hardships resulted from the ignorance of political and military leaders who had not foreseen the consequences of an adventure which placed the very existence of the country in jeopardy. The war was the culmination of an epoch of total falsity, one in which a defective social order had devalued and neglected an entire nation. A few intellectuals, members of the middle class and university students, were present at the front. Joined by young military officers, also victims of the drama which they had not created, they perceived that something fundamental was wrong and had to be put right. The seed of the revolution germinated from the common experience of the civilian and military youth in the war: a national consciousness was formed.

In the years immediately following the Chaco War, the banner of the young revolutionary nationalists who participated in the conflict was carried by two military officers who briefly occupied the presidency, David Toro (1936–37) and Germán Busch (1937–39). Although buoyed up by the forces of renovation, Toro was too weak and corrupt to survive. Busch, on the other hand, a strong military leader and a dedicated nationalist, was destroyed by bewildering dilemmas, indecision, and emotional instability. I was acquainted with these two military "socialist" presidents during their terms of office and played a modest role in each. They were succeeded from 1939 to 1943 by traditional military officers of essentially reactionary orientations.

Toro and Busch

Lieutenant Colonel David Toro, minister of government in the cabinet of President Hernando Siles, was appointed army chief of staff for the Chaco War. During the three years of that war, he showed himself to be more a politician than a military leader. After a series of government changes, Toro eventually achieved his ambition and seized power on May 16, 1936. Although he was careful to secure the support of the leading soldier of the war, Germán Busch, Toro soon revealed his political ineptness and his lack of any program. His government exhausted itself in superficialities and petty vanities. His days were numbered, and the instrument for his extinction was, in fact, Germán Busch.

My first contact with Busch occurred in 1930, at the time he was defending the Siles cabinet over which Toro then presided. On the night of June 28, Cadet Gustavo Maldonado ("Purito") and I, protected by a doorway, were fighting against a detachment of police who were shooting from a stable on Mexico Street in La Paz. Suddenly a detachment of soldiers appeared behind us. We mistakenly believed that they were a group of rebel cadets, but they were loyal forces, who disarmed us and sent us as prisoners to the general staff. The commander of this detachment was Lieutenant Germán Busch. Maldonado and I escaped and continued the struggle, and the rebel forces prevailed in the end.

Sharing the fate of other military officers who defended Siles, Busch was sent to the front when the government fell. At that time the front meant the Chaco, where the armed forces were engaged in reconnaisance required in those insecure times. Since Busch was born and raised near the jungle and liked the danger of combat, he was one of those who most distinguished themselves in these scouting expeditions. Outbreak of the war with Paraguay projected him into the midst of hostilities and he became more involved than most of his comrades.

My second encounter with Busch was at Kilometer 7 of Fort Saavedra, where he was commanding a special detachment. We spent several days together and recalled genially our fleeting intervention in the political episode when we served opposed causes in ignorance of each other. Thus we developed a mutual friendship and trust.

When the war was over and we had both been restored to our normal peacetime occupations, Busch assumed command of the cavalry division and later of the general staff, serving as one of the mainstays on which Toro depended to stabilize his government. After I returned to the job which I held before the war as deputy minister of education, we had our third meeting. I was in my office in the ministry one afternoon reviewing some files when the secretary announced the visit of Colonel Germán Busch. I had him come in immediately, greeting him with the affection of old comrades. "What a pleasure to see you, Camba. What can I do for you?"

He responded coolly, "I've come to question you. I've learned that in a meeting at the Hotel Rigolí last night you expressed disrespect for the armed forces and for me. I've brought along two pistols so that we can go outside and shoot it out."

Such a violent proposal caught me by surprise, especially since I had always had special affection for this friend and had never referred to him in derogatory terms. "I am surprised that you pose a challenge of this kind without assuring yourself of the truth. At least tell me the origin of this gross lie."

"The only thing that I can tell you," he said to me, "is that Dr. Roberto Bilbao la Vieja was at the meeting, defended me, and had an argument with you."

It was a happy coincidence that Bilbao, who was director of education, was in a room next to my office. I opened the adjoining door, invited him to come in, and requested that he confirm or deny the allegation. Bilbao denied the incident since we hadn't even been in the hotel, nor had he ever heard me speak in that sense. Busch withdrew, visibly affected and dismayed by his error and the injustice which he had almost inflicted on me. This episode cooled our relations temporarily.

With the advent of the Toro government, I resigned my government appointment and obtained a temporary position in a mining concern. One night in June 1937, I was walking toward my home after attending a movie in the Plaza Murillo. I was coming down Ayacucho Street when an automobile swept up beside me. It was Busch, driving an official car.

"And where are you going at this hour, Víctor? Get in—I want to talk to you. Later I will take you home."

Noting my reluctance, he insisted, vehemently. "I realize that you are offended, but I will explain. Get in and don't waste any more time."

We went up above the city and talked until the early hours of the morning. He was convinced that an intrigue of Toro's adherents had led to the injustice he had nearly done me. He explained that he had been slow to realize that Toro was using him as an instrument and that he could no longer support him. For this reason, he had decided to consult with his true friends. Considering the political events of the postwar period, we agreed about what was most fundamental: Toro was not the renovating force which the generation of the Chaco War required. He represented instead a return to the politicians who had failed with Siles. Moreover, he had promoted some of the corrupt and incompetent political and military figures responsible for the Chaco defeat. To all this was added the crime of having facilitated the employment, in the Ministry of Labor, of persons who, on the pretext of being communists, had refused to participate in the war. They included José Antonio Arze, Ricardo Anaya, and others.

"If I had the support of civilian forces, I would not permit Toro to continue for one day more," exclaimed Busch. Then he added, "I do not refer to traditional political parties, but to new forces."

My reply was categorical. Traditional parties no longer existed in Bolivia. They were buried in the war of the Chaco. The socialist factions formed from stagnant groups backing Siles had no political vitality, and the Communists of Arze and Anaya were merely opportunistic. At the moment there did exist one potential political force, not yet organized, but large enough to carry the moral authority needed to enter politics. I referred to the war veterans. The Veterans' Legion, organized after the war, was at that moment in the hands of some agitators who were trying to negotiate personal advantages, assuming powers to represent the Legion which they did not rightfully possess. One could take action and seize control of this institution; with its support, any political movement could be justified.

After an extended exchange of ideas, I presented Busch with a plan of action. A group of prestigious young people and real veterans would attend the next assembly of the Veterans' Legion. We would face the Legion's leadership and propose the naming of Colonel Germán Busch, the soldier who had most distinguished himself in the war, as the supreme chief of the veterans. If any opposition emerged, we would overcome it, by force if necessary; but I was sure that opposition would be weak. With such a title, Busch would be in a position to eliminate Toro and initiate a true government of reform.

The plan was fulfilled exactly, and the opposition of the incumbent leadership was almost nil. At the end of June 1937, a group of veterans came to Busch's home to report his appointment by acclamation and request that he take charge as soon as possible. On the following day, in the auditorium of the Ayacucho Academy, Busch was sworn in as supreme chief of the veterans. From that moment the days of the Toro government were numbered.

Busch's seizure of power on July 13, 1937, represented, in a way, the first attempt to introduce fundamental changes into the country. Busch intended to form his cabinet with a majority of the veterans who had participated in his nomination as supreme chief. We refused on the grounds of lack of administrative experience, but we did agree to form a kind of kitchen cabinet under the name of the Corps of Adjutants (*Cuerpo de Lugartenientes*). The twelve of us that formed this group were: Víctor Andrade, Mario Anze, Raul Anze, Eduardo Arze, Roberto Bilbao, Gustavo Chacón, Raul Espejo, Carlos Pacheco, Roberto Prudencio, Carlos Salamanca, Hugo Salmón, and Juan Valverde.

Our role was brief. A struggle immediately began between our group and the cabinet in which there were some ex-socialists who favored the deposed President Toro and one or two covert liberals. While we insisted on the necessity of prolonging the period of de facto rule in order to gain time for the organization of new political forces, the cabinet, led by Gabriel Gosálvez, pressed for the rapid convocation of a convention, thus avoiding the insurgency of these new forces. In this struggle the Adjutants were defeated, and Busch accepted our resignation. Some of us were placed in confinement, and most others simply stayed home.

The last meeting I had with Busch was several weeks before his tragic death. It occurred on August 6, 1939, at a public function of the social security administration, of which I was then director. (The post had been held for me by other officials during my period of confinement.) President Busch greeted me with affection, as always, and as we parted said, "I want to talk with you. Come and see me because I am caught in a maze of ambitions and lies that is driving me crazy."

"Send for me whenever you wish, Germán," I answered. "You don't know how hard it is to get past your admirers' barriers around you."

"I will put you in touch with my assistant."

He forgot about it and time ran out. A few days later, August 23, 1939, in one of the singularly mysterious dramas of our history, Busch was discovered shot in the head.

Busch's government was the first fresh breeze to enter the dark corridors of the national palace. Premature death saved a personality which was being smothered by the praise, manipulation, and bitterness of the Bolivian oligarchy. In his short time in office, Busch swung like a pendulum between the agents of the mine owners and the men who remained from the larger effort at renovation. The latter were weak personalities who did not even have the imagination or courage to resign. In any case,

Busch was the distant lighting which foreshadowed the revolutionary tempest then approaching Bolivia.

Quintanilla and Peñaranda

Carlos Quintanilla, as commander of the army, assumed the presidency without opposition after Busch's death. The leaders of the traditional parties hastily joined forces, forgetting past differences in favor of an arrangement called *La Concordancia*, a name that reflected their agreement on one fundamental point: to continue to maintain the status quo by wielding the power that had been temporarily snatched away from them by the short-lived government of Germán Busch. Quintanilla, won over by *La Concordancia*'s promise to present him with the rank of Marshall, collaborated enthusiastically and helped them to find an instrument for the realization of their goals. This instrument was General Enrique Peñaranda, whom the war had delivered from anonymity and during which he achieved the rank of commander of forces in the field.

It would be unjust to deny his personal sacrifice and his efforts in response to the call of history. Unfortunately, his lack of ability allowed him only to maintain a precarious balance among the professional ambitions and rivalries of the half dozen officers who coveted his position. He was kept ignorant of the fact that, as a result of the Japanese advance in the Pacific, Bolivia was enjoying for the first, and perhaps only time, the privileged position of sole supplier of tin to the democratic world. Bolivia, like the Esau of the Biblical legend, sold her birthright for a miserable plate of beans, for an invitation to Washington for consultations with world leaders in one of mankind's most crucial periods.

General Peñaranda was elected president of the republic in March 1940. If, on the one hand, he personified the army's defeat in the Chaco War, his personal good nature was well known as were his efforts in a situation which forced him to assume positions of command that were beyond his capabilities as leader, tactician, and strategist. Unfortunately, hopes that Peñaranda would reorder postwar political forces were not transformed into reality. Various independent citizens, however, myself among them, took advantage of the limited guarantees given by Quintanilla to present ourselves as candidates in the congressional elections. I was elected national representative from the Province of Sud Yungas.

The Catavi Massacre

The event that ignited the explosion of the political forces that had gathered during and after the Chaco War was the massacre of miners in Catavi in 1942.

Several years earlier, the mining industry that controlled the Social Security Administration (*Caja de Seguro y Ahorro Obrero*) had entrusted me with the management of that agency. I had been a frequent visitor to the mining districts where I learned of the potentially explosive situation caused by discontent among the workers. In connection with these activities, I participated in a Conference of Institutions of Social Security that was held at Santiago de Chile in September 1942. There I had the opportunity to meet Nelson Rockefeller, who had come not just for the conference, but on business relating to his position as coordinator of inter-American affairs for the United States government.

The first opportunity that I had to converse with Rockefeller, I spoke to him of the threat to Bolivian social stability caused by workers' demands in the tin mines. The company carried on its traditional resistance to them, supported by the government and the American embassy in La Paz. I went so far as to predict that if a solution were not found in time, the labor protest would develop into a strike which, as always, would involve the threat of violence. In the end the government, utilizing the army, would intervene, causing more bloodshed, followed by the inevitable political and social consequences.

I explained the situation to him because, as a result of contracts made after a conference at Rio de Janeiro in early 1942, contracts which were morally and materially linked to the war effort, the United States was at that time the only buyer of Bolivian tin. I proposed that, with respect to the future revision of the contracts for the buying and selling of tin, a special clause be included, stipulating that the price increase would be used for the direct benefit of the mine workers. This would be accomplished through the creation of a social assistance fund administered by a body having the tripartite representation of the government, the employers, and the workers.

Rockefeller was impressed with my presentation and indicated to me that, upon his return to Washington, he would contact the offices that were dealing directly with the matter. In the past, the mining companies had managed to embroil U.S. diplomatic representatives in everything related to the production of tin, arguing that since it was a strategic material, the United States was responsible for protecting its supply and normal production. In other words, any act that might paralyze the mines, in this case a strike, should be considered an act of sabotage against the war effort.

The U.S. ambassador to La Paz was then Pierre Boal, a man who suffered from a persecution complex and who wished to gain favor in the eyes of his superiors in Washington. To him it was inconceivable that a country which had proclaimed itself an ally and had declared war on the Axis powers would not compel its citizens to sacrifice themselves for the war effort. The flaw in his reasoning was that the burden of the sacrifice was being placed on the working masses who worked for day-to-day subsistence while the same sacrifice was not required of capitalists who continued to benefit from juicy wages, dividends, and hidden reserves. According to Boal, the miner must continue to work, the output of tin uninterrupted by protest, while the proprietors, protected by lawyers in Washington and London, would remain secure, both in their persons and profits.

The situation, however, was not so simple: the political forces which had germinated in the Chaco War were becoming conscious of their power. These forces were prepared to aid the workers in their just demands and to fight with them against the Bolivian tin superstate. On December 20, 1942, the tension erupted in the bloody incident at Catavi. The mine workers declared a strike, formed a group, and, when they walked out to protest, were received with shrapnel and mortar fire. Several hundred died that day, including women and children. The government admitted to only sixty-five deaths.

Political Consequences of the Massacre

In Washington there were unexpected repercussions. Ernesto Galarza, chief of labor affairs of the Pan-American Union, publicly accused Undersecretary of State Sumner Welles of having been one of the instigators of the massacre. Simultaneously, the progressive political circles which surrounded President Roosevelt voiced their disapproval of methods which tainted the cause of democracy. Thus the scandal assumed international dimensions to which the tin barons were unaccustomed; they could not conceal the bloody events in Bolivia. The incident was condemned by all political groups in Bolivia who did not belong to the alliance of old-regime parties supporting Peñaranda.

Nelson Rockefeller, on being informed of the accusations and scandal, may have remembered my unfortunately prophetic words. Possibly for this reason, officials from the American embassy in La Paz paid me a visit a few days later. Among them were members of the Board of Economic Warfare which, in those days, was strongly influenced by Vice-President Henry Wallace. I also ascribe to that conversation with Rockefeller the fact that when the U.S. government, in conjunction with the Bolivian government, resolved to send a commission headed by Federal Judge Calvert Magruder to investigate the causes of the massacre, I was invited to join it. Because I was a member of Congress, I could not serve on the commission, but I did provide it with data on the social situation in the mines and in other sectors of labor. I attended many of its meetings and participated in some of its trips to the mining districts. The commission published its completed report which, although very circumspect, pleased the mine owners not in the least. And Martin Kyne, a member of the commission representing the CIO of the United States, presented an even more categorical personal report.

As a contribution to the evaluation of the problem, I wrote a pamphlet containing my observations. Its publication coincided with my abrupt departure from the directorship of the Social Security Administration for having refused to withdraw my signature from a document demanding the government's explanation of the massacre, a document which I signed as representative from Sud Yungas. In this way my position with respect to current social problems was established, and any doubts about the existence of a Bolivian superstate controlled by the tin barons and run by their servile agents were erased.

The legislature of 1943 opened amid the tensions generated by the violence at Catavi. One of the first acts of the opposition parties was to present a report on the massacre containing a list of charges signed by various representatives, myself among them. The vote on this document was to determine the fate of the government. After a memorable debate a vote was taken, but the legal censure was not passed because of Deputy Messutti's unforgettable negative vote submitted in writing by the socialist deputy, Francisco Lazcano Soruco. The large minority vote for censure, however, ultimately proved definitive and marked the beginning of the end for the government.

Peñaranda could have saved the institutional structure of the country by seeking new political support and by forming a cabinet with the groups that had shown strength in Congress. Such changes would have produced subsequent changes in policy. Peñaranda had not only the constitutional, but the moral authority to do that. He did not belong officially to any political party and those who held power with him had used his name and reputation to gain office without any popular support. Nevertheless, he persisted in governing with the same combination of forces. As a result, those of us who were new to the political scene had no alternative but to overthrow the government by a coup d'etat.

2

Villarroel and the MNR in Power

The coup d'etat of December 20, 1943, marked the beginning of the national revolution. It was led by a group composed of military officers headed by Major Gualberto Villarroel and of civilians, the *Movimiento Nacionalista Revolucionario* (MNR), headed by Víctor Paz Estenssoro. I was active in bringing these two groups together as a result of my long friendship with Villarroel and my work in organizing the veterans of the Chaco War.

The Villarroel-MNR Alliance

My acquaintance with Villarroel dated from 1934, during the Chaco War. After the battle of Cañada Strongest, I was appointed adjutant of the Eighth Division which was then deployed along Cañada Cochabamba. The enemy, wisely trying to lessen the effect of its disastrous defeat at Cañada Strongest, was constantly harrassing the reorganized lines. The Supreme Command resolved to make a counterattack through the left flank of our army with a detachment formed by the Ayacucho and Castrillo Regiments. I was ordered to act as liaison officer at the front, and therefore presented myself to the commander of the Ayacucho Regiment, Colonel Roberto Ayoroa, and several of his officers. Ayoroa gave me a rude reception. "Since when does headquarters send us only 'college boys' for such an important position? Do you realize, Lieutenant, that the mission which you propose to carry out belongs to a higher-ranking career officer?"

Confused by such an unusual reception, I did not know how to reply; the questions seemed to defy response. Clearly I had not deliberately sought a mission which would be both dangerous and delicate. All I could say was, "Colonel, I am merely following an order from headquarters."

In a corner of the field tent an officer, clear eyed, of small build,

14

and showing signs of premature baldness sat up. He intervened firmly. "Colonel, there is no cause to reproach Lieutenant Andrade. He is only trying to fulfill the mission with which they have entrusted him. Here we are all Bolivians who do what we can, and it is not up to us as professional officers to reject the effort of the civilians who wear a uniform and who have earned their rank by sacrificing so much. On the contrary we should do everything possible to help them and welcome them here with open arms. . . ."

For several days after Villarroel's spontaneous intervention, I lived in his small field tent. He was commander of the First Battalion of the Ayacucho Regiment, and together we spent hours of profound emotion and anguish. An intimate friendship developed between us, interrupted only by his heroic death. In the course of that friendship, we had many opportunities to analyze national problems and the defects of our social and economic structure; we formulated plans for the future, hoping to collaborate in a common effort if destiny allowed us to leave the battlefield alive.

After the death of President Busch in 1939, the majority of young veterans who had followed Busch reunited to form an organization called *Estrella de Hierro* (Iron Star). We sought to bring together in one organization all the intellectual elite who had taken part in the Chaco War. At the end of October 1939, while serving as the leader of this organization, I was invited to represent Bolivia at the Regional Labor Conference in Havana. For this reason I entrusted the leadership of Estrella de Hierro to Dr. Roberto Bilbao. During my absence he ordered the official attendance of the group at a demonstration organized by *La Concordancia*. By so doing he placed the organization in a false position, since its very existence was based on nonconformity with the political parties responsible for the Chaco disaster. Confronted with this situation on my return from Havana, I had no alternative but to call for the dissolution of the group. So ended the ephemeral existence of Estrella de Hierro.

Meanwhile, Villarroel had been the guiding force in the formation of the military lodge, *Razón de Patria* (RADEPA), a group of young officers who had distinguished themselves by their competent leadership, their self-sacrifice, and their courage in the Chaco War. I was one of the few civilians who knew of the existence of this organization, due to my close friendship with Villarroel, its leader. To project the activities of RADEPA into the political arena, Villarroel and I decided to form a group in which both civilians and military might participate. So *Mariscal Santa Cruz*, which I headed, was born. In addition to the main cell in La Paz, branches were organized in Cochabamba, Potosí, and Sucre.

Peñaranda's refusal to modify the bases of his government was the final indication for both RADEPA and Mariscal Santa Cruz that the only recourse open to them was a coup d'etat. There was little doubt that the government would use the pretext of World War II to drown the opposition in blood. My role in this situation had a great influence on subsequent events. Convinced that the civilians who had gathered in Mariscal Santa Cruz were too few to give a new government the necessary political backing, I said to Villarroel and the members of the association that it was of vital importance to have the support of a political party whose policies had affinity with our ideals. We decided, with Villarroel's complete agreement, that it was necessary to invite the recently created MNR to join us. While this party did not yet have the support of the masses, its leaders were professionals and intellectuals of well-known capabilities and patriotism.

One August evening in 1943, I invited Villarroel and Víctor Paz Estenssoro to my home so that they could meet and, if possible, arrange some joint action. The meeting was successful, and on December 20, 1943, the MNR formed part of the first cabinet of President Villarroel.

Background to Nonrecognition

The coup d'etat of 1943, executed with exceptional speed and acumen, constituted the first total renovation of civilian and military leadership in conducting the nation's affairs. Villarroel, who had held the rank of major before rising to lieutenant colonel, was completely unknown to the public. People could not comprehend a government in which a figurehead connected with the mining superstate did not participate. Perplexity was even greater in diplomatic circles which had had no warning of the changes that were to be made.

Two prior events in the international sphere complicated the situation. One was the forged letter attributed to Major Elías Belmonte which was presented with much ado to the Bolivian Congress by the Peñaranda government. In this letter Belmonte supposedly informed the German embassy in La Paz that his friends were taking measures for a Nazi-style *putsch*, involving the use of bicycles in the city of Cochabamba. This absurd document, crudely conceived and written, nevertheless had served to unleash a furious persecution of the recently organized MNR.

Secondly, Belmonte was one of the most important members of the RADEPA military lodge. The document thus provided a basis for labeling any movement against Peñaranda as being inspired by enemy powers. Moreover, some of the civilian members of Villarroel's cabinet were portrayed as being involved in Hitler's supposed efforts to gain control of Bolivia, with the aid of Bolivian Nazis, and establish a center of resistance in the heart of South America.

It is difficult to understand how the foreign office of the most powerful country in the world could fall into a trap so poorly set by those whose only objective was to maintain their traditional stranglehold on the Bolivian people. Here for the first time, the weight of the immense international interests seeking to block the reform impulse of a generation was beginning to be felt in the worldwide struggle.

Few governments assume power with the handicaps faced by Villarroel. The colossal force represented in Bolivia by the *Asociación de Industriales Mineros* (Association of Mining Industrialists) reacted violently to the bold generation of Bolivians who had dared to organize a government without its permission. The groups of politicians removed from power now organized themselves, with financial aid from the mine owners, to overthrow these self-styled defenders of the fatherland who had the audacity to invade a field of action which the politicians had once monopolized. To this end the latter acted on two fronts: the domestic and the international.

On the domestic front they began the customary suborning of military officers and whispering campaigns fanned by clandestinely printed pamphlets which spread the most monstrous slanders about the public and private lives of members of the new government. The people, easily deceived, and disoriented by seeing new faces in the positions of traditional rulers, doubted the government's good intentions and promises, unaware that those who expressed them had proved their patriotism on the battlefield. The ignorance in which they were kept by their former rulers forced them to live in an atmosphere of doubt and suspicion. The young, well-meaning officers were unable to understand the people's state of mind. They could not conceive how the masses could continue to believe their old oppressors, appearing to long for the whip and bullets that they had received periodically from the henchmen of the great tin magnates and landowners. It was not surprising that some of the populace reacted violently, creating problems that complicated the situation for the new government.

On the international front, leaders of the old regime quickly activated the machinery of propaganda and the network of contacts which they had established long before to hide the reality of Bolivia and to discredit national values. They took advantage of the Belmonte episode and magnified the fabrication to such an extent that they caused the better judgment of the U.S. State Department to waiver, leading it to commit errors that had tragic consequences for the Bolivian people. They were also able to use the naiveté of some young American functionaries who were hiding out in the U.S. missions to Latin America and who wanted to satisfy their conscience by giving the impression that they were contributing to the war effort.

After the new government took power in December 1943, one of its first acts was to appoint Enrique Sánchez de Lozada as confidential agent in Washington. Sánchez had resided in the United States for many years and had even become a public official in the federal administration. The new government's lack of experience was probably the sole reason for this appointment. It not only was ineffective but meant the introduction of a Trojan horse into the tight ranks of the revolution. Sánchez became convinced that the only way of obtaining international recognition for the Villarroel government was through the substitution of the pseudocommunist *Partido de la Izquierda Revolucionaria* (PIR) for the MNR. Curiously enough, Sánchez owed his appointment to the pressure brought by Augusto Céspedes who, at the time, was secretary general of the government junta and one of the MNR's foremost leaders. I am convinced that Sánchez was aware of this fact. He did not, however, hesitate in proposing the expulsion of the man who had previously recommended him, nor in suggesting that José Antonio Arze, the captain of the Chaco War deserters, join a government composed of officers and civilians who had fought in that war.

The medicine proposed by the "confidential agent" was much too strong to be swallowed even by those inexperienced officers who knew little of international intrigue or the labyrinth of domestic political ambition. The far-fetched proposal was rejected and the undersecretary of foreign affairs, Fernando Iturralde, replaced Sánchez in Washington. He too could obtain no positive results and could not overcome the intransigent position adopted by Cordell Hull in response to the propaganda created by the owners of the tin mines.

The U.S. embassy in La Paz isolated itself completely, creating a *sui generis* situation in which its officers adopted the mentality of the besieged. The paranoia of Ambassador Boal led him to order all the high- and low-ranking functionaries of the embassy to leave their offices frequently during the day, go to a brick storage site, and secretly bring many of these bricks, wrapped in newspapers, into the embassy. He then began to build parapets where, in his fantasies, he would see his followers defending democracy to the bitter end against this creole brand of Nazis!

Meanwhile, the contracts for the production and sale of minerals and rubber had to be fulfilled to serve the needs of the United States, the war, and, naturally, the Bolivian treasury. For this reason relations were initiated with some officials of the Reconstruction Finance Corporation, bypassing the American embassy. The Americans responded very cautiously, as if dealing with medical patients under quarantine. The most open-minded of these officers, those who from the beginning sympathized with the true purposes of the revolution, were, undoubtedly, Phillip Kazen and Sproesser Wynn.

As 1944 began, Washington still had not recognized the Villarroel government, which had taken power only a few days previously, that is, on December 20. The Department of State was not content simply to withhold recognition itself. Instead, the U.S. government attempted to persuade most Latin American governments to adopt the same policy.

Bolivia and the War

United States disapproval of the Villarroel government needs to be understood in the light of the repercussions in Bolivia of World War II. The first military victories of Germany and Italy won admirers and fanatics who believed that Nazi fascism was a healthy corrective to the weakness of the democracies and a means to defeat communism. Political, academic, and military leaders split up into groups which hoped to profit from the results of the conflict in Europe. German, Italian, and Japanese immigrants organized and sought adherents to the totalitarian cause among intellectuals and other influential groups. Conservatives sought to capitalize on local distrust and dissension to magnify the effects of totalitarian propaganda and to identify it with many local movements. Moreover, the democracies were slow to counter totalitarian propaganda.

The struggle between the two sides took place in the schools, including my own. The American Institute, founded at the beginning of this century when the Liberals were in power, was supported by tuition and a subsidy from the Board of Foreign Missions of the Methodist Church of the United States. It met the needs of numerous Bolivian families who, in fulfillment of their liberal and anticlerical ideals, refused to send their children to Catholic schools. The fact that my father was a member of the Liberal party was one reason I had all my primary and secondary education at the Institute.

In the early thirties, when the Nazis seemed irresistible, another primary and secondary school was founded by the large German colony in La Paz with subsidies from the German government. Almost adjacent to the American Institute, the new German School had new buildings and new laboratories, a gymnasium, modern curricula, and libraries. An impressive portrait of Adolf Hitler adorned the entrance to the main lecture hall. The contrast with the facilities offered by the Institute was great since the income of the American school was too small to offer any competition. Students and alumni were painfully aware of this rivalry, especially when one day I was informed that the Board of Foreign Missions had decided to close the American Institute and sell the land and buildings because of the depression in the United States.

A half-dozen alumni who had some influence in the community met together to discuss the future of our school. If the Institute were closed, the German School, financed and controlled by the Nazi government, would become the main private lay school for Bolivian youth. It seemed senseless for the democracies to abandon such an important institution in the midst of a violent ideological struggle. We decided to communicate with the U.S. embassy in La Paz, but the first results were discouraging. We were told that the laws of the United States prohibited contributions by the state to religious organizations or institutions directly or indirectly. We were also reminded of the enormous defense costs being borne by the American government.

We decided to organize a secular Bolivian corporation so as to qualify for U.S. assistance. Our purpose was to preserve one of the most effective instruments of democratic influence in the conflict of ideas and systems. We also hoped to take advantage of this emergency to obtain from the United States enough assistance to offer to Bolivian youth a modern educational institution possessing educational equipment, libraries, athletic fields, laboratories, and scholarships for worthy but poor students. The Methodist Church rented all the buildings of the Institute to the corporation for one dollar per year, and we signed new contracts with all the teachers. Thus the school continued in operation. The government of the United States provided exactly what the Board of Foreign Missions had given before. Unfortunately, the U.S. government once more failed to realize the importance of this ideological and political struggle. The Institute survived but we did not realize our dream of making it a model primary and secondary school.

United States citizens in Bolivia were usually one of three types: officials, businessmen, or missionaries. Although there are exceptions, officials tend to act in an arrogant and overbearing way which cuts them off from the local community. Their private life takes place on a kind of cultural island, duplicating life in the United States. Officials meet with each other, speak only in English, read American magazines and publications, and eat imported foods. Finally, they send their children to schools organized to duplicate the American educational system, not only avoiding but also scorning native values and customs. Businessmen do the same, sometimes even more ostentatiously. The Methodist school, run by missionaries, was invaluable in neutralizing the influence of these two types of Americans. The missionary who came as a teacher was usually of humble extraction, possibly from a farming family in the Midwest. Sincerely modest, he made close friends and did in fact represent an important part of American life. His simplicity and austerity, due to low income and quiet temperament, placed him on a level where there was easy access to the Bolivian community.

In a society where the Catholic Church had sunk deep roots over the centuries, the missionaries usually abandoned evangelism and dedicated themselves to other significant activities. They were models of other styles of Christian life, thereby widening the horizons of religious thought. They struggled against intolerance and favored honest inquiry into spiritual values. Perhaps their most important contribution was facilitating truly democratic access to private education. In this sense, the American Institute did its part in helping win the war of ideas in World War II.

Hull's Famous Memorandum

In order to secure the diplomatic support of other American nations for the policy of nonrecognition against the government of Villarroel, Secretary of State Cordell Hull transmitted a memorandum of charges to the foreign offices of those governments in the hemisphere which had declared war or broken relations with the Axis. The U.S. plan was to make nonrecognition of the new Bolivian government a phase of the action against the Axis powers.

The charges were summarized in a telegram sent on January 10, 1944, to the U.S. missions concerned.[1] The MNR was described as an antidemocratic, anti-Semitic, pro-Fascist party which allegedly had received financial support from the German Nazis and was still influenced by them. Villarroel and some of his military associates were charged with holding views inspired by the Nazis and with having been closely associated with Major Belmonte who was believed to have been cooperating with the Nazis since 1941. The U.S. missions were instructed to inform the local foreign offices that in view of the foreign intervention in the Bolivian revolt of 1943, the U.S. government was unlikely to recognize the new regime. Meanwhile, Foreign Secretary Anthony Eden informed the House of Commons that Great Britain would not recognize Villarroel and would conform to U.S. policy in other respects as well. The only Latin American countries that avoided Hull's proposed collective action were Argentina and Chile; both recognized Villarroel before the memorandum was issued.

It is almost impossible to describe the impact that these events had on the state of mind of the young officers who had been the generating force of the revolution. They were motivated by patriotic ideals which grew out of the long hours of suffering and frustration in a useless and unproductive war. They were convinced that the country needed a good shaking to loosen the rotten fruit from its traditional limbs. However,

1. The text of the telegram was published in *Foreign Relations of the United States 1944*, Vol. VII: *The American Republics* (Washington, D.C.: Government Printing Office, 1967), pp. 430–32.

these officers were victims of the web of interests created by foreign influences. These influences harmed the people, that is, the Indians, workers, and lower-middle-class citizens who had shared with the officers the cup of frustration during the long years of the war. Now, in the critical moment, they could see that their most cherished hopes were to be crushed by the irrational manipulations of the eternal exploiters. These exploiters, as if by sleight of hand, had magnified a domestic confrontation into an aspect of the international power struggle taking place on the battlefields of Europe, Asia, and Africa.

In this situation, the politicians who obeyed the tin barons found conditions favorable for a counter-coup attempt against the revolution. To this end, they mobilized their lackeys and intensified the campaign of rumors, slander, and threats. They also instructed their followers within the armed forces to be on the alert. The PIR, which prior to that time had pretended to be negotiating its entry into the government, joined the conspiracy. In this tense situation, those responsible for the safety of the government overreacted: an attempt was made against the life of José Antonio Arze and Mauricio Hochschild, an Argentine industrialist of Austrian-Jewish background, was kidnapped. In the case of Arze, the attempt was a shot which served to resuscitate a political cadaver. The second incident gave the enemies of the new government an opportunity to represent it as composed of Nazi bandits who were using the situation to take advantage of Hochschild, the "peace-loving capitalist." In fact, he had remained in Bolivia specifically to become the key member of the conspiracy.

Each of these episodes might have been dealt with in a different way, but the atmosphere of isolation brought about by Hull's memorandum caused a tragic reaction which undoubtedly marked the beginning of the end for the pioneer government of Villarroel.

Resignation of Foreign Minister Tamayo

A few days after presentation of the Hull memorandum in January 1944, Boal left the country. Although Boal was a colorless, unimportant individual who had all the limitations of the typical bureaucrat, his attitudes were not so harmless. Desperate to conceal his ignorance and lack of ability, he did not hesitate to voice new accusations, declaring that the Bolivian revolution had been manipulated by the Argentine military government. This was another great fraud, exposed only when the new Bolivian government of July 1946 reestablished relations with Franco and pledged itself unconditionally to Perón through its jesuitical ambassador in Buenos Aires, Gabriel Gonzalves. After Boal left, Robert

Woodward took charge at the embassy. He was a genial, intelligent young man who was able to reach an adequate compromise between the restrictions imposed on him by Washington and the need to obtain first-hand information about the true roots of the revolution.

Soon thereafter, in February 1944, an event took place which served to identify me more closely with the international relations of the revolutionary government. Since December 20, 1943, I had occupied the position of minister of health, labor, and social welfare. It had been my intention to remain at that post for the period of time necessary to carry out the program which I had prepared many years before, when, as manager of the Social Security Administration, I had witnessed the tragic living conditions of the Bolivian miners.

Foreign Minister José Tamayo was a man whose honesty and revolutionary fervor could never be doubted. Motivated by the desire to lift the blockade of nonrecognition, and acting without any carefully preconceived plan, he sent a cable to our confidential agent in Santiago, Chile, instructing him to submit to the government of that country a proposal for independent recognition, thus forming a "southern bloc" with Argentina. The day after the cable was sent, President Juan Antonio Ríos of Chile publicly denounced that proposition, although without referring specifically to the Bolivian foreign minister's offer. In a carefully prepared speech he said that Chile would never be a part of isolated blocs within the continent and that its foreign policy would always be inspired by the international agreements for continental solidarity.

It was a bitter discovery for us to learn of the cheap victory which we had given the Chilean dignitary. No great amount of intelligence was necessary to perceive that President Ríos's phrase referred to the proposition of the Bolivian foreign minister. After all, in those days Chile was interested in obtaining $80 million (which it eventually got) for its metallurgical and hydroelectric plants. The undersecretary of foreign affairs, Eduardo Arze, confided to me his fears about this matter and showed me the text of the instructions sent to Chile. We agreed that this meant a step backward in our efforts to obtain a modification of the policy adopted by the Department of State. I immediately met with Villarroel who was also alarmed. He explained that he had not been consulted nor informed about the approach to Chile. We agreed that the action would only encourage the rumor already rampant on the continent that the Bolivian revolution had been inspired by elements and influences which were opposed to coordinated action in the war against the Axis.

Villarroel immediately called a meeting of the cabinet which convened that same night. He asked me to explain the situation. I did so reluctantly because I was convinced, and still am, that Tamayo's action was a result of his faith in the worthy cause he was defending. His desire to break the wall of isolation prevented him from perceiving the selfishness of his neighbors. I believe that one of the things that most influenced his error was the fact that Chile had hastily recognized the Farrel-Perón government, thus avoiding the pressure that the Department of State intended to use in order to isolate Argentina as it had isolated Bolivia. This step was bound to displease the North Americans, and so it was urgent that Chile make amends. Tamayo's proposition was an ideal opportunity, and the Chileans took full advantage of it. In this way, like schoolboys repenting their mischief, they avoided punishment and were rewarded with the $80 million treat.

There was no alternative but to accept Tamayo's resignation. For the sake of internal politics and the prestige of our government abroad, an immediate successor had to be found. When I proposed Enrique Baldivieso's name, I found great resistance and, instead, I myself was offered the position. I did not accept because I had my own plans for activities in the fields of labor and social security. However, I overcame the resistance of Villarroel and the other members of the government junta. That same night, the president's secretary, Hugo Salmón, visited Enrique Baldivieso to offer him the position of foreign minister.

My Role in Gaining Recognition

The diplomatic freeze between Bolivia and the United States proved to the latter that it could not, despite its immense power and size, completely avoid relations with my country. They had to be informally initiated through steps taken by representatives of semiautonomous North American offices such as the Board of Economic Warfare. Tin and rubber were needed for planes and tanks; the factories producing cannons and ammunition needed Bolivian tungsten; and other commodities, mainly foodstuffs for American soldiers, were required. In this way, the manual work of the Bolivian Indians of the Andes suddenly acquired a transcendental dimension for the life and the defense of that great nation. American functionaries had no alternative but to emerge from the hiding places built by Boal and rehearse their commercial smiles again. In these conditions, a labor conference in the United States appeared to be an opportunity to break the impasse over recognition.

My role in the recognition question began during the first few months of my administration as minister of labor. As representative of the government, I attended the meeting held to organize the *Federación Sindical de Trabajadores Mineros* (Mine Workers' Trade Union Federation), founded at a memorable gathering in Huanuni. For the first time, the mine workers felt that they were supported by their government in their desire to organize for social defense. Furthermore, for the first time in the history of Bolivia, those who held power showed a sincere interest in serving the people. The bloodshed in the struggle at Catavi had begun a new treatment of the class that, until then, had simply been an instrument for the politicians who used its suffering as a ladder, only to ignore it once they gained the comforts of power.

The International Labor Office called a world conference for April 1944, to meet in Philadelphia. This event offered an excellent opportunity to attempt again to convince Cordell Hull that he himself, influenced by the skillful propaganda of the Bolivian tin-mining oligarchy, had made a serious mistake. In my capacity as minister of labor, I traveled to the United States as a representative of the Bolivian government. I was now able to get in touch with high American officials and the main press agencies in order to make the truth known about the Bolivian situation. Until this time the revolution had been described only by the agents of the tin barons and by those who saw phantoms in any action which might disturb the quasi-mystical order which they deemed essential to the war effort. The fact that Hull's memorandum had not listed me among those classified as agents of the enemy put me in a favorable position to be heard. This was the most we could hope for at that time.

I traveled to Philadelphia with Enrique Saavedra, one of the leaders of the Catavi Miners' Trade Union, who was given credentials as representative of the Bolivian working class. In Philadelphia, I discovered that the Bolivian entrepreneurs had named Eduardo Fajardo as employers' delegate. Fajardo was an old classmate of mine in the American Institute of La Paz. For the first time, Bolivia appeared in a labor conference with full and authentic representation. Fajardo had all the credentials to represent the employers because he was secretary for the Patiño mines in New York. Saavedra was an authentic mine worker, elected by the Mine Workers' Federation. I had participated in the origins of the revolution and, being a member of the cabinet, was deeply identified with the forces which composed the government.

The first session of the conference had, in my opinion, a decisive impact on later events. One of the first reports announced a tentative decision contesting Saavedra's credentials, charging that his representation was fraudulent. My first reaction was to look for Vicente Lombardo Toledano, whom I had met in Havana during a similar conference in 1939. A discussion took place which lasted for more than three hours in the presence of Saavedra; of Licenciado Carrillo, who acted as Lombardo's assistant; and of Salvador Ocampo, well-known Chilean labor leader.

The fact is that at this time the South American labor movements were controlled by Communists. The North American workers, believing in the possibility of reaching conclusive agreements with the Russians as a result of their wartime alliance, were docilely following the example of those Communist leaders. Thus they were caught in a net which served exclusively the interests of the Communist International controlled from Moscow. What the good North American workers did not realize was that, even then, Communist strategy was aimed at increasing conflict between North and South America.

Lombardo was representing both the Mexican trade unions and an organization known as the *Confederación de Trabajadores de Latino-américa*. Some countries in which the organized workers were temporarily led by Communist agents participated in this organization. In most of the other countries, Bolivia among them, it had only the support of small committees composed of professional agitators, some Communist workers, and certain politicians willing to profit from trade-union activities. Lombardo, however, appeared to represent *all* the workers in Latin America and his word carried precisely that weight for the press and the organized workers of the United States. The problem for us was that Lombardo had connections with the so-called *Confederación Sindical de Bolivia*, a small group of a few politicized workers which, flaunting the high-sounding title of *Confederación*, claimed to represent the Bolivian workers. The group was heavily influenced by the PIR, a group with Communist and opportunist origins, which had sworn to fight to the death against the revolutionary regime after being denied admission to the new cabinet. It was, therefore, to be expected that Lombardo and his companions, one of whom was a prominent leader of the Chilean Communist party, Salvador Ocampo, would vigorously oppose admitting the genuine representation of the *altiplano* workers.

The decision of the conference on this question was bound to have exceptional importance for the negotiations scheduled with American officials for the recognition of the government. The rejection of Saavedra's credentials to the conference, especially by the labor group, would have meant the obliteration of the popular spirit which I intended to emphasize in my efforts to change the policies adopted by the former senator from Tennessee, Cordell Hull. Because of his stubbornness, a powerful lever was needed to budge him, and what better one could be conceived than the labor elements of the revolution? For that reason, I considered it fundamental that Lombardo and Ocampo should keep silent, at least on this matter.

The debate was long and trying. I even went so far as to remind Lombardo that in Havana, when the Mexican revolution was harshly attacked by the Cuban employers' delegate, I was the only non-Mexican delegate who defended that revolution. I had received a special note of thanks from General Heriberto Jara, then head of the Mexican revolutionary party. For the first time, I drew a parallel between the two revolutions. The final result of this first encounter was that Lombardo accepted my line of reasoning. Besides not objecting to the credentials of the labor delegate, he helped later to clarify the confusion created by the efficient machinery of the Bolivian reactionary elements.

The following weeks were ones of continuous movement for me between Philadelphia and Washington, the State Department, the Office of the Coordinator for Inter-American Affairs, Washington's press corps, the labor leaders, liberal groups; in short, every pertinent institution which I was able to reach during that time.

Any observer who penetrated beneath the surface of the typically diplomatic attitudes of the State Department would have realized that there were two currents among the high functionaries who participated in the formulation of U.S. foreign policy or at least that concerning the Western Hemisphere. Sumner Welles, who had been undersecretary of state until a short time previously, represented the "liberal" current which aimed at an eventual ideological understanding with the Soviet Union. The "conservative" current, whose spokesman was Cordell Hull, considered that the alliance and identification of interests with the Soviet Union were no more than a strategic necessity to achieve the defeat of the Axis powers.

On matters relating to the Western Hemisphere, Welles's group relied upon a young intellectual who was found dead sometime later, apparently thrown from one of the top floors of a New York hotel. His name was Laurence Duggan, and he was one of the first to understand the events taking place in Bolivia. He realized that the Bolivian tin-mining oligarchy had been able to project into the State Department a totally distorted image of the 1943 coup d'etat and of the participants in the new government. It took time to convince Cordell Hull, but once the initial resistance was overcome it was only a matter of time and making the right statements to the press.

The line of argument I pursued in conversations with high U.S. officials and in my press conferences was that the Bolivian revolution was a genuine popular movement which had overthrown a social system totally discredited in the Chaco War. The movement sought to eliminate from politics men who, instead of serving their country, served the interests of companies which exploited the tin and agricultural resources of Bolivia. These companies and their political allies used their economic power ruthlessly to subject the people to a bloody tyranny which culminated in the massacre at Catavi. By refusing to recognize Villarroel and encouraging others to follow that example, the U.S. government was encouraging the deposed economic and political forces and provoking civil war, the result of which would surely be bloody conflict and the paralysis of mineral production. I declared not only that the Bolivian and Argentine revolutions were separate, but that most Bolivians resented Argentina for closing its borders, an act of open cooperation with Paraguay during the Chaco War. Finally, I pointed out that much of the campaign against us originated with the Communists who considered us their true enemies for having seized the banner of social progress from their own hands. These arguments eventually prevailed over the "confidential information" supplied to the Department of State by the lawyers and lobbyists of the Bolivian tin-mining oligarchy.

Approximately a month after beginning my activities, Laurence Duggan, chief of the Latin American division of the State Department, announced to me that the decision had been made to send a mission to Bolivia. The mission would be headed by Avra Warren, U.S. ambassador to Panama, and it was assigned the task of preparing a report to form the basis of new consultations. Duggan's smile and the expression in his eyes belied his serious facade and were sufficiently eloquent to indicate to me that the matter was practically decided.

A scapegoat was needed to save face for the State Department. This was the role assigned by the Warren Report to the MNR, whose members in the cabinet were required to resign. The countermeasure adopted by the Bolivian government was completely justified. If, in order to explain the recognition of the Villarroel government, it was demanded that these civilians who had been accused of collaboration with the Nazis leave the cabinet, the logical countermove was to institutionalize the presence of the MNR in the government. In this way, moreover, the PIR Communist sympathizers' hopes of getting into the government through the maneuvers of men like Sánchez de Losada and Lombardo Toledano would be conclusively dashed. Following this plan, Carlos Montenegro, Augusto Céspedes, and Víctor Paz Estenssoro left the cabinet in order to qualify for the constituent assembly elections. The plan was carried out to the last detail. The MNR representatives left through the window, thus providing an excuse for the reconsideration of the previous nonrecognition policy. Then they returned through the door after the elections as a part of the constitutional government which was inaugurated on August 6, 1944.

On June 23, 1944, the revolutionary government, headed by Gualberto Villarroel, was recognized by most of the countries of the democratic world. It is pertinent here to make some additional comments on this episode. The principle of nonintervention in domestic affairs has been adopted after hard-learned lessons which prove that any type of intervention always produces negative results and does not achieve the desired aims. The United States not only refused recognition to the Villarroel government and later demanded that the cabinet consist of men who had not been listed in the Hull memorandum but, still worse, resorted to economic pressure. This was possible because the United States, owing to geographical factors and the war, was the sole purchaser of our minerals. These political and economic measures were all forms of intervention which seriously harmed the Villarroel government and had drastic effects on the future of Bolivia.

Although it has been said that nonrecognition is a sovereign act to which any country can resort, this is not the case when the country in question is a power which, because of its size and influence, can profoundly affect the government denied recognition and its entire people. In the matter of nonrecognition recommended by the January 1944 memorandum, the intervention was even more obvious and categorical because the power of a state which led the alliance of the democratic nations was being used. This power determined the attitude of the other nations, thus creating a vacuum for Bolivia as a whole, not just for its government.

It took the State Department many months to realize the grave implications of its unfriendly attitude toward a government which had made no aggressive moves whatsoever against the United States, or, for that matter, against any of the other powers participating in the war. This attitude and its consequences were based exclusively on information provided by self-seeking elements who were not defending any cause related to the war effort, but only their personal interests. The impact of this event appears even more overwhelming when one remembers that the revolution was based on the defense of the mine workers who were crucial to the extraction of the strategic materials in which the large powers were interested. Without exaggerating, it is possible to say that the Bolivian worker was a true soldier of the cause, whose function ran parallel to that of the soldiers who fought in the trenches, defending the ideals and interests of the Allies.

Finally, some countries tried to use the Bolivian situation to strike at Argentina which had refused to adhere to the continental decision of forming a single front against the Axis powers. This was part of the effort to attribute to the MNR similarities with the movement headed by Juan Domingo Perón. As frequently occurs in human affairs, when a weak mallet is used to hit a stronger object, the former breaks before the latter. Perón continued to govern Argentina many years after the infamous murder of Villarroel and the persecution unleashed against the 1943 revolutionaries.

3

My Appointment as Foreign Minister

After most of the countries of the allied world extended recognition to Villarroel's government at the end of June 1944, elections were held for a constituent assembly. At one of the assembly's first sessions in August, Villarroel was elected president of the republic for a four-year period. Meanwhile, I had returned to Bolivia at the end of May, satisfied that I had accomplished my assigned mission in the United States.

Soon after my arrival, I detected the first symptoms of disintegration within the revolutionary ranks. The absence of a firm policy on the part of the inexperienced minister of government was causing a schism in the forces which supported the government. Some of the military men, once they found themselves in power, underestimated the real strength of the popular masses. They drew unjustified conclusions from the sycophancy of a few professional politicians who attempted to take advantage of this flaw. The result was that these military men lost respect for civilians while acquiring a false notion of their own capabilities. They came to believe that the wisdom of all the economic, political, and social sciences was contained in the ministerial resolutions which they signed every day. In this way they developed a superficial concept of the art of politics: brute strength, money, audacity, and luck. They believed that once they had tightened the screws of police and military security, the success of the government would be assured. Internal politics were based on similar elementary and mistaken concepts. First there was acceptance of, and later subsidies for, a group of opportunists who wanted to destroy the MNR. These men saw an opportunity to encourage international opposition to the MNR.

The Committee for Political Coordination, organized at my suggestion before my trip to the United States, had ceased to exist, and the minister of government had remained as arbiter of the situation. His lack of experience. offered an easy target to his sly and malicious ad-

30

versaries. It was already too late to suture the deep wounds inflicted on the revolutionary body. Only the faith which I had in Villarroel and the intimate friendship which bound us together nurtured my hope that we would eventually find a remedy. This alone kept me at the side of the government.

The Plan to Increase Tin Prices

The Social Security Administration had been, for me, one of the ideal positions from which to observe the social reality in the mines, and, consequently, the reality of the entire country. Now, as minister of labor, I stripped myself of commitments which are often obstacles to honest action. Skeptical of the alleged intentions of the Bolivian Marxists who claimed for themselves the privilege of fighting for the forgotten classes, I developed an approach of my own which I have always considered reasonable. It has never been adopted because it violates the economic taboos which persist in Latin America.

This approach gave birth to a rather romantic plan which, however, clearly expressed the sincerity of the revolutionary government. Perhaps I proceeded naively, or rather, with the generosity peculiar to impulsive youth. Even now, after the experience gained from the hard lessons of reality, I am proud of the idea, although it was not understood fully in its time. Alarmed at the imminent danger of social instability, I formulated a plan based on one simple concept: to obtain an increase in the price of tin which would be used exclusively to improve the living conditions of the Bolivian worker. To carry out this plan, two basic agreements were required. One was that the owners of the mines accept certain limitations on their earnings, abandoning the notion that the war was an opportunity for a tremendous increase in profits. The other was that the buyers, in this case the United States, recognize as a new economic truth the need for the participation of the worker in the earnings of the company.

My expectations were unduly optimistic because I still thought that the appetite of the mine owners was not as voracious as some radical elements in my country had suggested. It did not take me long to discover that these companies believed any improvement in the living conditions of the workers to be a threat to their earnings and stability. Naturally, they sought an increase in the price of minerals, but only one that would boost their profits. If it did not, they would prefer to do without the increase. The companies reacted violently, for example, when I revealed, for the first time in Bolivia, statistics which described the tragic occupational risks the miners faced, risks which were products of the owners' negligence in mining safety. Their reaction was even more violent when, as member of congress before Villarroel came to power, I refused to support the government concerning its responsibilities in the Catavi massacre.

In any case, the idea had been expressed and neither bloodshed nor monopoly of the means of publicity were enough to keep it from the public consciousness. The revolutionary sectors were receptive to the basic tenets of the thesis presented by the Villarroel government in its demand for a readjustment of tin prices.

The plan, which could not be successfully opposed inside the country, was from the beginning sabotaged abroad by the mine owners. Regrettably, the ideal moment had passed for it to be received with any probability of success in United States. Secretary of Commerce Jesse Jones, a well-known reactionary, had won the battle within the administration against Henry Wallace who was practically deprived of all participation in the negotiations for purchases of raw materials abroad. Leo Crowley, one of the sharks of Wall Street, was placed in charge of the Foreign Economic Administration (FEA). The purchasers were assured of a lion's share in the negotiation of future contracts. The horizon on mineral negotiations appeared dark.

As a final concession to the remnants of liberal influence in the United States, the so-called labor clause in the contract was reluctantly accepted by the mine owners. If the meaning of this clause is examined in proper perspective, it represents a serious accusation against the Bolivian employers: it is only through a contract signed with a foreign power that the employer pledges to obey domestic social legislation. Would employers obey the laws only when they were worded to suit their whims and conveniences? Were the mine workers so defenseless against the power of the companies that only the compassion and humanitarianism of the buyers could force the employer to fulfill his social obligations?

My work in the Ministry of Health, Labor, and Social Welfare kept me constantly and completely involved. I was assuming that negotiations would proceed on the basis approved by the ministries of foreign affairs and economy. The fact is that neither of these ministries took charge of the drafting of the petition. Much later I discovered that both Baldivieso and Chacón followed advice from elements linked with the mining enterprises who recommended "noninvolvement" in such an absurd plan. This advice was bound to damage all possibilities of negotiating a revision of the contracts.

Up to that moment, the only constructive proposal to give a personal character to the revolution was this plan. While the ministries procrastinated, the country became increasingly concerned about the all-important contracts. President Villarroel himself finally took charge of the preparation of the historic petition. No amount of criticism of that document will succeed in destroying its essence; it is a milestone in the history of Bolivia. For the first time, a Bolivian government was asking that the workers obtain some direct benefits as repayment for their drudgery. For the first time, a proposal was made for worker participation in the value of production.

Approval of the plan was in the hands of a buyer who had flooded the world with his rhetoric of liberation from fear and misery. He was now given the opportunity to prove that such talk had not been mere lip service, uttered in moments of desperation to influence worldwide opinion. To use a term from card games, we were peeking at the cards held by North American capital.

The displeasure expressed by men like Jesse Jones and Leo Crowley was intense. In one dramatic moment, the hidden essence of a system had been stripped naked by one of the weakest nations. Although those affected by it strive to hide its intrinsic value behind a veil of oblivion, this event has had a profound impact. It has been the subject of many publications and comments. Robert Mathews makes a magnificent presentation of it in a pamphlet dealing with the so-called labor clause. In spite of its dry and abstract nature, this theme has also been treated as fiction by John Dos Passos in his novel about the New Deal dream, *The Great Design*. He suggests that this episode was one of the milestones signaling the moment when Roosevelt's policies began to lean toward Wall Street.

From this point on, gone was all hope that American public opinion had been sufficiently mobilized to dominate the great machinery operating from the skyscrapers of downtown New York. The repercussions were soon magnified in the usual way by the propaganda of the tin-mining oligarchy in La Paz. The United States was displeased. The negotiations were condemned to fail ignominiously. Groups of people gathering on street corners and around club tables were saying that the United States, in spite of its recognition of the government, would do everything possible to fight the proposal, including the imposition of an economic blockade. These pessimistic visions had two objectives. One was to encourage the opposition which was preparing the counterrevolutionary coup that erupted in November 1944. The other was to weaken the government, depriving it of the possibility of implementing policies designed to benefit the working class. Thus, the tin-mining oligarchy intended to convey to the people the impression that the new government, with its absurd ideas, had irritated the northern colossus and was leading the country into economic chaos. Even a person with few suspicions could see that this propaganda intimidated Baldivieso and Chacón, who chose to take no action concerning the problem.

Chacón skillfully evaded participation in the negotiations, relying to an unbelievable degree on help given by the greatest enemy of the proposal, Miguel Etchenique. Anybody acquainted even superficially with this man—former Patiño representative in La Paz, partner and confidant of the wizard, Alberto Palacios—would have concluded that he was the least appropriate person to represent the Ministry of Economics and the Mining Bank in the new negotiations. However, he was practically flooded with cables and notes in New York begging his "collaboration" in negotiations which, for the first time, were taking a truly revolutionary turn.

By the end of July, Baldivieso made his position known. He would remain in the Ministry of Foreign Affairs only until August 6. In the latter part of the year he would "accept" the position offered to him, that is, the ambassadorship in Washington, provided that the negotiations concerning tin sales were concluded by that time. He bluntly declared that he did not understand this matter and suggested that no one was better qualified than I for the foreign office.

The arguments used to convince me centered on the success of my earlier mission and on my political position equidistant between the army and the MNR. In view of the strength of these arguments, I had to give in although I would have preferred to continue in the Ministry of Health, Labor, and Social Welfare, where I had initiated a course of action which required further attention. However, the revolutionary government needed a man of the revolution in the foreign office, and that man had to be me. I accepted, therefore, with the understanding that I would remain in that position for a minimum of two years. My opinion was, and still is, that in order to make significant progress in fulfilling the aspirations of the generation frustrated by the Chaco War, at least this much time was necessary. Villarroel enthusiastically accepted my condition which, however, was destined to remain solely in the realm of good intentions.

The Bolivian Foreign Office

There were two urgent problems to solve in the foreign office: the appointment of chiefs of mission in our embassies abroad, and the reopening of negotiations for the adjustment of tin prices and the signing of new contracts more consistent with our rights. The first task was thankless, the second difficult. In the first case, Baldivieso's traditional affability had aroused many expectations among friends and enemies of the revolution. In the latter, we would have to face not only the North

American interests, but also the wounded pride of the tin barons and their representatives in Washington and London. Let us begin with the less important problem, the appointment of new chiefs of mission.

Although I had no great hopes concerning the efficiency and general quality of the foreign office staff, my first impressions were discouraging. It was made up of rather vain bureaucrats, smugly pleased that their suits were better cut than those of the ordinary public employee. They arrived at work late because, supposedly, they spent their nights at animated receptions. In the office they read the newspapers and pontificated on current society scandals. There were some who stood out for their ability, but they were few and far between, like beauty marks on a prematurely aging skin.

At that time, the new foreign minister would establish himself in the diplomatic service in the following way: he or his deputy would convene the staff of the ministry and deliver a short speech praising the "efficiency" of the service and the ability of the young "intellectuals" who formed the "diplomatic corps." Naturally, the speech was sprinkled with ritualistic phrases about patriotism and great responsibilities, historic missions, and diplomatic ability. Thus, the structure of that mutual aid and admiration society which is called Bolivian diplomacy remained intact. Later he would talk with newspapermen, particularly those who had ambitions to secure some post abroad, dropping phrases such as "difficult problems that require careful study by international mentalities." Then, subordinates who expected a well-paid assignment abroad would refer to the "genius" of the person responsible for the foreign affairs of Bolivia.

A mountainous country like ours, surrounded by high, enclosing ridges, gives us the sensation of claustrophobia. Thus, what sometimes cannot be obtained with flattery or gifts can be secured by an offer of a trip abroad on a diplomatic assignment. The resin of the tree of the foreign office seeps out into our missions abroad, carrying beyond our frontier this desire for praise and fawning. That is why a good diplomat, according to the mores of the time, was one who flooded the foreign office with newspaper clippings and personal references by friendly newsmen. His "reports" were prepared with scissors in such a way as to try beyond all endurance the patience of colleagues in La Paz who might have read them. These colleagues were willing, however, to inform the public that the negotiations taking place abroad were "progressing satisfactorily."

A few days after having taken charge in this ministry, I called a meeting of the entire staff and explained my ideas clearly. I said to them that, in the opinion of men with a high level of responsibility concerning public affairs, the least prestigious department in the government was the foreign office. Its mission—to devise and implement our foreign pol-

icy—was not being fulfilled because of the debonaire attitude and traditional laziness of its staff. I explained to them that, in my opinion, there
was no reason to give a privileged position to the officers of the foreign
ministry in relation to those of other ministries if it was not earned
through talent, studiousness, and hard work. I told them that appearances, although fulfilling hygienic and esthetic functions, do not compensate for the lack of substance. In other words, I wanted to work with
men, not with dolls. Most of the officers were stunned. The responsible
employees, and there were some, had a feeling of hope. They recognized
the possibility of initiating a period in which work, ability, and honesty
would be the only means of advancement in the maze of the so-called
diplomatic career. The others remained silent and disconcerted, hoping
that these announcements would remain words and nothing more.

One of my first responsibilities was to name the chiefs of mission
who had to represent the revolutionary government and the country
abroad. It is obvious that it was a matter not only of appointing persons,
but of incorporating them spiritually into a new political doctrine and
making them aware of their enormous responsibility. It is difficult for
me to find words to describe the attitude of certain people when they
realized that I was ready to make the appointments. I had never seen
so many hats tipped on my behalf, nor been the object of so much
bowing and scraping. Unknown relatives materialized who, in all probability, were not aware of my existence a few months earlier. My deliberately reserved attitude and my dislike for flattery baffled most prospective candidates.

It was no secret that the representation of our country abroad was
monopolized by a sort of union held together by a "gentlemen's agreement." Through this agreement, all the participating individuals pledged
to take common action so that whoever headed the foreign office would
always be a member of this strange society. If, for any reason, this was
not the case, they would act collectively to guarantee each associate his
sinecure as a member of an embassy. Moreover, they would use every
means within reach to show that anyone who did not submit to the
demands of the "agreement" was a failure whose mistakes were understandable since, after all, he was not a "career officer." There was never
in my spirit any desire to emulate these gentlemen, whom I always
considered a pompous but harmless group. However, after the 1943
revolution I realized that their position was totally opposed to the interests and objectives of the Bolivian people. What was this position of
theirs, so contrary to the interests of the fatherland? It was not their
political stance concerning the new regime, since most of them were
willing to change their attitudes radically in exchange for security in
their jobs. Their motives were deeper and more significant.

In the same way that Bolivians have been offered the fiction of a republican government, the rest of the world has been deceived concerning the true nature of Bolivian society. The major human component of this nation is basically the product of an indigenous American culture; the rest is almost totally *mestizo*. However, this population was usually represented abroad by a small elite composed of a few hundred families, descendants of European immigrants, and by others who naively and by self-deception believed they had erased completely all traces of Indian origin. It was not only a matter of physical appearance, however. These people tried to show the world the impossible through their conduct and culture; namely, that Bolivia was not a country composed of American Indians. This monstrous falsification did not fool anyone and only attempted to ignore one of the authentic traits which gives personality to the country and is a solid basis for national pride. It was naive to try to hide the very essence of nationality with a thin veneer. It merely served to illustrate to the world the curious and ridiculous ways of a country that copied, with little success, the style of other nations. Imitation of the distinguished Spanish *señorito*, the Parisian fop, or the British aristocrat was the best way to get ahead in this social class, typified by the diplomats who originated the "gentlemen's agreement."

The Bolivian oligarchy, composed of a few landowners and the three mining sharks, felt pleased and flattered that the country was being represented abroad by men totally estranged from the spirit of the country. They were thus natural allies. The landowners considered a country of Indians as a propitious field for receiving honors, decorations, and the fruits of an easy life. The mine owners saw it as a source of manpower for the exploitation of raw materials. For these individuals and their followers, the only role for the rest of the people was to live miserably in periods of peace or to serve as cannon fodder during war. To this minority, composed of diplomats who had their photographs taken in frock coats trimmed with gold, of owners of mining enterprises, of their lawyers and paid politicians, the nation existed only symbolically, in their checking accounts in banks in New York, London, or Zürich. The Bolivian fatherland merely provided diplomatic immunities, tax shelters, and the right to claim special treatment in the courts. They not only exploited the mines of the country and its plantations, not only capitalized on the blood, sweat, and tears of the Indians, but profited from their own role as diplomatic representatives of a country which they so deeply despised. That is why these diplomats resembled foreign mercenaries, and their representation was not only deceitful but contrary to the interests of the people.

It was difficult to shape a diplomatic corps from this material. Our long-held, false values have left such a profound subconscious impression that only the education of many generations will erase it. In making appointments, I sought men who combined revolutionary faith and a feeling of rebellion against the oligarchy with a knowledge of international practices, an understanding of their own personality, and the capacity for self-restraint. It was necessary to avoid exhibiting inferiority complexes or giving the impression of exaggeratedly improvised diplomacy. Upon reviewing the activities and performance of the appointed representatives, I believed that no better and more adequate selection could have been made. In this way, I formed a new team which carried out its work much more efficiently, in one of the most difficult moments for Bolivian international relations.

Much to my regret, I was not able to complete this task. Before three months had passed, it was necessary for me to resign as foreign minister for reasons which will be set forth later.

The Negotiations Stalled

Two factors heightened the urgency of completing the tin negotiations. One was that it was convenient for our hidden adversaries, the mine owners, to exaggerate the difficulties resulting from failure to renew the contract for the sale of tin to the United States. The other was the natural nervousness of the ministries of economics and finance in response to public opinion whose attitudes were magnified by a press subsidized by mining and other entrepreneurs. Both factors combined to exert pressure to formalize a new agreement which would include a readjustment of prices for the sale of tin.

Furthermore, shortly before the 1943 revolution, the negotiations had failed to the point that the Peñaranda government and the tin barons had decided to play a strategic card: the appointment of Manuel Carrasco as representative for both. The appointment fitted their needs perfectly since Carrasco simultaneously held two positions which qualified him for the job; he was president of the senate and chief of the lawyers for the Patiño mines. Thus it happened that this individual had gone to Washington in a dual capacity, to try to obtain what the then Bolivian ambassador, Fernando Guachalla, could not. The revolution found Carrasco in Washington, and the progress of these new negotiations was halted not only because of this conflict, but because of the long period of nonrecognition in early 1944. Once official relations were reestablished with Washington, the obvious step was to insist on the need to state the new viewpoint and arrive rapidly at an agreement.

The memorandum containing the position of the Bolivian government was presented to the Department of State by the chargé d'affaires.

The report that arrived and that undoubtedly had an impact on Mr. Baldivieso's morale was that the memorandum had been "received with displeasure" by the team of North American negotiators headed by the fearsome Jesse Jones.

The way in which the tin negotiations were carried out in those months of 1944 was absurd and contradictory. Chacón had been successful in assuring Miguel Etchenique's appointment as representative of the Mining Bank and the Ministry of Economics. There is no need to insist on Etchenique's counterrevolutionary position. The Ministry of Foreign Affairs was represented by officers who had been at the embassy in Washington since before the revolution. These elements, together with the representatives of the entrepreneurs, made up a unanimous group intent on sabotaging the government's plan to improve the lot of the mine workers who actually obtained the minerals from the Bolivian subsoil. It was therefore to be expected that the first news to reach Bolivia was aimed at preparing the counterrevolutionary atmosphere which erupted in 1944. This news was morbidly pessimistic concerning the possibility of obtaining an advantage in the future contract.

For these reasons, the ambassador's presence in Washington was urgently needed. The ministers of finance and economics shared this opinion. I begged the president to insist that Baldivieso travel to Washington, since his physical presence would strengthen the viewpoints expressed in the document requesting better prices. Villarroel called Baldivieso, and, in my presence and that of Jorge Zarco Kramer, minister of finance, asked him to go immediately to Washington.

Baldivieso explained that if the reason for his trip was the tin negotiations, he had to repeat that this field had never been his specialty. He had insisted from the beginning that these negotiations be centered in the Ministry of Economics, with my participation since I understood the matter in depth. He had asked the president for the ambassadorship in Washington with the understanding that he would go there once the negotiations had been concluded. Furthermore, personal matters would prevent him from traveling until January of the following year.

Upon receiving Baldivieso's answer, we exchanged confused glances, and I believe that we all had the same question in mind: why had he chosen the ambassadorship in Washington if he knew that the prime issue to be discussed was the tin sales contract and that the ambassador to the United States had to take responsibility for those negotiations?

Baldivieso formulated a *sui generis* proposition. The fact that I accepted was even more curious and naive. In my capacity as foreign minister, I would travel to Washington to preside over the contract negotiations. Once these negotiations were completed, Mr. Baldivieso would arrive to take charge of the embassy. Since I saw no other solution, I accepted the strange proposal. However, we had to sound out the Department of State to establish its reaction to a visit by the Bolivian foreign minister for this purpose.

The result of this sounding was adverse to Baldivieso's proposal. The acceptance of a mission headed by the foreign minister himself would amount to an initial concession. The U.S. chargé d'affairs in La Paz received instructions to discourage the foreign minister from making the trip. Once we knew these results, we met again in the president's office where I insisted that it was necessary for Baldivieso to make the trip immediately. Upon his firm refusal, the president had no alternative but to accept his resignation.

The MNR leaders, who at the time were not members of the government, had been given the inside story on this matter. Víctor Paz Estenssoro visited the president and expressed his view that this mission was of utmost importance to the country's foreign relations. The ambassador to Washington occupied a strategic position because he could support the revolutionary process or deal it a heavy blow by identifying with the adverse stance assumed by the Department of State. It was imperative to defend the revolution abroad; if our representative were to become a simple spokesman for the foreign press, the revolutionary process would be weakened and confusion created.

As a result, I was needed in Washington to head the Bolivian mission. I had to change my plans once more and assume a responsibility which was all the more delicate since most of the supposed experts in the matter were prognosticating the inevitability of its failure. As I left for Washington, the supporters of the revolution had hopes for the success of my mission while the revolution's adversaries predicted my failure.

4

The First Mission Begins

It is difficult to describe my emotions on assuming a position that had not been part of my immediate plans, but was one on which Bolivia's political future depended. I knew that behind my back there were ripples of envy and predictions of doom by those who claimed the right to monopolize international negotiations and sought to assure my mission's failure in advance. I left Bolivia under the cloud of my opponents' wrath and professional diplomats' resentment. I was but weakly supported by my colleagues in the government, many of whom viewed the possibility of success in my efforts with skepticism. Some of them appeared to favor the breakup of the revolutionary coalition, thereby permitting the return of "experienced" diplomats.

I arrived in Washington two days before the election of Franklin Delano Roosevelt to his fourth term in the White House. The evening on which the results were being announced on the radio, I was with Carlos Víctor Aramayo, one of the tin barons. He was in Washington to represent the large mining companies in the negotiations. I saw him grow pale with anguish as the defeat of the Republican candidate became evident. His expression was like that of a croupier who sees the bank has been broken. Aramayo's features reflected defeat, helplessness, and hatred. We were on opposite sides not only in Bolivia's domestic politics, but in the struggle between the exploited and the exploiters.

Stettinius and Rockefeller

After his electoral victory, Roosevelt took a long rest in the South. For this reason I did not present my credentials until December 20, 1944, but I did, like every new ambassador, visit the secretary of state a few days after arriving in Washington. Stettinius and I took an instant liking to one another, and a friendship developed which was extremely advantageous for my mission. He was a relatively young man considering the average age of U.S. officials. He had a good build, somewhat angular features, and completely white hair. His small blue eyes left an impression of generosity and integrity. It was obvious that he was neither a professional diplomat nor a veteran politician. Nor did he have the appearance of an intellectual or an academician. On the contrary, he had the typical gestures and manner of a successful businessman, the product of a tradition of leading industrialists in whose world making friends was as important as making money. Because he had been concerned with large affairs, he had the capacity to take an interest in the smaller concerns of humble people.

How different was his conduct from that of the businessmen of our semicolonial countries, accustomed to treating people as if they were slaves. Our rich acted as despots toward the weak while fawning upon the powerful. Stettinius, who had been the president of United States Steel before entering government service, was unaffected and straightforward, without pretense or sham. He may or may not have been capable in matters that were not his specialty. He may have erred or hesitated in difficult moments because he had to serve in one of the most trying periods of the war. As a man whose strength derived from humility and who transformed power into generosity, Stettinius embodied the best of the United States and brought honor to his country.

Stettinius was not only my friend, but also my teacher, helping me to understand the North American temperament and the way to deal with it. He taught me that in the United States the most important thing is to get to the point, stating directly and clearly the interests that one is defending and the needs that one is trying to fulfill. He also made me understand that there is nothing more dangerous and, above all, futile than deception. A government with enormous sources of information, the United States almost always discovers deception. In dealing with North Americans, the truth should be viewed as good strategy as well as a moral obligation.

But Stettinius taught me something else: North American businessmen, accustomed to fighting for every cent from the time they learn to walk, nevertheless have a humane side which is sensitive, generous, and sentimental. The trick is to touch these emotions without wounding them, thus obtaining seemingly impossible concessions which reflect a generosity unparalleled in other countries.

The key to being a good North American administrator is knowing how to find the right men to realize one's objectives. Stettinius was a master at this in the State Department. He was able to organize a team which served to fulfill the objectives of U.S. policy, especially in Latin America.

He chose Nelson Rockefeller as assistant secretary of state for relations with Latin America. He could not have made a more opportune and satisfactory selection in keeping with the temper and principles of U.S. policy toward the rest of the continent. It was necessary to give concrete meaning to the Good Neighbor Policy without clashing with the new course of the Roosevelt administration. The government needed the full cooperation of American capital for the war effort, but business had demanded an end to the radical innovations of the New Deal. It was therefore necessary to form friendships based not on fear, but on goodwill. Expectation of wonderful gifts should be replaced by the development of mutual cooperation, beneficial to all.

Rockefeller had acquired experience in his work as coordinator of inter-American affairs and had demonstrated profound goodwill and concern through his private activities in Latin America. He was a central figure in the effort to obtain continental cooperation for the war effort. Rockefeller could be considered as a symbol of the new approach of the modern American capitalist to countries with semicolonial economies. His actions as well as his words showed respect for the rights of those nations to a better life. In the days of the Morgans and the Vanderbilts he might have been labeled a dreamer and a radical. Now, big capitalists had to realize that they were not as invulnerable as their pride had led them to believe. If they wanted to survive, they had to adopt a new attitude toward the community and to become more socially responsive. Nelson Rockefeller belonged to this new generation; throughout his public service he tried to follow the dictates of social conscience.

Rockefeller was blessed with youth, dynamism, personal attractiveness, intelligence, and prestige, but handicapped by a name which was controversial in America. He was a question mark for the majority of the men who were watching the State Department's new team. As it turned out, the appointment of Rockefeller was the most effective of the Roosevelt administration in respect to Latin America.

At a luncheon given in honor of Nelson Rockefeller during the San Francisco conference in 1945, I was asked to say a few words about him. On that occasion I said that destiny plays extraordinary tricks, sometimes allowing men to transform adverse prejudices into instruments of good for themselves. For many years in Spanish America, the name of Rockefeller went hand in hand with the concepts of fear and suspicion. It signified indiscriminate use of the power produced by economic strength and, for this reason, it was the target of the animosity of those who attributed their poverty to industrial exploitation.

By 1945, that name had acquired another meaning. Continuing the humanitarian activities that his father and grandfather initiated, Nelson Rockefeller has transformed this name into a promise of cooperation, understanding, and humanitarianism. No longer does the name Rockefeller exclusively represent rivers of oil and the exploitation of concessions for American capital; now it is synonymous with the struggle against epidemics, with the possibility of better education, and with helping the poor to better their living conditions. In this manner Rockefeller acted as a true patriot because he tried to establish relations between the United States and our countries upon solid and permanent foundations, based on dignity and mutual respect.

For the position of chief of the Division of American Republic Affairs, Rockefeller chose Avra Warren who, until then, had been ambassador to Panama. This was the man who had helped to arrange U.S. recognition of the Villarroel government. Now, at his new post, he demonstrated a truly exceptional character. He was the standard-bearer of a new school of thought in relation to Latin American policy, based on sensitivity toward and respect for the virtues and defects of other cultures. It maintained that the United States should not try to set itself up as the teacher of democracy, but should rather demonstrate its virtues by example.

Besides having the astuteness of a true diplomat, Warren was a realist. He was one of the men who had best understood the meaning of the Good Neighbor Policy. He did not have the lyricism, the arrogance, nor the pretension of Welles, nor was he an intellectual like Larry Duggan. But Warren, a mature and informed observer, was an exceptionally capable diplomat.

The Department of State

As a newcomer to Washington, I learned of the strength as well as the inefficiency of the gigantic machinery of the State Department. It is often impossible to discover who makes the final decisions on policy. The foreigner is left with the impression that no official has the self-assurance nor sufficient authority to resolve issues on the spot no matter how simple or insignificant they might be. As a consequence, the prevailing method seems to be to divide responsibility among committees or other collective bodies which act in mysterious ways. Their decisions are not always wise because their members, often serving only temporarily, hold differing views and represent widely dispersed agencies of government. This method is exasperating when action is required on economic matters.

A curious contrast exists between the North American diplomat in a foreign country and the official who works in a division of the State Department. It is equally interesting to observe the transformation which the official undergoes if he moves from the State Department to an embassy. In Washington the tradition of democratic simplicity prevails, reflecting the style of U.S. political leaders, be they president, secretary, senator, or Supreme Court justice. But the North American official found outside the country, especially in other American republics, adopts a domineering and patronizing air. He seems to expect others to be agreeable, make conversation, and come to him. He places himself in a seat of honor from which he expects to receive the homage and petitions of everyone else.

The United States as a nation has grown up schooled in the virtues of selling commodities, ideas, policies in its own interests. The strange thing is that the selling goes on in Washington and not in U.S. missions abroad. On this point the North Americans are very different from the English, who act abroad as true agents of their country. The Americans, on the other hand, show no desire to create an atmosphere favorable to the policy of their country. They give the impression that the fact of being American, with the great influence that their country has on the entire world, is more than enough to establish their position. The result is that they frequently create fear instead of friendship and attract vested interests rather than affection. In addition, their "friends" often turn out to be those who profit in their wake, personally enriching themselves with their aid and who, therefore, are quick to abandon that friendship when the flow of aid is checked.

The November Executions

I had been in Washington less than three weeks when I had to intervene in an extremely unpleasant political matter which was about to change the course of events completely. I am referring to the attempted coup of November 20, 1944, and the executions that followed it, and its repercussions in Washington.

It was, I believe, on my last day in La Paz that I went to say goodbye to President Villarroel. I had to wait for a few moments in the antechamber because he was in conference with a group of army officers. Once the conference had ended, Colonel Francisco Barerro and Colonel Armando Fortún, among others, left the presidential office. I spoke briefly with Fortún, who told me that the general staff had been informed of a conspiracy involving several officers on active duty. He informed me that the president refused to give credence to the reports and was unwilling to take the necessary measures.

I then spoke with the president who confirmed what I had just heard. He commented on the difficult situation of a president who was unable to verify the accuracy of accusations that were so frequently made. He spoke of his aversion to violence and persecution and of his mistrust of the informers, who generally were inspired by personal interests and vengeance. He blamed them for the misery that the oppostion had to suffer and also, in some cases, for the fall of governments. For my part, I expressed to him my fear that the opposition was preparing a surprise attack. I pointed out the double game of the opposition who, while conspiring against the government, made an outcry in the international press when the government took steps to protect itself. This was surely affecting the credibility and prestige of the government. I concluded by telling him that I understood the situation fabricated by our adversaries. The government was obliged to let them plot, protected by the external pressure now being mobilized in favor of the exploiters of Bolivia.

I strongly urged Villaroel to bear in mind that Bolivia could not oppose the public opinion of the rest of the continent. Unfortunately this was still controlled by our enemies because we lacked the necessary force to impose our policies and make them independent of the criticism of interested groups. Time was needed to lay the foundation for the struggle to win over outside opinion. In the meantime we must proceed with special caution, trying to harmonize the internal control required by the revolution with the postures which had to be maintained abroad.

Since I was sure that Villarroel shared my ideas, my principal concern was that such thinking should influence the security organizations. I had reason to believe that the officers who composed these units had become extremely presumptuous, acting independently of the political responsibilities they owed the cabinet. They were not aware of the external factors nor of our country's dependence on them.

Errors and offenses by the weak are magnified; impunity, it seems, is always enjoyed by the strong. In most societies, for example, it is expected that a humble woman wear an immaculate integrity as a badge of her poverty. If she parts from conventional virtue by committing a sin, society vents its fury on her. If, on the other hand, the sinner enjoys the prestige of money and family, and knows how to keep up appearances, society not only pardons or ignores her sin, but praises her with prestige and poetry. The poor, however, must live subject to the chains of social convention.

Weak nations suffer the same fate. In exchange for the right to a sovereign and independent life, even though it may be the freedom to die of starvation, they must subject themselves strictly to the norms of conduct established by the more powerful nations. As long as the activities of a weak nation do not affect the interests of the great powers, they are not made subject to international political ethics. If a dictator supported by mercenaries sacrifices the lives of hundreds of peasants and workers on the altar of his ambitions, it does not matter as long as he leaves untouched the interests and concessions obtained by citizens of the great foreign nations. Let the dungeons of the dictator be filled with human blood; let women and children shed rivers of tears under the whip and shrapnel of paid assassins. Nothing will arouse the so-called continental conscience as long as that suffering serves to maintain the concessions given to corporations listed on the stock exchanges of New York or London.

Let the press be restricted or seized. Let radio announcers be beaten by bullies in the studios. Let political prisoners be killed in the prisons and women abused in the streets. Let thousands of workers be massacred with artillery and aircraft fire. Let thousands of peasants and their families be driven to swamps infested with snakes and tropical fevers. Finally, let the vote be denied to 90 percent of the nation's electorate. All this came to pass in Bolivia after the assassination of Villarroel. What is more, according to the propaganda of the mining interests, these measures were not contrary to democratic principles nor to the four freedoms proclaimed by Roosevelt.

If, however, a movement arises which opposes the centuries of servitude, and if it seizes power, then every instrument of investigation is put into play to make a microscopic analysis of its actions. A revolutionary government is not permitted to do anything which departs from the canons of superficial and strictly formal democratic procedure. In order to survive even temporarily, it must present itself garbed in virginal innocence, totally defenseless against slander, insults, and subversion.

Take, for example, the political party, the regime, or the leader who attempts to side with the great national majority; who dares to question the existence of privilege in the hope of creating opportunities for the majority of a nation's citizens; who conceives and proposes to carry out a plan which might be able to save the common people from their poverty and ignorance; who valiantly repudiates privileges due to race, religion, or birth; who proposes to uplift the masses without any condition other than hard work and right conduct. Such a party, government, or leader must come to terms with the problems raised by these revolutionary designs, and above all, with the web of international interests expressed and defended through control of public communications media. It is not enough to be on the side of justice in this modern world. It is absolutely essential to possess the means to make oneself heard, with a voice that can reach from pole to pole and circle the globe. This voice still belongs to the powerful, to those who form part of that invisible international society which is stronger than all the international pacts between nations.

Nevertheless, men continue to fight and die on the painful road toward liberation. Behind every advance guard destroyed by shrapnel or slander, new waves of men arise, advancing along the road strewn with heroic dead and washed by the blood and tears of generations. That which seems to defy explanation can be explained thus: force is not enough to subject a nation indefinitely. The sense of liberty and justice is part of the divine spirit that breathed life into man. The eternal struggle between good and evil begins in human consciousness and reaches its culmination in the collective life.

Realistically confronting the task of representing my country in negotiating a better basis for its economy, I knew then, as I know now, that each step would be as minutely analyzed as if the fate of the world conflict depended on it. The U.S. and European press does not have sufficient space to treat the domestic problems of every large country, and much less to concern themselves with the "small Latin American countries." It would, however, magnify our errors and, naturally, ignore our successes. Bolivia was the subject of dispute and therefore should proceed with caution. Although these are not the exact words, they are the thoughts that I expressed to Villarroel on saying good-bye.

During the afternoon of November 20, a journalist friend informed me that he had just received news of a revolt in Oruro followed by the execution of several figures associated with the previous government. Because I had already received direct reports, that was not news for me. What was surprising was the confidential information that a person linked to the American government shared with me moments later: groups in the State Department who had opposed the recognition of the Bolivian government were now preparing a memorandum to the foreign offices of the continent proposing the reimposition of the diplomatic quarantine on the Villarroel government. That piece of news proved to be true.

My conduct in more than forty years of public life, years in which I have been pursued and never pursuer; in which I have been imprisoned and exiled, but never jailer nor exiler; in which I have pardoned and done favors for those who have unjustly attacked me, should clear me of any suspicion of cruelty. But I must say that when I compare the attitude taken by our adversaries at that time to their later conduct, only my faith in the existence of an ultimate justice saves my spirit from total collapse.

The ten men shot in Oruro and Chuspipata have since been covered over by the bodies of workers, women, and children, all innocent. The ten were sacrificed to satisfy the appetite of those who profited by their death, and of those who, having hidden themselves away during the fray, came out to avenge themselves when the danger had passed.

For the Welles, the Bradens, and other U.S. officials of their ilk, the shooting of these ten citizens shook the foundations of civilization. On the other hand, the thousands of workers massacred in Catavi on one earlier, and two later occasions; the thousands of peasants killed in unprecedented butcheries; the prisoners dragged from their cells to be lynched in the public square by a group of hired and drunken terrorists; the holocaust of blood and the implacable hatred of the "democratic government of students, workers, and professors"; the murders, the disregard of the most elementary principles of human decency, the orgy of blood and death—all this failed to move civilized sentiment which yet cried out, with understandable furor, against the shootings of November 20, 1944.

My intuition told me the real purpose of the international scandal that was being stirred up. Therefore I decided to confront the situation directly. He who knows the State Department realizes that it is little short of impossible to make an appointment with the secretary of state in less than twenty-four hours' time. Luckily, Americans are not ruled by protocol, and when they find their interests and aims are not directly affected, they are inclined to tolerance. I was fortunate to find a man of Stettinius's caliber. He granted me an interview for ten minutes; I spoke without interruption for one hour and a half.

I began by telling him clearly that I was not justifying the violence, but was, rather, explaining the antecedents that culminated in the critical days of November 1944. The Chaco War had profoundly affected the spirit of the generation that had to bear the weight and the mistakes, the immorality and stupidity of the leaders of the previous generation. The thousands of men who died of hunger and thirst, the thousands who dragged their fleshless bones across that South American desert, were symbols of the ineptitude of the politicians and military officers who conducted that war.

If the war had been painfully bitter, the reality of peace was even more so. The astuteness of the leaders and the tiredness and lack of unity of the followers allowed the rise of another group of profiteers who did their best to complete the destruction. In the face of this spectacle, the country's true servants—those who were scarred and mutilated in the defense of national territory; those who suffered the anguish of three long years of a war without direction or meaning; those who had left friends and brothers rotting in the immense solitude—had all withdrawn like snails into their shells and let their bitterness grow.

The revolution of December 20, 1943, was a ray of light for those souls that had been submerged in darkness. For the first time they saw the ousting of traitors and the honoring of those who had sacrificed themselves to defend the fatherland. The counterrevolution of November 20,

1944, was a challenge to their very souls and obscured their perspective of the law. Their response was to punish the guilty. But the really guilty ones were at the time well hidden as usual, waiting to see the outcome of the plot. So several who had no reason to pay, paid with their lives. By preparing a memorandum which was aimed at intervention, the State Department seemed to be offering protection to the exploiters of my country. The merchants of pain and human misery in the tin mines would redouble their efforts to overthrow the government, and civil war would break out. Thousands of bodies would be added to the dead of Oruro and Chuspipata, increasing the human sacrifice for the sake of the economic interests of the tin barons.

Stettinius, who was far from being a radical but had considerable political insight, comprehended the truth. The proposed memorandum for international consultations with respect to Bolivia was tossed into the wastebasket.

My First Interview with Roosevelt

The Office of Protocol of the Department of State informed me that the president of the United States, Franklin Delano Roosevelt, would receive me on December 20, 1944. Although I was prepared for such an event, I was still impressed by the idea that in a few hours I would shake hands and converse with the man of the epoch. He was the most famous and powerful political figure of the century and the man who has left the greatest mark on the history of the American continent. And Roosevelt in person corresponded to the Roosevelt that I had imagined.

A limousine stopped in front of the Bolivian Embassy on Massachusetts Avenue, and out stepped an enchanting old gentleman, George T. Summerlin, smiling and silent. He had been for many years director of protocol. He was small, gentle, and elegant in his dark suit, and he looked like a Protestant minister.

This is one of the few opportunities that one has to ride in a White House vehicle. The huge carriage with bronze ornaments, the escort of grenadiers, the fanfare of military bands, the curious crowds that throng to see an ambassador's cortege pass—all are absent in the land of the Yankees. The substitute is this luxurious limousine, driven by a tall chauffeur with a good-natured air and an impersonal manner. The ceremony is the same for the ambassador of all the Russias, of the Duchy of Luxembourg, or of the people's government of Bolivia.

After taking off my overcoat and handing my hat to the receptionist, I entered a large vestibule with a great oval table in the center. I exchanged courtesies with an army colonel, probably one of the president's aides-de-camp, and then the elderly Summerlin directed me to a door.

In the brief instant that it took me to cross the room, I was reminded of the first time that I went to the town of Llallagua to see the engineer, Pickering, general manager of the Patiño mines. A Mr. Garrett, tall, fat, and ceremonious, served as the North American magnate's Summerlin. He shrouded the interviews that his boss granted in more mystery and solemnity than I found in my first interview with the president of the most powerful nation in the world.

Behind the door that Summerlin had pointed out, in a large oblong room, behind a desk covered with papers and statuettes, sat Roosevelt.

"Mr. President, I have the pleasure to present to you the ambassador from Bolivia," Summerlin said, as if reciting a prayer.

"I am very pleased to receive and greet you, Mr. Ambassador," said Roosevelt, extending his hand to me and inviting me to sit down next to him. Summerlin retired silently from the room.

"I believe that we must exchange something, Ambassador," the president said.

"That is so, Mr. President," I responded. "Here are my credentials that authorize me to be ambassador to your government, and here, in this other document, are my thoughts on what is for me a solemn and unforgettable occasion."

"Thank you very much, Mr. Ambassador. Here you will also find my thoughts." Saying this, he handed me an envelope.

The magic of his smile was undeniable. It was not the smile of the professional politician which ends in a grimace. It was a genuine smile, warm and cordial, not detractive from the strength of character visible in his manner. He seemed to radiate an irresistible magnetism. Whoever has been with Roosevelt has been in the presence of an extraordinary man.

Nevertheless, behind his smile and the eyes that reflected intelligence and goodness, one could perceive internal turmoil. Deep circles surrounded the sockets of his eyes. His broad forehead, furrowed by wrinkles, revealed an infinite weariness. It was not necessary to be a doctor to realize that the power and glory would very soon exact their price. His optimism and vitality were in tragic contrast with the fatigue that was bearing down on him.

Although he made no mention of the period of nonrecognition, his attitude confirmed what his written speech said about me. He knew my past and received me as a true friend. He expressed to me in a few words what was worrying him intensely: the war effort. It was necessary to mobilize all spiritual and physical forces to defeat the enemy. He described in broad terms the sacrifice of the North American people and their determination to continue indefatigably in pursuit of victory. Very subtly, he asked my opinion about Bolivia's cooperation in the war effort.

Briefly I explained the value of the contribution of the Bolivian mine workers. I also told him of the hard struggle against the jungle to extract rubber and quinine. I have always been convinced of the great contribution, in time of peace as well as of war, of the thousands of workers who suffer from silicosis and tropical fevers, of the thousands who have been buried in the bowels of the earth or in the heart of the jungle. Therefore it was not difficult to express my thoughts discreetly but vehemently.

Roosevelt spoke of his anxiety over the appearance and rise of totalitarian ideas in America, giving me an opportunity to offer a brief interpretation of hemispheric politics and sociology, which were what brought me to Washington. Latin America has always been a sounding board for European thought and the European drama. Such was the case of the French Revolution, of Marxist philosophies, and of totalitarian systems and practices. However, these reflections are limited to intellectual circles or serve briefly as a platform for political opportunism. The social and economic structure left by Spanish colonialism and the wars for independence is still the only one in existence. This is one of the reasons why, after almost one hundred and fifty years, the Latin American revolutionary process is still incomplete.

The true conflict is regional, stemming from political systems which do not represent the aspirations of the majority of the people. It is the struggle of the masses rising to the call of an industrial civilization which promises abundance and ease. They are rising up against the remnants of a feudal agrarian system and what is perceived as semicolonial exploitation in the extraction of raw materials.

To defend themselves against this advance, which began to gain momentum after the First World War, the conservative forces labeled their opponents as instruments or members of a conspiracy of nations that were striving for international political domination. Thus this movement was branded periodically as Communist, Nazi, or as belonging to some philosophy or political system which constituted a threat to the American community of nations. In this way the conservatives have been concealing their real position, alarming the unwary who did not understand the roots of the conflict, and frequently obtaining the indirect support of international public opinion.

I do not pretend to deny the existence of Fascists and especially of committed Communists, who in certain instances act as agents of foreign governments. However, I maintain that political programs associated with these ideologies sometimes are an expression of popular aspirations and concepts about how to organize community life. In other words, they represent aspirations rooted in the culture and tradition of the continent, roots which many theoreticians have tried to ignore or conceal.

Roosevelt's clear eyes expressed something to me that gave me assurance throughout the rest of my mission. He seemed to be interested in my uninhibited treatment of matters that fell outside the framework of this type of interview. I noticed an attitude of encouragement and sympathy. Was I, perhaps, repeating some of his own ideas which had led him to become the first North American revolutionary since Lincoln? When Summerlin entered, indicating discreetly that the alloted time was up, the president signaled him to wait a little longer. I stayed just a few more minutes, anxious not to abuse the president's courtesy. Summerlin's expression of consternation, as he entered for the second time, told me that it was time to leave. Once again we shook hands warmly and I left the room, comforted.

At that moment I met my friend Guillermo Belt, ambassador from Cuba, who was also going to present his credentials. Outside the White House some reporters were waiting. Upon seeing me they took pictures and asked me for a statement. The only thing I said was, "It is symbolic for my country that the president has received me on the very day on which Bolivia is celebrating the first anniversary of the people's revolution."

5

World War II and Bolivian Tin

Franklin Roosevelt deserves full credit for repudiating the "big stick" policy formulated by his cousin Theodore. In doing so he swept aside a century of fear and distrust which had divided Latin America and the United States. In a sense, by the Good Neighbor Policy, the United States established itself as a champion to liberate the masses from need, oppression, and slavery.

Roosevelt's reversal of U.S. policy toward Latin America had magnificent and immeasurably favorable results—for the United States. They were most evident in the contrast between Latin American policy in World War II and World War I. In World War I, except for a few governments under U.S. military occupation or direct fiscal control, most Latin American countries remained neutral or were frankly sympathetic to the Kaiser and his allies. In World War II, after the policy of nonintervention had been put into practice, most Latin American countries joined the United States in the war while the outcome was still in doubt.

The Good Neighbor Policy paid off even more for the United States in its economic relations with Latin America. During World War I, Latin American trade with the Central Powers continued; the blockade did not eliminate it completely. Prices of strategic raw materials went up as a result of high demand. In World War II, since Latin America's political position had already been decided in favor of the United States, economic agreements became part of the bargain. Prices were frozen by contract and, theoretically, since the Anglo-Americans were the only buyers, the prices were to be fixed by "common agreement." The history of the negotiations for the sale of tin is an instructive example of how "common agreement" was reached between Bolivia and the United States.

The Bolivian Miner

When I arrived in Washington as the new Bolivian ambassador in the fall of 1944, the long shadow of the Catavi massacre of 1942 still hung over the negotiations for a new tin contract. Since Bolivians had fresh in their minds the humanitarian phrases used by Roosevelt and Wallace, and since the latter still was vice-president and head of the Board of Economic Warfare, the mass murder at Catavi could not be hidden behind the usual silence and lies. Moreover, the event was linked to the war effort and to the Bolivian commitment to provide strategic materials. Other sources of tin, in the Far East, were blocked by Japanese control of the Malay straits. The Bolivian mine workers, the only ones who could work the mountain pits at an altitude of 12,000 to 15,000 feet, had thus acquired exceptional importance.

In the United States, men who had a humanitarian and liberal outlook were asking themselves if the methods employed at Catavi should be used to obtain war materials in the fight for freedom. Even those indifferent to the rights of the poor countries shuddered at the possibility that this only source of tin would be jeopardized and that the intensive production needed in those moments would not be continued. Consequently, there was unanimous reaction in favor of investigating the reasons for that mass murder. President Peñaranda was labeled by public opinion as a murderer, and Undersecretary of State Sumner Welles was accused publicly of supporting criminal policies. For me, the much-glorified solidarity of the Americas appeared about to reach the people themselves. It was under these circumstances that the United States sent the Magruder Commission to investigate and to report on conditions in the Bolivian mines. Was the United States willing to do something effective in this matter? If we, the Bolivians, had opened the doors of our house to such a mission to show them our misery, it was not because of exhibitionism nor the desire for sympathy. It was important to answer a basic question: Was the United States partly responsible, and, if so, did it have an obligation to remedy the problem? The answer seemed to be yes.

In the first place, Patiño Mines Enterprises Consolidated, Inc., is a corporation organized and registered in the state of Delaware, although it is well known that every cent of its capital has come from the sweat of the Indian miners and the sale of the tin they mine. Yet the company enjoyed the status of an "American company" which demanded and obtained the support of the diplomatic and consular representatives of the United States. The strange thing was that its owners posed at times as

North Americans in order to gain U.S. protection and at others as members of the Bolivian diplomatic service to avoid payment of certain taxes in the United States and Europe.

Second, and more important, the United States had obtained at the 1942 conference in Rio de Janeiro a virtual freeze on raw material prices for the duration of the war. The Bolivian government agreed to continue supplying tin ore without knowing whether prices in general could also be stabilized. Later, prices for other goods and services rose disproportionately due to shortages of manufactured products and to speculation. As a result the United States could not escape responsibility for the serious deterioration in the living conditions of Bolivian workers caught in the price squeeze.

Moreover, wages were extremely low in comparison to the gross value of production, particularly if we take into account the fact that work in the Bolivian mines is basically manual. I proved this in a pamphlet published in 1943, using figures, not subsequently challenged, based on the salary records of the companies themselves. The largest item in the cost of production for Bolivian tin was "administration and implementation expenditures." Each enterprise maintained an army of decadent European aristocrats who led a life of luxury devoid of work. While North American and British magnates endured a period of austerity, those French and Spanish playboys, supported by the tin barons, continued to collect and spend millions.

Meanwhile, the effort to achieve maximum production of strategic materials such as tin fell mainly on the shoulders of the Bolivian worker. The tin miners were as important as the soldiers in the front lines, and they should have received the same treatment and consideration that was given to the defenders of the democratic cause. I am convinced that many U.S. leaders believed that their country shared responsibility for the social situation in the Bolivian mines. Otherwise, sending the Magruder Commission would not have made sense. It would have amounted only to an impertinent intrusion, making our misery even more painful and pathetic.

In the personal report which I submitted after the tragic Catavi events, I upheld a fundamental concept. If we were going to depend on the goodwill of the companies or the existing fiscal arrangements to solve social problems, the workers and peasants would remain in misery, neglect, and ignorance. The high rate of infant mortality would continue to be the main cause of stagnation in population growth. If the sole wartime buyer of our minerals, the government of the United States, would allow a just increase in the price of tin, this increase should not serve only to augment the entrepreneurs' profits. It should be used to carry out a plan of social welfare designed to solve the problems identified in the reports by Judge Magruder, Mr. Kyne, and myself.

Another aspect of this problem relates to the allocation of profits to capital and labor. Capitalist theory holds that the greatest incentive for production is profit paid on invested capital. Without earnings, industry loses its dynamism and depression follows immediately. My question was: Why should the profit motive apply only to capitalists? Why not acknowledge that the worker who contributes his labor also responds to profit incentives?

The Bolivian case is a good illustration of these two extremes. The role of capital is especially related to the recovery, concentration, and transport of ore, to exploration, and to administration. Ore is obtained by the worker with his hands, either by opening the vein itself or by picking out pieces of shattered rock. Why then did North American negotiators always maintain that providing incentives to the owners was the best way to increase production? If instead the worker were to receive an incentive in material compensation, it was logical that he would also increase his output.

From the moment Jesse Jones and Leo Crowley took charge of U.S. mineral purchases, the worker was relegated to a secondary position where his ambition and need for incentives were not recognized. The worker had to be satisfied with being a simple cog in the machinery of production, and the owner only oiled it to obtain maximum returns for himself.

We had to negotiate a new contract with individuals who, to a greater or lesser degree, believed the traditional theories. They were not willing to accept the thesis of the Bolivian government and in their hypocrisy gave a distorted interpretation of the situation: the implementation of plans for social welfare was Bolivia's concern; the United States, true to its new nonintervention doctrine, should not meddle in internal affairs.

The First Tin Contract

When I began conversations with the Department of State and the Foreign Economic Administration (FEA), I discovered that the atmosphere had been prejudiced against the Bolivian government in a way that defies description. The Hochschild kidnapping, the attempt against the Communist agent, José Antonio Arze, and the shootings of November 20 —all presented in a lopsided and partial manner by our adversaries—had contributed to the formation of a black legend about the new government. In the eyes of some Americans, we appeared as a group of adventurers who had taken power to murder, confiscate, and dismantle the industrial apparatus of the companies. In the eyes of others, our policies were directed by Argentina with the purpose of blocking the war effort.

Our positive qualities were deliberately ignored. The fact that we wanted to protect the main elements in production, the workers, was not taken into account. Nor was the fact that, due to the confidence inspired in the workers by the new leaders of the nation, social peace had been achieved, meaning an increase in production. Finally, our extraordinary efforts to cooperate with respect to other strategic materials, such as avoiding contraband in rubber, were not recognized. The moans of the oligarchy which had been removed from its long-held position of absolute dominance in the country had, unfortunately, a greater impact, and it became the object of sympathy.

An official who acted as spokesman for the FEA in matters related to the purchase of minerals exerted a malevolent influence in the negotiations. He was Alan M. Bateman, a metallurgical engineer and former university professor. As a result of his professional specialization, he was called upon to act as principal representative of the United States in the negotiation of mineral contracts. If the only disadvantage of his character had been a one-sided technician's point of view, there would have been a possibility of arriving at a reasonable understanding. Bateman was not an ordinary technician, however, but one who was intoxicated by power and delusions of grandeur. The influence and power of the United States went to his mediocre head.

It is possible that there was a trauma in his past, a product of the anonymity of a professorship which permitted him to exercise no greater power than failing lazy and inept students. In his new capacity, he suddenly emerged from anonymity and discovered that he held in his hands the destiny of millions of individuals. The exercise of this authority made him drunk with power. If his arrogance had been known to the average citizen of the United States, it would have caused shame and revulsion. This person exercised authority against defenseless peoples, assuming dictatorial and insulting attitudes; he attributed to himself the powers of a supreme judge concerning the needs and conduct of the sovereign nations upon whom he attempted to impose sentences. Bateman was the prototype of those who exercise authority that they have neither earned nor deserved. Although he represented the government of the United States, I have always denied, out of respect for the great people of that country, that he represented the true values of American citizens. As we will see later, the arrogance which made him lose perspective also became the rope with which he hanged himself, only to return to anonymity. Nobody now knows who Bateman is, and it is only because of the need to discuss the tin negotiations that I will provide additional information about him.

An American engineer in Bolivia got into a fistfight with a mine worker. Bateman, encouraged by the mine owners, sounded the alarm. He exaggerated the danger to the lives of engineers working in the war effort and demanded special protection for them. His strange conclusion was that in these conditions it was not prudent to increase the price of tin. I was forced to put him in his place. The protection of American citizens in Bolivia should not have been the concern of Mr. Alan Bateman, but of the United States embassy in La Paz; the norms of international law were designed for matters of this kind. To link the price of tin to the personal conduct of workers and owners was an act of the most reprehensible coercion.

It was not necessary to go very far in the negotiations with Bateman and others to realize that the central thesis of the Bolivian government could not prosper. That an increase in the price of minerals could directly benefit the workers was a pill that the new FEA team found hard to swallow. In view of this, we had no alternative but to make our presentation for the record. In the future we decided to limit ourselves to efforts to obtain a better price.

Among the many interviews which I had with North American executives, one worth describing was with Leo Crowley, appointed by Secretary of Commerce Jesse Jones to replace Henry Wallace as chief of the FEA. In the feud between the two giants, Wallace and Jones, as frequently happens, we Bolivians were the ones who suffered most. They called each other names and accused each other of being liars. President Roosevelt had to settle the feud; he lifted Jones's arm, and thus the Bolivian tin miners were thrown back into their hopeless situation.

Crowley was a Wall Street financier. He had an imposing appearance, with a big face and hard, severe features, crowned by totally white hair. There was no sign of kindness in him. He gave an impression of being able to observe things coldly, with a total lack of feeling. Crowley's physical appearance was the stereotype of the shark of Wall Street.

When Crowley received me in his New York office, he kept me waiting for a long time. His purpose was apparent. Informed of the vehemence of my arguments, he realized that I had no qualms about calling a spade a spade. Furthermore, he knew that I had had the audacity to unmask the responsibility of the mineral purchasers concerning social conditions in Bolivia, a country which was completely defenseless in the face of a monopolized market. Therefore Crowley instructed his aides that the Bolivian ambassador should be kept waiting to "cool off." What he did not know was that this did not cool me off because I would have waited not only half an hour but an entire year to tell Crowley our reasons for demanding a better price. If his tactics were a show of strength, my position was too weak to feel it. When there is no resistance, one does not feel the strength of one's opponent. Whoever strikes a paper wall wastes his time. Since I was in no condition to strike back or to put him down during the interview, his action amounted only to a breach of courtesy. I waited as long as Mr. Crowley saw fit.

He received me in the company of another official. On his desk was a stack of papers, and he had a pencil in his hand. It was obvious that he wanted to show me that my visit was an unwelcome intrusion and that it should not last a moment longer than necessary. During my explanations and demands, he confined himself to listening with a disdainful expression, turning his attention at times to papers which had no connection with the matter under consideration. He asked no questions, offered no answers. His silence seemed to indicate that next to the billions of dollars he was handling at that time, my problem, that of the people of the Republic of Bolivia, held no interest for him whatsoever. However, I could tell that his attitude was largely an act, because I knew that Mr. Crowley could not help being interested in our rubber, tin, wolfram, etc., even if the values assigned to these materials did not quite match the nine-digit figures to which he was accustomed.

Fortunately, I know the social structure of the United States fairly well, and Mr. Crowley did not impress me as typical of the business community or other privileged sectors in the United States. As a comparison, I recall the openness, generosity, and cordiality of John Snyder when he was President Truman's closest associate. I have met rich and powerful men: the Rockefellers, Chryslers, Kaisers, and others. None of them adopted the attitude of a great tyrant. Rather, the impression these men conveyed was that the exercise of power filled them with fear of the Lord; they did everything possible to avoid excessive pride. That is why when I met Crowley, I understood the case of Alan Bateman.

The truth was that the process we were experiencing was not a "negotiation" because one of the parties had no alternatives. We Bolivians couldn't eat our tin, wolfram, or antimony. We needed to sell them to buy products which our people needed to live: food and manufactured goods. The other party, the United States, which also represented Great Britain, held all the cards in its hands. It could wait, or so it seemed, longer than we could. It knew our weaknesses: our total lack of fiscal reserves, and the permanent sabotage which the government suffered at the hands of the mine owners. We could not present a united front. The hostility between the tin barons and the people was our greatest disadvantage, putting us at the mercy of the purchasers.

The problem will be better understood when I describe later negotiations. Concerning the first contract, in addition to the disadvantages already mentioned, we had that of time. We had been exporting for more than a year without a contract. The producers demanded a fixed price in order to maintain production; the government needed to know the price of minerals in order to calculate its revenues and plan the budget. Credit, prices, salaries—in short, every possible aspect of our economy depended on a solution.

The considerations pertaining to workers' conditions were a separate issue embodied in the so-called labor clause. We intended to convert this provision into a true instrument for achieving some of the objectives with respect to the miners that we had sought earlier. In the meantime, we channeled the negotiations exclusively toward obtaining a better price, justifying our claims by referring to increases in the costs of production. These were caused by an increase in the cost of living which made it necessary to raise employees' salaries, and by higher transportation and insurance rates than in the prewar period. The scarce supply of vital materials made them all the more valuable, and the government needed the revenue to carry out its programs effectively.

The "negotiation" had the character of a petition, an appeal to equity and to the need to maintain production at acceptable levels. The buyer knew the limits of our resistance and was aware of the extent to which our political and social stability depended on his small payments for our tin. With an almost mathematical precision, he would apportion just enough money for us to survive and continue working without having to take desperate measures.

There were some factors, however, which favored our side. The United States desperately needed the minerals. It neither wanted nor could afford to risk a breakdown in the mines. Moreover, there were men in the U.S. government who believed that the Bolivian revolutionary government should be given the opportunity to carry out its programs successfully. Unfortunately the influence of these men was insufficient on two consecutive occasions as we shall see.

The unfavorable factors were many. We could not survive without selling our minerals, yet we had no buyers but the Anglo-American powers. The mine owners wanted the government to fall even more than it wanted a price increase. Finally, some of the North American negotiators believed that some nations were condemned by fate to suffer a subhuman level of existence, in order that the more powerful and privileged nations might sustain a high standard of living. Because these men supported the existence of privileged nations, they did not care about injustice or inequity among the people of a country like Bolivia.

Clearly the best strategy would have been for the government and mine owner representatives to present a united front. However, the producers' contribution was more negative than positive. They limited themselves to blaming the Bolivian government for the increase in production costs, criticizing "higher taxes" and the imposition of "social obligations." Because it was not convenient to their political ends, they failed to mention that without using any force whatsoever, work in the mines had been sustained continuously without any strikes. The mine owners' tactics strengthened the opposition since it was easy for them to argue that the Bolivian government was trying to make the purchaser bear the brunt of bad economic and social policies.

What were the tin barons seeking? Did the overthrow of a people's government have priority over an increase in the price of tin? Why did they avoid bringing up the real reason? The rise in the cost of living was due to the world war, which had increased the cost of producing minerals. This phenomenon could not be attributed to the government's labor policy nor to Bolivia's internal problems. It had its origin in events beyond the control of any government, in this case one which opposed the substitution of guns for whips as an instrument of production.

The principal argument of the mine owners was that taxes and the policy of social assistance were going to "kill the goose that laid the golden egg." But they were unwilling to admit that this, in reality, was the policy of the Peñarandas, Hertzogs, and Urriolagoitias, who would use bullets and bombs to destroy systematically the only ones who could work the mines: the miners themselves.

In spite of the warnings of the mine owners, the representative of the Mining Bank, and other members of the delegation, we finally obtained a price increase. The price was raised from $0.62 per pound, which had been paid before the revolution, to $0.635, to be retroactive to January 1944. This decision did not satisfy me completely, nor did I consider it equitable. However, it was the best we could hope for under the circumstances.

The War Effort in Bolivia

Bolivia's contribution to the war effort deserves further explanation. The prices of manufactured goods, which had a decisive influence on the cost of living, were governed almost exclusively by the law of supply and demand. The huge demand for tires, for example, had placed them almost out of reach; the scarcity of structural steel raised the price to 1,500 Bolivian pesos per hundred pounds in the market in La Paz, while the price theoretically should not have exceeded 400 pesos. In contrast, the prices of minerals, rubber, quinine, and other products which we were exporting were regulated by the agreements of the 1942 Rio conference where the Latin Americans yielded to the rhetoric of the

Padillas, Aranhas, and others while the Anglo-Saxons contrived to control the cost of the war and turned us into contributors but not beneficiaries. The wartime price controls operated as a funnel, with Bolivia at the small end.

Our sacrifice would have been justified if at the end of the war we had participated in the victor's prosperity. On the contrary, we found ourselves treated like poor relations who were shown the door because the party was over. North American officials were saying, "The honeymoon is over!" What honeymoon was this? Our relationship with the United States never yielded such benefits. We Spanish Americans, with Latin imagination and passion, had become enamored of diplomatic rhetoric in the early war years.

The men who received our protests had another favorite saying: "Uncle Sam cannot continue to play Santa Claus indefinitely." Viewing these episodes more objectively, could the amounts that the United States spent in Latin America be considered gifts from Santa Claus? A few examples should suffice. Bolivia sold approximately 9 million kilos of rubber to the United States over a period of three years during which the precious substance was intensively grown and harvested for the war effort. As a concession, the "contract" permitted us to sell 500,000 kilos of rubber to Argentina, which was paying $5 per kilo, as compared to the $2 per kilo paid by the United States. In this transaction alone, our gift to Santa Claus approached $30 million. The sum does not include what was paid on the black market, which so seriously corrupted Bolivian border officials.

One might argue, of course, that these prices were possible only because Indonesia and Malaya had been occupied by Japan and other means of producing rubber had not been perfected. This is true, but it does not change the fact that a truck owner in Bolivia had to pay ten times more than the prewar price to replace his tires and, therefore, had to adjust his freight rates according to these prices and not to those idealistically agreed upon in Rio de Janeiro.

I recognize the right and the obligation of North American diplomats to defend their country's interests in such matters using any ethical means. I do not, however, accept the idea that the United States in any instance played the attentive bridegroom on his honeymoon, or that it played Santa Claus. The United States was an inflexible negotiator, unwilling to part with a cent. We, on the other hand, had been put off our guard by charming speeches only to find out too late that we were unprepared for the ensuing confrontation.

We were also frequently reminded of the North Americans' sacrifices in the war effort and of the thousands of bodies strewn on the battlefields of Iwo Jima. I, like all those who have defended their homeland in time of war, am aware of how much those great sacrifices meant. However, participation in a cause which involves heroism and suffering is a far cry from a struggle over commercial rights and interests. Aircraft and tank manufacturers, whether or not they had sons at the battlefront, coldly continued to negotiate their contracts and to make profits in their businesses. A general's pay continued to be higher than that of a common soldier although the latter was the one fighting in the front lines. In other words, commercial and hierarchical considerations remained despite the wartime economy.

While minerals are our livelihood, their value is nothing in comparison to the human resources which we might have had to contribute. It is impossible to put a price on men's lives, whether they die from the explosion of a grenade or from lung disease in the mines. Our minerals acquired exceptional value when other sources of supply were cut off from the democratic world. In the end I believe that no one would have dared to hint at the possibility of insurance for us in case the allied nations found a substitute for tin. Perhaps we would have been brushed aside with no choice but to scratch about in our mountains for other ores.

When one is on the edge of an abyss, being in a ditch is a privilege.

The Strange Mr. Bateman

The first contract that I negotiated was relatively short-lived. Although we obtained retroactive terms, the United States committed itself only until June 1945. The price increase that we had obtained was opposed by Bateman in his untiring efforts to deny us our rights. I perceived him to be the real external enemy of the revolution, hoping to use tin as a lever to support our domestic adversaries. If his directives and desires were not followed to the letter, it was only because I was able to have his decisions countermanded by the State Department, where I had the understanding and friendship of Nelson Rockefeller.

Bateman showed his true colors and revealed his concept of our country in a curious episode. A U.S. citizen, N. Altschuler, who apparently had several friends in the offices of the FEA responsible for minerals, had acquired a tungsten mine near La Paz. It was a good mine, but he had to invest in the construction of access roads and the installation of a hydroelectric plant. In order to obtain the necessary credit, he needed sales contract guarantees. Judging from Altschuler's own statements, Bateman granted him this guarantee orally, without having the legal authority to do so. So Altschuler ended up with debts which he would have been able to settle if things had gone as expected. But in the middle of 1945, the FEA declared that it had completed its tungsten purchases. This resulted in Altschuler's sudden bankruptcy.

Whether it was simply an act of desperation or because he thought he could count on the active support of his friends in the FEA, Altschuler commited a serious offense, punishable by the penal codes of every nation. He sold notes in New York for $150,000 without having a cent in assets. One of these notes was bought by the Central Bank of Bolivia and another by a private broker. The explanation for the purchase, given by the manager of the Central Bank to the board of directors, was that Altschuler seemed to enjoy the full support of the FEA and for that reason his credit was honored.

Altschuler had simply swindled $150,000 and compounded his offence by fleeing with the money. The defrauded parties pressed suit. The charges were sustained in court and plans were made for the extradition of Altschuler, who had been detained in Lima. The request for extradition by the Bolivian supreme court was already in the hands of the Peruvian authorities.

At about this time I encountered Alan Bateman at a reception given by the Chilean Embassy in Washington. Bateman made a special effort to speak to me in private. Knowing that only a very important matter could make him act in such a manner, I gave him his chance in one of the embassy's small salons. He began to talk to me on the eternal subject of tin. To my surprise his tone was soft and persuasive; if I had not mistrusted the man so much, I would have thought that, for some reason, he had been converted to our cause. But suddenly he came to the point.

"This matter of Altschuler, Mr. Ambassador . . . I am extremely worried because I have been informed that the extradition papers have arrived in Lima. I believe that something could be done. . . ."

"I do not understand what it is that is worrying you, Mr. Bateman. It is a question of a judicial procedure taking its normal course."

"You know what I am referring to, Mr. Ambassador. If Mr. Altschuler is taken to Bolivia, he will probably be assassinated."

"I find your way of thinking alarming, Mr. Bateman. If you have any information about some plot against the man's life, which is within Bolivian jurisdiction, you will do us a great service in revealing everything you know."

"I do not know anything, Mr. Ambassador. . . . I only fear that Mr. Altschuler's life will be in danger as long as he is in the custody of the Bolivian police."

"I must remind you, Mr. Bateman, that you have no right to offend the honor and respect due to institutions of my country. I must also remind you that there is a United States Embassy in La Paz which will be able to take action in the event of a denial of justice or a lack of security. We deal with you only about contracts for the sale of tin."

"For that very reason," insisted Bateman, "I ask you to intercede. If you want, you can block the extradition process, making the parties concerned withdraw their complaint."

"I should not continue to discuss this matter with you, Mr. Bateman, but I will be frank with you. I cannot afford the luxury of making an enemy of you since we are subject to the power you wield in the purchase of minerals. My denouncing your interference in this matter to the State Department could place you in a difficult position, but they might let you continue in the discussions about the tin contracts. Therefore, the best I can do for you is to forget momentarily your insults to the administration of justice in my country and simply inform my government of the content of this interview."

"So Altschuler will be left to his fate?"

"Not to his fate, but to the proceedings and findings of justice. However, if you and your friends in the FEA are so concerned about his fate, why don't you invite the withdrawal of the complaint by canceling the debt?"

So ended this attempted pressure tactic by Bateman. I had to swallow my just indignation at being unable to avenge insults to one of my country's institutions. The happiness or the misery of many families still hung on the word of this peculiar personality.

The Collaboration of Stettinius and Rockefeller

I had great hopes for the second round of negotiations and did not want to see them destroyed by an imprudent act. Convinced of the partisan position of the FEA, I realized that the most effective way to counteract its attitude was through systematic work in the State Department. In spite of Bateman's authority, if the department took an interest in the matter, its influence would be decisive.

Throughout early 1945, I worked tirelessly to bring the leaders of the State Department around to our point of view, not only gaining the personal friendship of Stettinius, but directing his attention to the problems at hand. Taking care not to bore them with such a complex problem, I methodically sought to lay the groundwork for a favorable decision by the secretary of state and the assistant secretary, Nelson Rockefeller, once we arrived at an impasse with Bateman, as I knew we would. Fortunately, these two men, Stettinius and Rockefeller, were prepared to open their minds to the truth and were, moreover, respectful of the rights of others. They belonged to the new generation of capitalists who know that if capital is to maintain its rights it must remember its obligations to society. They recognized that an intransigent position on the part of capital facilitates class struggle and generates violence, and that for capital to isolate itself behind defensive bulwarks in the middle of a dynamic society would bring on the destruction of that society. These men believed then and believe today what Nelson Rockefeller said in a speech in 1949: "In this combination of social objectives and capitalist incentives this country [the United States] has a creative, dynamic force that can be effective throughout the world in serving the needs of the people."[1]

The outlook for the new negotiations, which were to begin in June 1945, seemed bright, even though Bateman would continue to be the spokesman for the FEA. We were informed that he believed a price increase or even the stabilization of present prices to be unsuitable. Given our increased production costs, we would be at a comparative disadvantage with Malaya once production there was resumed.

The decision of the State Department was needed to overrule Bateman. It was reached as a result of an interview which I had in San Francisco on June 14, 1945, with Stettinius and Rockefeller.[2] At that meeting I expressed my concern about the renewal of the tin contract as a means of assuring social and political stability in Bolivia. I explained that tax revenues from tin were essential for completing our long-term plan of development and meeting our social and economic problems, thereby avoiding a serious crisis. Secretary Stettinius expressed his sympathy and support for my point of view, and, in my presence, composed a telegram to the Department of State to that effect.

The Consequences of Roosevelt's Death

All this seemed to indicate that we would have complete success this time in our negotiations. Meanwhile, however, a tragic event had taken place: the death of Franklin Delano Roosevelt. My first reaction was simply one of personal sorrow because I admired this great statesman. Later I understood that his death would mean hunger and desperation to the miners of my country.

In spite of Roosevelt's death, the San Francisco conference, convened

1. "Material: Men Against Men—The Problem of the Underdeveloped Area," speech delivered at the Mid-Century Convocation on the Social Implications of Scientific Progress, Massachusetts Institute of Technology, 1 April 1949.

2. A record of the conversation is in *Foreign Relations of the United States 1945*, Vol. IX: *The American Republics* (Washington, D.C.: Government Printing Office, 1969), p. 579.

to draft the Charter of the United Nations, continued its deliberations. In the next chapters I will refer to those events and my role in them. While Stettinius dedicated all of his energies to assuring the success of this conference, political forces and pressures were mobilized to meet the new situation in Washington. Was it a continuation of the events of the Democratic party convention in which Harry Truman had been designated the vice-presidential candidate, putting an end to the hopes and ambitions of James Byrnes? Was it, perhaps, as some informed sources reported, that upon the death of President Roosevelt the colossal figure of Cordell Hull rose up again, blaming Stettinius for the change in policy toward the Argentine government? After the conference of San Francisco ended, I was stunned to see the headlines in U.S. newspapers: "The resignation of Secretary of State Edward Stettinus has been accepted. James Byrnes is the new secretary!" The scaffolding I had constructed so laboriously collapsed.

Whatever the reasons for this untimely change, the opponents of the policies of recognition of the Villarroel government and reestablishment of relations with Argentina returned to the State Department. Carl Spaeth was back with greater determination than ever. Soon afterward, Spruille Braden replaced Nelson Rockefeller as assistant secretary of state for Latin America, his aggressive policy towards Argentina putting all that we had achieved in Chapultepec and San Francisco in grave danger. Avra Warren was humiliated by being sent as ambassador to New Zealand. In like fashion, all the other high functionaries who belonged to the team formed by Stettinius and Rockefeller departed, one after the other.

Before the new team took over, the officials of the Department of State who had served under Stettinius eloquently showed the extent to which they were prepared to resist the punitive position of the FEA. In a letter to Leo Crowley on June 28, 1945, Undersecretary of State William L. Clayton described a reduction in the price of tin from $0.635 to $0.55 per pound as excessive in view of the continuing demand for tin for the war and as a violation of international agreements reached at the Chapultepec conference. Clayton proposed that the reduction be only to $0.60.[3]

As mentioned above, the secretary of state himself had sent a telegram from San Francisco endorsing the steps that Bolivia was taking to better its contract for the sale of tin. Those who know the levels at which these matters are discussed can appreciate the value of this gesture by my friend. One can understand why I was optimistic, in spite of Bateman's position, until I found out that Stettinius was no longer secretary of state.

3. Ibid., pp. 580–82.

I had one last recourse: to get to know the new secretary, James Byrnes, as soon as possible and obtain support from the outgoing secretary. Stettinius was good enough to introduce me to Byrnes with generous expressions about me and my contribution at the San Francisco conference. But it did not take long for me to realize that Byrnes was a completely different figure who wanted to give the impression that he had his own ideas and objectives and was not about to let himself be influenced by anyone. Once again I had the sensation that an abyss was opening before me.

Reality surpassed my fears. The Department of State did not want to intervene in the negotiations and gave Bateman a free hand. His arrogance increased and, believing himself fortified by the new situation prevailing in the Department of State, he set himself up as a dictator. That epithet may seem extreme: how can the spokesman for a democratic government which was fighting for freedom against totalitarian dictatorship be converted overnight into a dictator? Although it may seem incredible, that is what happened.

The Bolivian representatives gathered for new negotiations, since the old contract ended on June 30, 1945. The Mining Bank was represented by Jorge Alborta. The large mining interests had Mauricio Hochschild, who represented his own interests, and Jack Bowers, who represented the Aramayo Mines. Patiño was selling to Great Britain under the same conditions governing the contracts with the United States. The medium-sized mining interests were represented by Jorge Zalles; and I, as ambassador from Bolivia, presided over the delegation.

We were summoned to Bateman's office which was located in one of the temporary buildings constructed during the war in a beautiful park near the banks of the Potomac River. He received us, more puffed up than ever, surrounded by some of his assistants. After striking a solemn pose, he ordered one of his secretaries to read a document which was, in effect, an ukase.

The document, which was very long, can be reduced to the following: I, Alan Bateman, in name of the government purchasers, have decided that the price of tin shall be $0.635 until such and such a date, and that it shall then decrease periodically until it reaches, by the second half of 1946, the price of $0.585. Also, I have determined that the penalties for the presence of impurities in the ore be thus and so. . . . Then he added emphatically: "If one of you wishes to dispute these decisions, I have arranged for three chairs to be placed out there under a tree. I can assure you, however, that I will not occupy one of those chairs."

In spite of having been duly prepared to confront Bateman's temperament and attitudes, this edict left me completely dumbfounded.

Unable to believe my ears, I requested a copy of the document and the shorthand notes of the meeting. The other members of the delegation who had traveled thousands of miles to defend their points of view were left thunderstruck. Even Hochschild, who had worked so hard to turn Bateman against the government of Bolivia, realized that he had been wielding a double-edged sword. The ukase of the mineral czar affected not only the government of Bolivia, but also the mine owners.

One learns when dealing with the North Americans to think twice before answering even once. Loss of control or a violent reaction are advantages for one's adversary, unless one has a purpose in feigning anger. My natural reaction would have been to reject violently such impudence, branding his attitude as dictatorial, worthy of Hitler or Mussolini, throwing the ukase in his face. But it was apparent that Bateman had come prepared for such a development and planned to convert any gesture into a pretext for avoiding discussion of the matter. With studied calm, I simply requested the adjournment of the meeting, citing our need to inform ourselves in detail about the document. When the session was adjourned, Bateman insisted once more that he would not attend other meetings in which the orders that he had given would be discussed.

It is difficult to conceive of an individual so arrogant that he is unaware of the norms governing relations between sovereign nations. Bateman had decided to assume the role of dictator of the Bolivian economy. Perhaps he hoped to use this case as a precedent for assuming an equivalent role with other countries who found themselves obligated to sell minerals to the United States. The Chapultepec agreements on equitable treatment, the concilatory attitude of the North American delegation, the treaties on juridical equality of states, the necessity of maintaining the continent's economic unity, the Inter-American Economic Council—everything which had been patiently elaborated in multiple continental meetings wasn't worth the paper on which it was written for the magnificent and irrepressible Alan Bateman.

It would have been possible to create a scandal by appealing to the press and members of the United States Congress. But this road was filled with dangers because it would have begun a struggle which the weak would lose. The serious interests of the Bolivian people were at stake, and domestic politics, always uncertain in our land, made me adopt a more prudent course which turned out to be the most appropriate.

Bateman Defeated

My first step was to request an interview in the Department of State to confirm the official points of view expressed by Bateman. As the North

American spokesman, he went to that interview trying to bully us with his manner. I could not help but smile at his perplexity when he saw that my object was not to initiate nor to insist on a discussion of tin, but rather to formulate certain questions in order to obtain an official ratification of the position that he had taken. He did it with unparalleled arrogance. Once again he repeated that phrase about the "three chairs under the tree" with which he seemed to have fallen in love, and emphatically reiterated that the conditions laid down in the meeting meant "take it or leave it!"

Then I asked him, not as a public official but as a mineral expert, if he believed that Bolivia could survive without working the tin mines, and if we could sell the product of our mines to a third party. His answer was sharp and swift. "Negative on both counts."

I paused deliberately for a long time, as if I were attempting to find new arguments. When the silence began to become embarrassing, I limited myself to thanking him very courteously for having attended the interview. I took care to show him that I had not defied his "order" by trying to force him to occupy one of the chairs under the shade of the old tree along the Potomac, nor by discussing the details of the tin contract, a subject forbidden by Mr. Bateman himself.

While we were getting up out of our seats and preparing to leave the room, I noted moments of hesitation on Bateman's part. I believe he had just realized that his overconfidence had led him to lower his guard. That is how I caught Bateman and freed myself of a dangerous adversary. This was not, however, a personal feud. It was necessary to counter the blows without wounding the self-esteem of the person behind them. The counterattack had to be muted but effective.

I pretended for several days to forget about the tin and the contract that had been presented to us. In my own mind, I clung ardently to the question of principle, leaving aside the details of Bateman's ukase. I adopted the stance of a questioner representing a small country seeking to clarify in advance his position vis-à-vis a superpower, in this case the United States.

Should we be prepared for a new type of dictatorship? Did the attitude of the North American spokesman signal the first step in the modification of the juridical structure of the continent, based for so long on the equality of states? Would the United States set itself up from then on as the governing entity for economic and political questions in America? If such were the case, did we small countries have the recourse of appealing to the other branches of the United States government? If we found ourselves subject to the authority of an executive official, would we have the right to petition Congress or the United States Supreme Court? Upon what law or authority was the jurisdiction which Mr. Bateman was trying to exercise founded?

I pretended to believe that Mr. Bateman was not acting on his own and had not exceeded his authority. His actions could possibly be the result of new policies adopted by the United States following the victory over Germany. I therefore sought to clarify the situation and, at the same time, inform my people of the changes. Nonetheless, I believed that I had found a contradiction between the attitude of Mr. Bateman and what had been set forth and signed a few weeks earlier at the conference in San Francisco and in the Charter of the United Nations. Did this mean that the United States had resolved not to ratify the charter?

These and other questions made the friends of the FEA and the officials of the State Department shudder. I took care to emphasize that my questions were meant to confirm what seemed to follow from the attitudes of the FEA spokesman. I added that these were preliminary questions leading to a formal statement to the department on behalf of my government.

On August 6, 1945, Henry C. Ramsey, chief of north and west coast affairs in the Department of State, came to the embassy to greet me on my country's anniversary. I told Ramsey that both the content and form of Bateman's proposal of July 23 were unacceptable. I explained that I was cooperating with the mine owners to make a joint protest and expected their agreement on the maintenance of prices at their current level. I pointed out that prices for tin would have been much higher if they had not been controlled. Nor did I believe that prices for Bolivian tin should be reduced simply because tin from Malaya might become available in the near future. Although I believed that nationalization of the tin mines would be an error, it was a measure which the government might be forced to take in the ensuing crisis. Ramsey made my views known to his superiors, as a memorandum of this conversation later revealed.[4]

The final result of this episode was that Alan Bateman disappeared suddenly from the Washington scene. Someone said that he had requested retirement and had gone fishing for trout in the Allegheny Mountains. I never saw him again, nor did he ever play a role in subsequent tin negotiations.

Conversations were resumed with other officials of the FEA. It was officially recognized that the "form" of the U.S. offer had not been correct and did not represent the policy directives of the FEA. Since U.S. officials were placed in a defensive position, it was easy to arrive at a negotiated settlement: the extension of the contract for one year at the

4. Ibid., pp. 584–87.

same price. At the end of that period discussions would be resumed to determine whether it would be necessary to increase or decrease the price according to the then existing conditions. That was how the third contract was negotiated.

The denouement of this episode was that Bateman's dire predictions about the fall in the price of tin did not come true. As official spokesman for the United States, the eminent expert, Mr. Bateman, maintained all through the negotiations that the price of tin on the world market would go down to $0.50 per refined pound during the year 1947. He also predicted that once controls were eliminated, the tendency of prices would be downward, because by that time work in the Malayan mines would be fully under way. The reality was different. In 1947 the price of tin rose to $0.73 per pound and the tendency toward higher prices continued until 1949 when it reached $1.03 per pound of refined tin.

6

Setting the Stage for Peace

As 1944 was drawing to a close, one could feel the ebbing of the strength of the Axis powers. The Allies, on the other hand, grew stronger day by day, and there was an acceleration in the rhythm and impetus of their military effort. In anticipating victory, they recognized the necessity of establishing the foundations of a new international order and creating an organization to replace the League of Nations, which had been incapable of preventing aggression.

Current in world opinion were many themes about how to establish an effective new international organization. Among these were the beliefs that the stronger nations should have greater responsibility, that it was essential to provide for an international executive authority whose powers and strength would be sufficient to avoid conflicts and impose peace, and that an international armed force should be organized which would be capable of putting down any threat to the peace. In addition, there was support for broadening the jurisdiction and powers of the International Court of Justice and accepting the principle of compulsory jurisdiction.

Dumbarton Oaks

In this atmosphere, complicated by clashing political philosophies, the need to create a means to reconcile those differences and facilitate peaceful coexistence seemed even more urgent. The four great powers—the United States, the Soviet Union, England, and China (France was still occupied by the enemy)—decided to hold a meeting of specialists to formulate the bases for the constitution of a new international organization which would replace the "feeble and unsuccessful" League of Nations. This meeting was held in Washington, D. C., at Dumbarton Oaks during August, September, and October of 1944.

The deliberations of the delegates were carried out in strictest secrecy.

The rest of the world was merely informed of their outcome without having been invited to participate in the study of the theoretical foundations of the new organization. Even when the Dumbarton Oaks proposals had been distributed, what the designers expected to be done was not clear. Were changes to be suggested? Did they expect simple commentaries, or did they merely want to test world reaction to the proposals? These and other questions induced the Department of State to hold a series of meetings in Washington with the ambassadors of the other American nations in order to study the document.

By the end of 1944, several countries had submitted their commentaries and proposed amendments to the Dumbarton Oaks draft. The proposals sent by the rest of the countries ranged from simple praise to, as in the case of Mexico, an entire reworking of the Dumbarton Oaks design. The meetings were held without defining their scope or specifying the objectives to be pursued.

Although the outcome of these meetings was inconclusive, they did afford us the opportunity to meet the man who was behind the conception of Dumbarton Oaks. He was Leo Pasvolsky, a naturalized U.S. citizen from Russia. From that time until after the San Francisco conference, he was the silent figure in the background who seemed to determine U.S. views.

Pasvolsky was then in his fifties, short, and decidedly round of face and body. This rotundity did not suggest obesity, but rather the firmness and agility of a tennis ball. He resembled a priest dressed in street clothes, with a smooth and affable manner which did not completely disguise his pride in his own ability and in the power that he wielded. He spoke correct English with a strong European accent, in a soft and monotonous tenor voice. His reasoning reflected his technical command and vast knowledge of international affairs.

Pasvolsky's central thesis, which generally coincided with that of the Russians, was that the international organization should call for the abolition of all other international bodies. The chapter on regional arrangements was merely a temporary plan which would mean the slow death of the Pan-American Union and of the inter-American system in general.

The meetings began with the reading of the project and of the commentaries sent by the other countries. From the beginning, Pasvolsky played the part of official defender of the Dumbarton Oaks project against all attempts at reform. We all thought that the purpose of the meetings was to adopt new points of view in order to perfect the design. Therefore, when there was objection to the name "United Nations," in that it had been adopted for the war and not for peace, I proposed that the new organization's name be left until the end, not only of these preliminary meetings, but of the conference. Perhaps the world, itself, would give it an appropriate name. I recalled that it had been impossible to give a special name to the war, although President Roosevelt had suggested the adoption of a name which would express the goal of liberation. The world continued to call it the "Second World War."

There was a feeling of displeasure among the diplomats upon realizing the purpose of these meetings, although the displeasure was diplomatically concealed. Everyone continued to attend, without much enthusiasm, and with the only apparent motive of taking notes on what the great powers made known through Mr. Pasvolsky.

Bolivia had not elaborated any commentary or suggestion for revision of the Dumbarton Oaks proposals. The reasons were the long period of nonrecognition and the well-known weakness of the foreign office in matters requiring depth and dedication. In the end, we turned out to be the most realistic since the concerns of the other countries were ignored, their judicious studies ending up in the wastebasket.

In one of these meetings I brought up the need to define a practical objective which would go beyond simple indoctrination in the goals and content of Dumbarton Oaks. I suggested making a resumé of the coinciding points of view of the American nations for the Chapultepec conference. After their discussion and approval there, they would be presented to the San Francisco conference as an American opinion. It was to be understood that the United States would commit itself to sponsoring such views before the other great powers. My suggestion was supported enthusiastically, having adherents even among the U.S. advisors. However, Pasvolsky, who saw in this a threat to the integrity of the original project, employed all his influence to see that the plan was not accepted, probably acting according to some agreement among the great powers.

At this point in the sessions, the central theme that the Chilean delegation would take in San Francisco appeared. Marcial Mora, the intelligent Chilean ambassador to the United States, vehemently affirmed the necessity of including the phrase "respect of international treaties" in the chapter on the objectives of the new organization. While I had always believed Bolivia to be a country whose only defense of territorial or other rights lay in respecting international treaties, I realized that the Chilean embassy had its own particular ends in mind. It was in this way that one of the most interesting episodes of the San Francisco conference began. Chile was not defending this idea in any broad sense nor promoting peaceful coexistence within the law. Instead, its purpose was to put an end to the possibility of the revision of the treaty of 1904 which had walled off Bolivia. I communicated all of this to the foreign office, maintaining that we should concentrate on distinguishing between the terms "revision" and "respect," which have no true connection. The two terms operate separately, neither complementing nor excluding one another.

The Chapultepec Conference

The American nations should at this time have been formulating resolutions concerning the transition from war to armistice as well as trying to fit the inter-American system into the design of the world organization drafted at Dumbarton Oaks. The preliminary question was how an American conference could be held within the system when tradition and previous agreements provided for the participation of *all* American nations, irrespective of the legal status or diplomatic recognition of their governments. The Argentine republic, which at the time was diplomatically isolated, nevertheless had representation in the council of the Pan-American Union. Could an American conference be held that excluded one of the republics affiliated with the system?

The problem was solved by setting aside the Pan-American Union and having the government of Mexico extend invitations to attend a Conference on Problems of War and Peace in Mexico City. This name, because it was artificial and temporary, has been forgotten. The conference has been better known as the Chapultepec conference, taken from the name of the picturesque hill where the castle, dating from Mexico's imperial period, is located.

The host country extended invitations to every nation that had declared war on the Axis. There were some that had broken diplomatic relations but not yet declared war. They hastened to do so, and thus could attend the meeting. In this way, an inter-American conference was held without the presence of Argentina. The meeting began on February 21, 1945, and lasted for three weeks.

Our entire delegation had already departed from La Paz when the Department of State called me concerning a matter which showed how deeply the international slander had wounded us. Avra Warren, chief of the division of American republics of the Department of State, told me that the U.S. government had been informed that there was an Axis agent among our delegates. He requested that that person be removed immediately from the delegation if we did not want to face an unpleasant situation in the preliminary sessions of the conference. Convinced of the falsity and slander of the report, I positively refused to transmit such a message, indicating that we certainly would prefer to withdraw the entire delegation. I appealed to Warren's personal knowledge of Bolivian domestic politics. After a discussion which saved the day, I was able, with much relief, to have the request withdrawn.

Given our antecedents and our role as a delegation from a revolutionary government at an international meeting, it was important for us to take a position in accordance with our national prestige. In these cases, positions of honor in a conference chamber carry special meaning, both for the country's self-image and for its international reputation.

My initiatives had an unexpected effect. When Foreign Minister Chacón went to interview one of the most influential delegates, he was informed that that person was prepared to support the candidacy of Bolivia for the presidency of the Commission of Social Affairs if, in view of his international reputation on the subject, the position were filled by Ambassador Víctor Andrade. The Bolivian foreign minister immediately accepted this proposal, demonstrating his realization that personal interests should be secondary to the larger objectives of the revolutionary government. Following my advice, he called a meeting of the entire delegation to tell them what had happened.

In this meeting, Carlos Montenegro, the Bolivian ambassador to Mexico, stated his vehement opposition to such an arrangement. He did it in the name of the MNR, expressing the opinion that, since the head of that party was a member of the delegation, he could not permit him to be shunted aside. Either the commission should be headed by Víctor Paz Estenssoro or the offer should be refused.

Since such an uncomfortable situation had been created within the delegation, I asked the foreign minister to decline the offer, expressing our appreciation. He returned announcing that he had arranged appointments as secretaries of the economic and social committees. Paz and I carried out these assignments.

The Chapultepec conference had, apart from the Argentine question, three major items on its agenda: further measures for the prosecution of the war; arrangements for a postwar international organization; and the consideration of economic and social problems in the Americas.

The main achievement of the conference with respect to the first item was a resolution on reciprocal assistance and American solidarity, known as the Act of Chapultepec. The central provision of the act was that any attack by a state against another American state would be considered an act of aggression against the other signatory states. It constituted the basis for a defensive alliance. Two aspects of the act represented a step forward in the peace-keeping arrangements of the hemisphere. It went beyond the Havana declaration of 1940, making its provisions equally applicable to aggression originating within as well as without the hemisphere. It also made specific provisions for the application of sanctions, and, for the first time in inter-American agreements, provided for the use of force. The act took effect immediately because the signatory nations were at war with the Axis powers. It also constituted the basis for the Treaty of Reciprocal Assistance signed at Rio de Janeiro in 1947.

With respect to the second item on the agenda, it will be recalled that the Dumbarton Oaks draft proposals for the new international organization were drawn up without Latin American participation. Nor did they provide for the autonomy of the inter-American system. According to these drafts, for example, regional organizations could not take enforcement action without authorization from the proposed Security Council. As a result, there were fears that the inter-American system, which had demonstrated its vitality and relative efficacy for half a century, would be sacrificed on the altar of a new organization whose own efficacy was in serious doubt.

What should be the spirit of the decisions adopted in Mexico City regarding the Dumbarton Oaks proposals? Should there be an effort to formulate American points of view and act collectively to secure their adoption? The United States had clearly decided not to adopt specific measures in Mexico City. We were given to understand that it could not commit itself to modifying an agreement of the four great powers. Since the United States later changed its tactics in the discussions about Article 51 of the United Nations Charter, one wonders why a careful consideration of these questions could not have been undertaken at Mexico City in the hope that reason and justice would find their champion in a united America. Instead, the work of the committee in charge of discussing the relation between the inter-American system and the new world organization proved fruitless and unimportant.

One of the most important results of the Mexico City conference was the common action of the Latin American republics at the San Francisco conference later that spring. There they strove to save the provisions of the Act of Chapultepec and effect their inclusion in Article 51 of the United Nations Charter, which provided a second line of defense in the event that regional peace-keeping mechanisms failed.

The discussions on economic and social questions in Mexico City foreshadowed the continuing contrasts between U.S. and Latin American interests. The United States was fearful of higher prices for raw materials while Latin Americans wanted to liberate themselves from the yoke of foreign goods and dependence on the exportation of a few commodities. Differences also arose regarding the role of "free enterprise" and government. Moreover, the United States and Bolivia presented different proposals for representation on a future inter-American economic and social council. The United States proposal, which prevailed, favored representation by governments, while Bolivia proposed tripartite representation by government, worker, and employer delegates. Bolivia's position was based on the belief that Latin American industrialization required not only agreement between governments, but readjustments within internal national structures.

Much attention was also given during the conference to the absence of Argentina. The United States was finally forced to accept the unanimous Latin American position that Argentina's reincorporation into common continental efforts should be facilitated. The United States agreed to invite the Brazilian foreign minister to Washington to help find a solution to the Argentine problem.

Preparations for San Francisco

After the conclusion of the conference in Mexico City, we turned our attention to the conference in San Francisco to be convened on April 25, 1945, to consider and approve a charter for the new postwar international organization. With almost impertinent insistence I petitioned the foreign office to appoint the Bolivian delegation well in advance. Two principal reasons prompted me to do this. I knew beforehand the importance of this conference, not only in terms of our participation in the drawing up of the charter, but in terms of what the delegation's role could mean for the prestige of the revolutionary government. It was therefore my duty to create the best possible atmosphere for the personalities who might form the delegation. I was anxious to know whom the government would appoint to the delegation so that I could begin to use my influence to obtain some leadership posts at the conference. It is well known that preceding every international conference there is intense activity by all participating nations to obtain honorific or strategic positions. Those who hold such positions have an advantage as they maneuver toward national political objectives.

I was invited to several meetings in Washington designed to arrange the formal aspects of the conference, but my participation was limited because the foreign office did not give me the necessary information. To the many inquiries about whether I would be part of the delegation, I was unable to reply either affirmatively or negatively. The insecurity, anxiety, and uncertainty in which the Bolivian politician lives is proverbial. This is due not only to his opponent's activities, which are unscrupulous, but to the actions of our own colleagues in government, who often do not hesitate to set traps. I knew that I was opposed on two fronts, by some leaders of the MNR in our Congress and by our press, which was dominated by sectarian feelings. I was also acquainted with the intrigues of displaced persons from international companies.

Although our work began in an atmosphere of confusion, I nevertheless had frequent conversations with my good friend, Senator Arthur Vandenberg. I encouraged him in his noble effort to ensure that the United Nations Charter contain specific provisions for the revision of international treaties that had been imposed by force. Those treaties were potentially negative elements which could undermine the peace, the peace that the new organization was to preserve.

The close contact that I maintained with Secretary of State Edward Stettinius and Assistant Secretary Nelson Rockefeller went beyond formal relations between public officials. These friendships allowed me to obtain the promise that the United States would back the Bolivian delegation's bid to chair one of the committees. Nelson Rockefeller mentioned the committee which would study the Economic and Social Council. To this and other overtures, I had to respond evasively because any affirmation about my role in the delegation, had it later been proven unauthorized, would have made matters worse.

When I received a cable informing me that I had been named head of the delegation just two days before the opening of the conference, I hesitated to accept the appointment. Only my deep love for my country, the responsibility that I had assumed from the time that I participated in the overthrow of the previous regime, and the friendship and respect that I had for Villarroel persuaded me to accept. I have never been able to discover the reasons for the delay. The Bolivian delegation was thus composed of the following: Víctor Andrade, head of the delegation; Carlos Salamanca, Luis Iturralde and Eduardo Arze Quiroga, delegates; Walter Montenegro and Mario C. Arroz, secretaries; and Joaquín Aquirre and Julio Quiroga, attachés.

During the preliminary meetings in Washington, I was promised the chairmanship of the committee which was to study and draft the powers of the Economic and Social Council. Meanwhile, I had received instructions to propose an amendment to the charter authorizing either the Security Council or the General Assembly to revise international treaties which might endanger future peace. Therefore, I had to maneuver quickly to obtain instead the chairmanship of the committee which would deal with the treaty-revision issue.

I took advantage of the interest that the Indian delegate showed in the committee for the study of the Economic and Social Council. I hastened to call on him to inform him that we were prepared to yield the chairmanship in view of the important role India should play in future economic and social problems. Because of this action, we obtained the support of both the United States and Great Britain for the chairmanship of the committee that was to study the political and security powers of the General Assembly. In this committee the touchy subject of the revision of the treaties would be treated. I was elected by the steering committee and ratification in the plenary session took place without further difficulty.

In view of the number of attending nations and the high quality of the delegates, I consider election to preside over a committee to be an unforgettable honor for me and for my country. However, it is one thing to be chosen for a position and a title and quite another to perform at the level required by such a post. The questions to be discussed were difficult. The men whom I would have to call to order were giants on the world scene. I was also well aware of the difficult and challenging problems which resulted from rules of procedure, multiple amendments, and different languages. Tact would be essential to avoid incidents.

The delegates who attend international meetings do so passionately, with the objective of enhancing their national and personal reputations. These international encounters often become real battles in which nations defend their respective points of view. Delegates are depersonalized, they stop acting as individuals and become champions of the views and values of their countries. The heavy pressures that are brought to bear are strange to the novice in these matters. Enormous sums of money are spent on receptions and public relations for what a superficial examination would call merely satisfying a nation's vanity. Something much more important is at stake. According to the quality and character of their representation, the various countries acquire positions that later affect their capacity to achieve foreign-policy objectives.

The delegate of a small country has a tremendous disadvantage because his influence is determined only by his good judgment, courage, and resourcefulness. The delegate of a great power, however, speaks with the backing of great military and economic power. The words of Stettinius, Molotov, or Eden were always considered to be important although they were often only repetitions of something already said. The mundane comments repeated by a representative of a small nation were lost in anonymity and obscurity. The boldness of the concepts put forth by a delegate from a small nation had to be carefully measured because if they appeared imprudent, the resulting ridicule would threaten his country's international position.

The Press at San Francisco

A delicate and important aspect of the San Francisco conference was relations with the world press. There were more than three thousand newspapermen in the city on the lookout for news. The reporter is interested in three kinds of news: first, exclusive and sensational news; next, commentary on the development of events; and last, anecdotes or human interest stories about important persons. The flamboyant or vain delegate often erred by providing too much of the last type of material, deceiving himself if he believed that such an approach would increase his country's prestige. On the contrary, it could evoke laughter or pity. A delegate who talked too much could be responsible for errors in stories, and newspapermen might begin to ignore him. Therefore the news had to be reported carefully; one's colleagues also depended on it. There were items that should not have been reported because, while they may not have been "state secrets," their premature disclosure was a breach of faith with the other delegates. Although the "newsy" delegate was momentarily praised by the press, mistrust very soon caused him to lose his sources of information.

As president of one of the committees, I had to hold a press conference almost daily in the central auditorium of the Veterans of Foreign Wars Building where the committees met. I realized that it was better to tell the press in advance that there was no news than to keep the reporters waiting anxiously, only to speak of routine matters or subjects which had no news value. This was appreciated by the press, especially the big papers and major wire services. They were also glad to be given advance notice of the possibility of sensational news. In this way, they could get ready to send out major stories.

Sometimes newspapers picked up stories almost intuitively. They would assign several reporters, who, taking advantage of friendships developed during the conference, tried to put two and two together. When a delegate became aware of this, it was best to level with the journalist, who appreciated candor. Sometimes this meant informing him of the impossibility of making a statement yet, sometimes simply giving him immediately what he was looking for. By carefully considering these matters, one could acquire influence with the press. A representative of a great power could occasionally afford the luxury of being indiscrete and hostile; the representative of a small country had to conduct himself just right.

I was fortunate that my press conferences were always well attended, in part because they were held in English, and because I took care to keep the content interesting and to satisfy, as much as possible, the reporters' appetite for news. I believe this is the reason that the U.S. press, often brusque, uncongenial, and overbearing with the representatives of small countries, treated me exceptionally well. One of the most important daily newspapers said of my first speech before the plenary session that of the dozen speeches given, mine was the only one that contained constructive ideas for universal peace.

The *San Francisco Chronicle*, the largest newspaper on the West Coast, said in reference to my second speech, delivered on June 21 in the plenary session that had been called to hear the results of the labors of the Second Commission: "It is the best speech that has been given in the nine weeks that the conference has lasted. . . ." One who knows the American press, its frugality with praise and its moderation in editorial comment, will understand this as an exceptional compliment. *La Prensa* of New York also called attention to the *Chronicle*'s treatment of my speech.

When the new president of the United States, Harry S. Truman, arrived in San Francisco to attend the closing of the conference, all the delegation heads were at the airport to greet him according to strict protocol. As was expected, hundreds of photographs were taken as the president extended his hand to each delegate. The goodwill of the press toward me is demonstrated by the fact that the photograph of the Bolivian delegate shaking the president's hand was the one used for distribution throughout the United States and in the major magazines of the world.

I point these things out, not from vanity, but to show what can be obtained by respecting and studying the human spirit. The Bolivian delegation had been provided with only a bare subsistence. Not a cent was left over to pay for receptions or for the publicity that other delegations had. It was not possible to demand of the country what it did not possess. Therefore, the Bolivian had to be perceptive and work especially hard to achieve what others could sometimes secure with money.

Memorable Breakfasts

The day after our arrival I received a note from Nelson Rockefeller inviting me to have breakfast every morning in his apartment. I thought this was merely generosity on my friend's part, but afterward I realized it was something more. Every morning he invited different heads of delegations, according to the subjects being discussed at the conference. In this way he was giving me the opportunity to learn at first hand things to which I would not otherwise have had access. Moreover, it was extremely instructive to get acquainted with the men representing the different countries; there was no more strategic way to find out the objectives of their policies.

Every delegate wishes to anticipate events in order to keep his government informed and give the impression of being well situated. There was nothing more useful to me than those breakfasts in Nelson's apartment. They were something of a sacrifice because I went to bed late and wanted, with all my heart, to stay in bed, but the call of duty and the need to take advantage of the occasion overcame my desire to rest.

Two other U.S. advisors also attended these breakfasts. One was Avra Warren. I have considered him one of the few Americans to grasp the true political situation in Latin America and for this reason to have deserved the confidence Roosevelt placed in him. Another advisor was lawyer John Lockwood, reserved, analytical, and extremely intelligent. The Ecuadorian ambassador, Galo Plaza, also attended, and both of us, while soaking up this wealth of information, brought up problems or concepts which led to a healthy exchange of views about conference developments.

The Chairmanship of the Conference

Early difficulties over the candidacies for the chairmanships of commissions and committees having been overcome, the first conflict causing a real sensation was the dispute over the chairmanship of the conference as a whole. Although it apparently had no more than formal importance, the dispute revealed Soviet global strategy for the first time.

After several unofficial meetings, a consensus was reached to follow precedent, that is, the delegate of the host country, in this case the United States, should preside. As a result, the attitude of the Soviet Union in the first session of the steering committee was disconcerting. To the proposal that the chairmanship should belong to the host country, Mr. Molotov, minister of foreign affairs and head of the Soviet delegation, reacted promptly. With precise, curt phrases he flatly opposed the proposal, maintaining that the four sponsoring countries, the United States, the Soviet Union, the United Kingdom, and China, ought to preside on an equal footing.

The state of tension caused by this confrontation of giants preparing themselves for combat made the first session dramatic. The dreamers and romantics, and present as well as past victims of conflicts between the powerful, exchanged glances of consternation, anguish, and fear. The world held its breath as the two most powerful nations came face to face in the global arena. Rebel opposition formed to "stop the Soviet 'colossus' now."

As in many other diplomatic scenarios, out of the confusion arose the voice of the representative of the United Kingdom, the glamour boy of the conference, the elegant Anthony Eden. With skill and subtle tact, he proposed a compromise: four chairmen would be elected, but three of them, by common accord, would withdraw in favor of the distinguished and eminent delegate from the United States. The first session was adjourned without arriving at any agreement.

The Latin American delegates had a special meeting in Nelson Rockefeller's apartment and decided to propose the following solution: to name the U.S. delegate as chairman and the delegates of the other sponsoring powers as vice-chairmen. The U.S. delegate, by a gentleman's agreement, would preside only over the opening and closing plenary sessions. Ezequiel Padilla offered to propose this compromise the next day.

When the session was convened, Molotov once again insisted on his position. He reasoned that since the four powers were sponsors of the conference, they were equal. He openly referred to Russia's role in the war, claiming the respect due to her sacrifice. He declared that she was not prepared to let anyone else take first place in the future leadership of the world. Padilla asked to speak next and, in his own special way, gave a carefully elaborated speech, proposing the idea agreed upon the day before in the Latin American group.

Molotov, upon hearing the translation, could not disguise his displeasure. He immediately stood up and exclaimed rudely and aggressively: "The Mexican delegate has delivered a memorized speech and therefore has not answered my arguments. He brings up traditions and precedents which are not being questioned nor discussed here. I ask that he respond to my arguments and not say things that he has memorized."

There was great consternation in the hall. No one had expected such a violent and aggressive response. Did Molotov know what had long been a subject for comment in Latin American circles, that Padilla always memorized his speeches? Was such an allusion merely a coincidence? The fact is that it produced a shudder in the assembly, while the perplexity of the previous day increased.

Another incident demonstrated the Soviet position regarding small countries. When the irrepressible delegate from Honduras, Julian Cáceres, spoke on this issue, merely repeating ideas which had already been expressed, Molotov interrupted him, exclaiming disdainfully, "Honduras thinks this way . . . but Russia thinks otherwise." His words and gestures left no room for doubt that he wanted to point out the smallness of Honduras in comparison to the immensity of the Soviet Union.

There were many possible explanations for the Soviet attitude. Undoubtedly they wished to establish that the Soviet Union was a power on which the destiny of the world depended, that it would give way to no one in matters of prestige and authority, and that its word should be decisive in the solution of any problem. What was probably more disorienting for the other delegates was that the Soviet Union had been expected to take advantage of the San Francisco conference to establish itself as the champion of the small nations, thus neutralizing the great influence of the Anglo-American bloc. It had been expected to follow the pattern of the Communist struggle and try to present itself as the defender of the rights of the masses. In doing so, it might please the nations whose emerging political parties saw socialist theories as means of combating the influence of capitalist countries. In other words, it was expected that the Soviet Union would proselytize among the nations at San Francisco as had the Third International among the working masses of the world.

Soviet conduct had opposite results. The small nations shuddered in terror and met together to offer greater resistance and defend their rights. Whether due to the skill of British diplomacy or to Russian ingenuousness, England came forward to raise the arm of the United States, the champion, who defended the sovereignty of small nations, their rights, and their contribution to the war against the Axis. So, at least in this episode, the countries considered to be typically imperialistic turned out to be the defenders of the colonial or semicolonial nations against the advances of a new imperialism.

If it was the objective of the Soviet Union to frighten the rest of the world, it admirably succeeded in San Francisco. What I have not been able to understand is what the U.S.S.R. hoped to gain. If its purpose was simply to establish its claim to leadership in the postwar world, it did so by losing the goodwill of the small nations.

Once again the skill of the United Kingdom in effecting a compromise was demonstrated. Eden, speaking with studied simplicity, as if he were proposing a friendly toast at a golf club, proposed a solution which was finally accepted: four chairmen would be elected, but the U.S. delegate, besides being one of the chairmen of the conference would also preside over the steering committee and the executive committee. In this way he would retain virtual control of all the work of the conference. As practical men who cared more about results than form, the Anglo-Americans appeared to have given way but in fact carried the day.

Two scenes complete this portrait of Soviet tactics at the conference. During the impasse about the chairmanship, when the hall was in a tense mood, Molotov suddenly exclaimed, "I want to know what the French delegate thinks about this controversy." Every face turned towards Georges Bidault. Imaginations conjured up a vision of France in turmoil as extremist elements marched forward at an irresistible pace. Here was France, her economy prostrate, needing U.S. aid more than ever before. France was caught as in a vice between two giants.

Bidault pretended not to hear the question. He remained immobile, deaf to Molotov's request. Those seconds were an eternity. Time stopped; the world balanced on a needle. The French delegate said nothing; the unanswered question hung in the air like mist, dissolving in the distance.

The other unforgettable scene was the Czechoslovakian statement on the chairmanship issue. Jan Masaryk, son of the Czech patriot who fought so hard for his country's independence, also found himself caught in a vice. His country bordered the Soviet colossus while his interests and values inclined toward the West. His appearance conveyed the presence of a volcano within. His eyes, darkly circled, were those of a man condemned to perform an act completely opposed to his convictions or to die. He rose slowly from his seat with gestures totally unlike those of the Masaryk I had known earlier in Philadelphia. With a barely audible voice he read a statement supporting the Soviet position. Were his manner and facial expressions deliberately designed to impress the Americans, letting them know that such a statement was imposed by the circumstances? The spirited Masaryk, an orator who never used to lose an opportunity to demonstrate his perfect English and to assert his personality, remained silent and neglected during the rest of the conference. The final act of this drama took place in Prague when Masaryk's broken body, found under the window of his house, again posed an unanswered question for the future.

Argentina Versus Poland

One of the first good opportunities to determine the position of the participating countries was the dispute over the admission of Argentina and Poland. The coup d'etat of 1944 in Argentina removed General Pedro P. Ramírez from the presidency and put General Edelmiro J. Farrel in his place. The U.S. government began the machinery of consultations and then denied recognition to this new government, persuading the majority of American countries to follow suit. Bolivia hastened to reestablish diplomatic relations, and Chile, Paraguay, and Ecuador recognized the new government almost simultaneously in order to free themselves from the consultation process.

As mentioned above, the Chapultepec conference had to take place outside the framework of the Pan-American Union so that the Argentine government would not have to be invited. Argentina's absence was significant because at that time it was the most important country in Latin America, one with whom all the other countries had ties of many kinds.

The ambassadors of Chile and Ecuador, Marcial Mora and Galo Plaza, along with myself, were conscious of the atmosphere in the Latin American community. Taking advantage of our personal friendship with Secretary of State Stettinius, we held a confidential meeting with him and Rockefeller during the Chapultepec conference. We communicated the reality of the situation, saying what other nations hesitated to express openly: if Argentina's absence had been lamented at Chapultepec, it would be even more tragic in San Francisco, where America should present a united front to the other blocs already being formed. After an exchange of opinion, and observing the good humor of the secretary of state, we suggested that it was necessary to request the assistance of the other great Latin American country, Brazil. So, Foreign Minister Léon Velhoso was invited to visit Washington as soon as the Chapultepec conference was over.

In Washington, a small committee of eight Latin American ambassadors was organized, myself among them. With Velhoso presiding, we held several meetings in Blair House, the guest house on Pennsylvania Avenue across from the White House. We finally reached agreement, and Galo Plaza and I immediately prepared a brief memorandum of five points in which Argentina would agree: (1) to break relations with the Axis and declare war; (2) to take effective measures to eliminate espionage and Nazi activities within her territory; (3) to adhere to the economic warfare measures agreed upon at Chapultepec; and (4) to subscribe to the Act of Chapultepec. In return the United States would promise to sponsor the recognition of the Farrel-Peron government by other Latin American governments and promote her admission into the new world organization. Nelson Rockefeller took this document immediately to the White House and within half an hour he returned with the document bearing the initials F.D.R., signaling its approval.

Following the Chapultepec conference, Argentina fulfilled her part of the bargain and was recognized by the American countries that had not already done so. The next move was up to the United States: to obtain an invitation for Argentina to attend the United Nations conference in San Francisco.

Meanwhile, Soviet sponsorship of a new government in Lublin worried the United States and Great Britain because it meant the exclusion from Polish soil of the Polish government-in-exile in London. Reacting strongly, the allied governments sent declarations to every nation at the conference, and Stettinius left no doubt that the United States would not recognize the Lublin regime. In an early meeting of the steering committee, the United States proposed that the delegate of Argentina be admitted to the conference since Argentina had declared war on the Axis. Simultaneously, the Soviet Union proposed the admission of the Lublin government, clearly hoping that both governments would be admitted as a compromise.

When the western governments refused that trade-off in the steering committee, the Soviet government opposed the admission of Argentina at one of the first plenary sessions. The final vote was overwhelmingly in favor of admitting Argentina and rejecting Lublin's bid. The twenty-one votes of the American states were supported by the British Commonwealth and by Asian and Middle Eastern countries. The tense debate eliminated optimism about future harmony among the great powers and suggested the necessity for strengthening the regional system in the Americas.

The Argentine delegation, presided over by the elegant and genial ambassador, Miguel Angel Cárcamo, was warmly welcomed by the Latin American countries but was received coldly by the countries that had been predisposed against her. Argentina did not play a significant role at the conference, and the delegation's participation was discrete and timid. It seemed to want to pass unnoticed. What a difference from the position the Argentines have adopted at other international conferences! The concessions they had to make to obtain a seat at San Francisco were a severe blow to Argentine pride, but as true statesmen they drank the bitter cup and awaited the future quietly.

What caused the United States to adopt such a severe policy toward Argentina? In his memoirs, President Truman explained that U.S. refusal to recognize the Farell government for over a year was because of its pro-Axis activities and because it had not fulfilled its commitments for hemispheric defense. He explained that after Argentina had declared war on the Axis, the United States recognized the government, and supported its readmission into the inter-American system and to the United Nations conference for the sake of continental solidarity. For the great majority of Latin Americans, the State Department's position was not very solid since it appeared to be severely punishing an American country for defending its neutrality. May it be that an independent attitude on the part of an American country can be characterized as insubordination?

Anecdotes of San Francisco

The majority of the Latin American ambassadors traveled to San Francisco from Washington in the same plane. Nelson Rockefeller and Dr. Leo S. Rowe, director of the Pan-American Union, traveled with us. Almost all of us stayed at the St. Francis Hotel. As soon as our rooms had been arranged, we accepted Nelson Rockefeller's invitation to meet in his apartment to converse before the social round began. To our surprise, we discovered there that the suitcase of Galo Plaza, the Ecuadorian ambassador, contained several bottles of Scotch whiskey, a liquor of incomparable value during the war. It was not available in stores or bars because of restrictions on its export by the United Kingdom.

Rockefeller called the hotel desk and requested a waiter to bring luncheon menus, a portable bar, and set-ups. When the waiter arrived and we had ordered lunch, the host asked him to prepare some cocktails, asking each guest what he wanted. We noticed a peculiar embarrassment on the part of the waiter, who exclaimed, overcoming his timidity, "I cannot mix cocktails because I do not belong to the bartenders' union. If I did, I would be invading the territory of another union." Hearing our expressions of surprise and amusement, he turned to Galo Plaza. "You are an American. Help me explain this to these foreigners [including the only North American, Rockefeller]. We have orders to do everything possible to see that their stay is pleasant, but one thing I cannot do is ignore union rules." One of the ambassadors who was not affiliated with any union acted as bartender and this incident was closed.

Another entertaining episode occurred during the discussion about what the official languages of the conference should be. After a laborious informal debate, it was resolved to adopt five official languages: English, French, Spanish, Russian, and Chinese. English and French were adopted as working languages.

In one of the frequent meetings of the Latin American delegates with Nelson Rockefeller, the Brazilian ambassador, Carlos Martins, proposed with great emphasis that Portuguese also be adopted as an official language and requested the support of the other American delegations. He offered as proof the argument that Brazil had nearly fifty million inhabitants, that it covered the largest area of any American nation, and that it had participated in the war with an expeditionary force. Some members of the North American delegation responded that although his reasons were very respectable, the inclusion of Portuguese would evoke an equivalent demand by the Arabs and Indians. They asserted that this would cause problems for the secretary's office since it would be necessary to improvise the translation into unforeseen languages.

Most of the Latin American delegates remained silent since no one wanted to support a case which had little chance for success. The exception was the ineffable Julian Cáceres, the Honduran ambassador in Washington. He was the essence of tropical exuberance, completely undaunted by the prospect of being ridiculed or committing an indiscretion. Believing that he was pleasing the American delegation, he attempted a special argument to convince the Brazilian delegate to retract his demand.

"My dear colleague Martins, I do not understand why you insist that Portuguese be adopted as an official language if Spanish has already been included among them. They are twin languages! You see, my distinguished colleague, when you preside over the sessions of the council of the Pan-American Union and give one of your eloquent speeches, I and the rest of the representatives of Spanish-speaking nations find that Portuguese is the same as Spanish."

"One moment, my esteemed colleague," Carlos Martins responded.

"You understand me when I speak in the Pan-American Union simply because I have always spoken in Spanish as a gesture of courtesy toward my Latin American colleagues."

Don Julian, as usual, was not upset, and joined the general amusement at this unexpected end to the debate.

7

The Issues Joined

The United Nations conference in San Francisco used as its working document the Dumbarton Oaks proposals, together with later amendments suggested by the conference's great power sponsors. The conference was divided into four main commissions: the first for the preamble and the first chapter of the proposals; the second for the powers of the General Assembly and the Economic and Social Council; the third for the Security Council; and the fourth for the International Court of Justice. These commissions were divided into committees where the real work was done and whose operation occupied more than 90 percent of the conference.

Committee II/2

After closely examining the matters on the agenda, I concluded that the most important controversies would be over the powers of the General Assembly, particularly those related to security. Therefore, I considered it advantageous to acquire an influential position in the Second Committee of the Second Commission (II/2). Luck was with me and I was chosen to be chairman of that committee.

Among the forty-nine delegates on Committee II/2 were people of international reknown and influence. Without a doubt the dominant personality was Senator Arthur Vandenberg, the most important member of the Foreign Relations Committee of the U.S. Senate. Andrei Gromyko, Soviet ambassador to the United States and later foreign minister, represented the Soviet Union. The chairman of the Australian delegation was Herbert Evatt. The eminent Professor Dehouse represented Belgium, and Prime Minister Peter Frazer, New Zealand.

Vandenberg chose Committee II/2 because he was most concerned about the powers to be assigned to the General Assembly. He maintained that the General Assembly of the United Nations should be a town meeting of the world. Vandenberg wanted the countries to be able to meet in an international public forum to express their opinions freely and to defend their rights.

Vandenberg's life and work are a model for those who aspire to participate in domestic and international politics. I remember him with great affection and gratitude. In the last session of the committee he proposed a special tribute and the award to me of the gavel that I had used during our two months of deliberations. He also praised me in the U.S. Senate when the ratification of the United Nations Charter was being discussed. These actions, however, are not so much the reason for my admiration as are his intellectual capacity and the extraordinary force of his personality.

Andrei Gromyko, the mysterious Russian, is difficult to describe and evaluate. He then had the appearance of a precocious disciple, a dedicated representative of the new school of Soviet diplomats. His face reflected a permanent seriousness, never crossed by a smile. He had sad, dark eyes which seemed to be fixed on the distance. Nothing moved him; his facial muscles never contracted in surprise, joy, fear, or anger. Expressing neither satisfaction nor fatigue, he was the consummate poker player. His speeches were carefully considered and meticulous. I never heard him improvise. When he had to make some correction on the spur of the moment, he did so with the care and precision of a tightrope walker. He was not an orator; his exposition was clear, cold, and monotonous.

The second Soviet delegate to the committee was a young professor from the Ukraine. Thin and dark, he had the mien of a seminarian. He functioned masterfully as Gromyko's double, barely concealing his innate suppleness and vitality. He, too, was a product of the diplomacy of the Bolshevik Revolution. Extremely discreet, they both obeyed orders like soldiers, their gestures revealing not the slightest personal reaction. Rigidly disciplined for collective efforts, their concern for detail went to extremes. They never tired of insisting on a point when they did not understand its meaning, nor did they hesitate to raise endless questions, whether it pleased or displeased others. Seeming to move in an atmosphere of permanent mistrust, they were always on the defensive. Even the most innocent and simple proposal had to undergo their suspicious scrutiny so that no hidden provisions might injure Soviet interests.

Herbert Evatt, Australia's minister of foreign affairs, was a man whose robust personality made him something of a loner. Although Deputy Prime Minister Ford was the head of the Australian delegation, Evatt was continually speaking and acting on his own. Only Evatt, of course, could do this, since besides representing an important element in the

Australian cabinet, he was exceptionally dynamic. He attended sessions of four or five committees a day, informing himself on all the details and proposing plans and procedures with a vigor that evoked wide admiration. He seemed more like a prosperous and honest shopkeeper than a British diplomat. Although thickset, rough mannered, and carelessly dressed, he lost his peasant ways when he spoke from the floor and was revealed as a leader of the masses.

Evatt used this world forum to play politics in the grand manner, increasing Australian prestige and making his views stick. His success was unparalleled. Although he was practically unknown when the conference convened, he emerged at the end as a true world leader of the age. He overshadowed his own delegation and his Commonwealth colleagues, MacKenzie King of Canada and Marshall Jan Smuts of South Africa. In spite of their prestige and experience, they were ignored like two old politicians who had gone out of style, as the rugged figure of the Australian emerged on the world stage.

The New Zealander, Peter Frazer, could not conceal his rivalry with Evatt. He attempted to follow his example but achieved only a poor imitation. He had neither the character nor the charm of his Australian neighbor. Evatt's unaffected style consistently evoked congenial responses, while Frazer was coldly received at nearly every turn.

The United Kingdom was represented in the committee by Mr. Dingle Foot, the epitome of the British civil servant: courteous, subtle, and extremely discreet. He participated in debates prudently, following parliamentary procedures in the style of his country. Alternating with Foot in the committee was Professor C. K. Webster, an elderly man with carelessly combed hair who resembled the professorial stereotype portrayed in novels and films. An eminent historian and authority on the Congress of Vienna, he was also the author of two volumes on the influence of Great Britain on the Latin American independence movement. He was a poor speaker, often confused by words and concepts, but he was invaluable to the work of the subcommittees because of his inexhaustible knowledge and his mastery of the written word.

Two delegates from Latin America, Eduardo Zuleta Angel of Colombia and Padilla Nervo of Mexico, distinguished themselves. Zuleta was a historian whose fluent Spanish was precise, calm, and correct. A pompous speaker, he liked to hear himself talk, reiterating his ideas and overloading them with metaphors. He had a sharp mind with the insight of a Latin American lawyer. He defended his point of view, often the opposite of our own, with vehemence and passion. Padilla Nervo was the supreme pragmatist. Oratory did not interest him, and in this respect he differed from the chairman of his delegation, Ezequiel Padilla. Padilla

Nervo always found a solution to problems, no matter how intricate. He had great knowledge and experience in the affairs of international organizations, and this proved of great value in the work of the committee.

Impasse Over the Assembly's Powers

Among the most important issues discussed in our committee was the scope of the subject matter with which the General Assembly could deal. Would this great international tribunal be limited as to the character and extent of its business? An amendment introduced by Australia tried to respond to this question, proposing, in effect, that the General Assembly discuss and make recommendations respecting any subject concerning relations between nations. The amendment was submitted to the committee under the prescribed procedures and the vote took place without further discussion or opposition. A few days later, however, the Soviet delegate dramatically reopened the matter. He said categorically that Russia did not accept the text of the amendment.

A question of procedure arose. The amendment had been approved in all its stages and the time had passed for proposing its reconsideration according to the bylaws of the conference. Consequently, the majority of the representatives opposed reopening the discussion, attempting thereby to overrule the Soviet objection. In response, the Soviet delegate assumed an unyielding position and declared that his delegation would not sign the charter unless the approved article were removed.

As chairman of the committee, I was caught in a difficult and critical situation. On the one hand, the position of Australia and of the other countries, who maintained that the matter was closed, was just and deserved a favorable ruling. On the other hand, realizing the gravity of the Soviet position, I saw the danger of being overruled by some arrangement made outside the committee among the great powers and of thus being rebuffed. I had to find a solution which would reconcile the two extremes: maintain the prerogatives of the chairmanship while protecting myself against the possibility that the matter would be reopened in spite of the committee's vote.

It was obvious that the conference would not be allowed to fail over a procedural question, and with this in mind, I held back my decision. In a dramatic session, the Australian delegate Evatt created a sensation, upbraiding the Soviet delegation. Showing no emotion, the Soviet delegate responded as though repeating a litany, "Mr. Chairman, Russia does not accept the Australian amendment in the form that has been approved."

Evatt returned the attack with admirable vigor. He explained the significance his proposal had for the democratic procedures of the organization. He attacked the Soviet position on secret treaties and secret protocols so passionately and eloquently that he won the hearty applause of most of the delegates. The Russian delegate remained impassive. He did not refute any argument, nor give reasons nor replies to the various questions posed. Once again he repeated, "Mr. Chairman, Russia does not accept the Australian amendment in the form that has been approved."

The delegates of Egypt, Belgium, Mexico, and several other countries arose and demanded that I put an end to the matter and pass on to the next agenda item for the day. I looked at the delegates of the United States, Great Britain, and France, and saw in their faces expressions of sympathy. They remained silent, indicating that some sort of compromise might be in the wind but that it was my obligation to enforce the rules of the conference.

I found the solution and said more or less the following. "Fellow delegates, as far as this committee is concerned, the matter of the Australian amendment is closed and I cannot permit its reconsideration, as the position of the Russian delegate would require. However, for difficult cases in which we come to an impasse that could endanger the success of the conference, there is a steering committee to which we will refer the matter. If the steering committee decides to discuss the matter, it is within its rights to do so. If that committee resolves to entrust to us the task of finding a solution, I believe that our obligation is to do so." Raising the gavel and striking the table with authority, I continued, "The chair rules that the reconsideration proposed by the Russian delegation be referred to the steering committee."

It was a happy solution reflected in the relief felt by the other forty-eight delegates. Everyone seemed to be satisfied with the compromise although no one dared to interpret the true motives of the Soviet position. I have the impression that the Kremlin feared unlimited discussion in the General Assembly because such discussion might involve issues where international affairs impinge on domestic policies. Take, for example, the matter of immigration. Several countries have adopted and continue to impose discriminatory measures. An open discussion of this subject would place many countries in an embarrassing position, since it is not easy to reconcile such restrictions with declarations of liberty, equality, and democracy.

Now that this matter had been temporarily resolved in Committee II/2, there was a great effort behind the scenes to make sure that there would be no opposition in the steering committee to reopening the matter. At the meeting of this committee—formed by the chairmen of the delegations and presided over by Stettinius—it was found that the great powers had agreed to reopen the question. The committee approved by a unanimous vote, but it was still undecided where the matter should be discussed. The chairman proposed that the question be returned to Committee II/2 for solution. All the delegates turned their glances to me as Stettinius submitted his proposal to a vote and then said, "I believe that it is unanimous, but to be sure, I ask that those who oppose this motion raise their hands."

In all the room only one arm was raised: mine. Sincerely spontaneous, this gesture won the sympathy of all the delegates. They realized the immense difficulty of the task entrusted to me and interpreted my gesture as a good-humored protest. Stettinius asked me to stand and proposed that the conference delegates give me a round of applause and, thereby, a vote of confidence. The chairmen of the delegations stood and gave me a standing ovation.

I will never forget that scene: surrounded by delegates from fifty countries, among whom were figures of world renown, I was profoundly moved by the applause which they offered affectionately and enthusiastically. My action had served to reduce the tension, but their applause was also a tribute to a representative of a small country which was striving to cooperate in this worldwide effort.

The arduous work then began and I found myself obliged to maintain a frantic pace. A subcommittee under my chairmanship, formed by the delegates from the United States, Russia, Great Britian, Australia, Belgium, and Mexico, was charged with drafting the article that would define the powers of the General Assembly. We examined every word in the dictionary trying to find a formulation acceptable to all. At times it seemed that our efforts would prove futile. We were proposing a formula that had to be submitted to Moscow. It was a strange situation in which we were really holding discussions with persons on the other side of the globe. We advanced inch by inch in what seemed to be an interminable journey. At times discouragement beset us and we needed to summon all our patience. We would meet again and once again irreconcilable positions would be taken.

Meanwhile, the other committees' work had been completed. The whole conference, more than three thousand people, had their eyes on my committee. The press anxiously tried to discover the true reasons for the conflict, but I knew that premature publicity would only hamper prospects of a solution, and so all the members of the subcommittee were sworn to secrecy. Several days passed with meetings in the morning, afternoon, and evening. They began in an atmosphere of pessimism in the face of the tireless resistance of the Russians, for whom time was an ally. At last, after a tortuous ordeal of ten days, we arrived at a formulation that was incorporated as Article 10 of the U.N. Charter:

The General Assembly may discuss any questions or any matters within the scope of the present Charter or relating to the powers and functions of any organs provided for in the present Charter, and, except as provided in Article 12 [referring to powers of the Security Council with respect to the maintenance of peace and security], may make recommendations to the Members of the United Nations or to the Security Council or to both on any such questions or matters.

The Revision of Treaties

The Dumbarton Oaks proposals made no reference to the problem of the revision of international treaties. This was a subject that greatly interested many countries, and especially Bolivia because of its loss of access to the sea under the treaty of 1904, which concluded the War of the Pacific.

No matter how strong and convincing, the arguments presented by small nations were unlikely to achieve the incorporation of this principle into the charter without support from one of the great powers. Therefore the first step was to obtain this support. Luckily for Bolivia, an ally of the first magnitude appeared. He was none other than the American senator, Arthur Vandenberg. He was a man of exceptional influence, given the difficulties of maintaining a united front for furthering the war effort. He was also the most important U.S. delegate at the San Francisco conference.

If one wished to imagine the archetypal statesman, no better model could be found than the real Senator Vandenberg. He had the appearance of an Anglo-Saxon patrician. Tall and broad shouldered, he had an honest, kindly face covered with lines carved by many years of intense living. On first acquaintance he evoked admiration, respect, and affection. His clear blue eyes radiated goodness and sincerity. He spoke with the assurance of a veteran politician and an experienced parliamentarian. His voice was virile and his gestures had a natural dignity. His thinking was straight and clear, without subterfuge or compromise. He therefore had the courage and the habit of expressing his ideas with dazzling clarity.

Vandenberg was born in Grand Rapids, Michigan. He was editor of a newspaper in his native state as well as being an illustrious lawyer and author of several historical studies of Alexander Hamilton. When he first came to Washington in 1928 as senator from Michigan, he embodied the dominant attitudes of the Midwest. In other words, he was an isolationist who believed that the destiny of the country would best be served by a policy of looking inward, letting the world face its periodic crises without the participation of the United States. Nonetheless, Vandenberg was an intelligent and honorable man. He made great efforts to assure the Democratic administration of Republican support for the war effort and later seized the problem of worldwide justice and peace with the same passion, skill, and dedication that he had displayed when he advocated isolationism. He became a true champion of the organization of a new world in which justice would triumph over force and tyranny.

Vandenberg was influenced not only by the failure of the Treaty of Versailles and the League of Nations to prevent such acts of aggression as the invasion of Ethiopia, but by events on our own American continent. Among these was the War of the Pacific, which had resulted in the unjust denial to Bolivia of access to the sea. Should several generations of Bolivians live enclosed by their mountains because of a war brought about by the ineptitude, immorality, and provincialism of its leaders? Can the greed of a nation which attempts to solve its economic problems by despoiling a neighboring country be condoned indefinitely? This region of the Pacific coast lacks water and other essentials to human life. Is it, therefore, indispensable to the lives of the peoples of Peru and Chile? Must Bolivia impassively await economic strangulation and be kept from its rightful place among nations?

The great American, Arthur Vandenberg, rebelled against this glaring injustice. He saw that one of humanity's greatest obligations is to rectify the wrongs of the past. International treaties imposed by force engender problems that impede mankind's peaceful progress. They create situations which systematically deny the ideas which the United States propounded in leading its people in one of the most intense war efforts known to history. So, the great senator formulated a declaration which moved world opinion: he would employ all of his influence to see that the U.S. Senate did not ratify the United Nations Charter unless it provided for the revision of international treaties that were based on injustice and endangered world peace. Vandenberg's position would have been decisive if total opposition to it had not arisen from another great power, the Soviet Union.

Ever since the first meetings of the conference, the Soviet Union had opposed the inclusion of any article related to revision of international treaties. Its delegates presented impressive arguments. They said that Germany, which would sign treaties ending the war, could eventually resort to such an article to avoid complying with the treaty obligations. It was impossible to convince the nations terrorized by Nazi invasions that Germany had not needed the dispensation of international law to break the commitments made at Versailles. There was a desire at the conference to create an international security instrument that would prevent repetition of the aggression which had culminated in World War II.

The difficult negotiations with the Russian delegation, which threatened to withdraw from the conference if the charter did not satisfy its interests, resulted in a compromise known as the Vandenberg Amendment. It was officially presented by the sponsoring powers and then approved in Committee II/2. This amendment, incorporated into the body of the charter as Article 14, provides:

Subject to the provisions of Article 12, the General Assembly may recommend measures for the peaceful adjustment of any situation, regardless of origin, which it deems likely to impair the general welfare or friendly relations among nations, including situations resulting from a violation of the provisions of the present Charter setting forth the Purposes and Principles of the United Nations.

With agreement among the great powers on the Vandenberg Amendment, the problem of treaty revision was practically resolved as far as the drafting of the charter was concerned. It was important, however, during discussions in Committee II/2, to prevent any change in its wording and to establish the basis for its interpretation and application in the future.

The position assumed by Vandenberg encouraged the revisionist nations to present, in their turn, other amendments. They did this not because they were certain of approval, but rather to affirm the principle and reinforce the spirit of the Vandenberg Amendment. The countries presenting draft amendments which were favorable to the revision of treaties were: Belgium, Bolivia, Brazil, Ecuador, Egypt, and Mexico. The countries which represented a united front against specific mention of treaty revision were principally the U.S.S.R. and her Eastern European satellites, and, in America, Chile, Colombia, and Peru.

Bolivia proposed several amendments concerning the power to revise international treaties within the General Assembly and the Security Council. We were able to separate the concept of revision from the proposals presented by Chile about "respecting" the treaties, demonstrating that in all societies, respect for law does not prevent the creation of the legal means and instruments for its modification, revision, or abrogation.

Upon its return home, the Chilean delegation made statements which were received with skepticism, even there. It asserted that its action had prevented the specific mention of the revision of treaties. Everyone knew that this question of principle had been resolved by the compromise among the great powers. It was also known that Vandenberg had said that he accepted the clause "any situation, regardless of origin" because he considered it to be even broader than the specific mention of treaty revision. It clearly covered situations involving the existence of an unjust treaty or one signed under duress.

The Chilean delegation focused its efforts on obtaining a special mention in the charter of "respect" for international treaties as a counter to the revisionist thesis. This concept, however, is mentioned in the preamble of the charter in such a way that it correlates with the Vandenberg Amendment. The preamble calls for the establishment of "conditions under which justice and respect for the obligations arising from treaties and other sources of international law can be maintained. . . ." Such a formulation allows for situations in which certain treaties produce burdens that are too heavy to be borne indefinitely by a community. In such cases the world organization could take the necessary steps to reestablish these conditions so that the obligations created by a treaty could be maintained.

During the plenary session which considered the results of our work in Committee II/2, a confrontation occurred between the Chilean delegate, Manuel Maza, and myself. Commenting on the importance attached to the Vandenberg Amendment by the countries supporting the revisionist thesis, I pointed out that weak countries feel more acutely than strong countries the burden of unjust and insecure arrangements which, sooner or later, require a solution. They can never agree to the limitations imposed on international politics by vested interests. They have faith in justice. That is why they subscribed to Senator Vandenberg's amendment and agreed with him that Article 14 should not be interpreted as preventing the consideration of the revision of treaties by the General Assembly.

I argued that provisions for the revision of treaties do not imply the failure to fulfill them, but, rather, that they take into account the need to reconsider obligations that cannot be honored. Direct and friendly negotiations would be preferable; the world organization should intervene only where efforts to reach a friendly and equitable understanding have failed and peaceful relations between states are endangered. I concluded that the Bolivian people, encircled by the Andes, looked to the future with the faith that the world organization would someday study the problems arising from Bolivia's landlocked condition and recognize her right to associate with the rest of the world through free access to the sea.

After complimenting me on my contribution to the deliberations, the Chilean delegate expressed the view that my preoccupation with revisionist problems prevented the committee from benefiting fully from my "intellectual resources" and "wisdom." He claimed that Senator Vandenberg was more inclined to emphasize the implementation of a treaty. With reference to boundary treaties, he emphasized that once in effect, they became a historical fact. He added that "when there are military victories, the subject is terminated by the imposition of force." That Prussianism resounded loudly through the conference, whose purpose was precisely to condemn brute force.

That phrase and the attitude it represented did not escape the attention of the newspapers. They gave my speech a prominent place, wrote large headlines about Bolivia's landlocked situation, and commented favorably on our cause.

The Veto and Regional Arrangements

The theory upon which the newly founded world organization rests implies certain limitations on the sovereignty of small nations. Responsibility for the preservation of peace lies principally with the great powers, whose agreement and unanimity are the only effective guarantees of world peace. An opposing vote or the nonconformity of one of these great powers paralyzes the work of the organization. In other words, the great powers reserve for themselves the power to oppose and override measures which they consider to be contrary to their objectives, interests, or inclinations. The small nations have six seats on the Security Council, but their individual or even their collective action would not be able to influence a decision even though their interests might be deeply involved. So the smaller nations have limited sovereignty because of a freely accepted juridical principle.

Although this principle was derived from the political realities of World War II, the concept of the complete sovereignty and juridical equality of all nations had been maintained as one of the pillars of international law and coexistence among nations. The veto, which the great powers have reserved for themselves in the United Nations, has put an end to this fiction, and has recognized inequality among nations as a juridical principle of the new international order.

The positions of the great powers with respect to the veto varied. The Russians took the most aggressive line, pointing up the weakness of the smaller nations. The Americans were the most persuasive, keeping in reserve the veiled threat that the charter would not be ratified if it did not contain the veto. The British worked silently, behind the lines, leaving combat at the front to others. A variety of arguments was advanced in support of the veto. Since the war had been won principally by their effort and sacrifice, all the great powers should belong to the world organization. The exclusion of any one of them would mean another war, perhaps in the near future. If the veto were not written into the charter, the parliaments of the great powers would not ratify it, thereby nullifying the new organization. The conclusion from this line of reasoning was that the small countries should rely on the great powers to keep the peace, just as they had relied on them to win the war. Finally, the great powers could not and would not limit their sovereignty by subjecting themselves to the decisions of the majority.

During the Chapultepec conference in the spring, Secretary Stettinius had revealed that one of the agreements reached at the Yalta conference in February concerned voting procedures in the Security Council. It was decided that the *sine qua non* for any decision by the Security Council was unanimity among the great powers. In other words, the opposition of one of them would suffice to defeat a resolution. This constituted the essence of the veto power which the great powers now claimed for themselves.

The objections raised by the other countries, medium-sized and small, were numerous, ranging from those based on the principle of juridical equality to romantic arguments derived from an emotional interpretation of the meaning of democracy. The great powers, accused of acting dictatorially and of employing the methods of the Fascists whom they had just defeated, remained imperturbable.

What worried the American nations most was the implied threat to the inter-American system. Unrestricted veto power would destroy this system with one stroke of the pen by permitting the interference of a power from outside the continent. The principle of America for the Americans was being eroded, and the inter-American system was about to be absorbed into a new organization whose effectiveness was subject to discussion and doubt. The Dumbarton Oaks plan had recognized the existence of regional agreements only as a negotiating ploy to avoid flying in the face of tradition. Regional organizations were really to be converted into mere branches of the world organization.

More important than the threat to continental tradition was the proposal that the unanimous vote of the five great powers be required for the investigation of matters which could affect peace even though the investigation did not involve the use of force. This meant that an act of aggression by one American nation against another could go unpunished if one of the great powers vetoed the investigation.

The United States was committed to support the unrestricted veto and worked vigorously to obtain Latin American backing. The Bolivian delegation worked hard to limit the veto, trying to make the U.S. delegation realize the danger of putting the inter-American system at the mercy of extracontinental powers. Let us suppose, for example, that Bolivia were attacked by a stronger country seeking to strip us of our mineral wealth. While our people have shown their willingness to die to defend their homeland, they have neither the leadership nor the material strength necessary to win a war against even the weakest of our neighbors. If the Dumbarton Oaks proposals had prevailed, the aggressor nation would only have had to secure backing from one of the powers possessing the veto in order to stop any action directed at keeping the peace. The aggressor could then continue his plan of conquest. To avoid a worldwide struggle, the interests, rights, and happiness of Bolivia would be sacrificed. Such a situation might mean that war would occur only between small nations, while large nations would jockey for position in advance of potential world conflicts.

In spite of its imperfections, the arbitration provided by the inter-American system is the best instrument we have been able to devise to deal with the threat of armed conflict between two American states. One of its practical advantages is that because of the great disparity in power between the United States and Latin American countries, the former can exert its influence on the latter with roughly equal intensity.

The only way Latin America can make the world cognizant of its prestige and influence is to federate in a single nation. Until Latin American nations grasp this central truth, we will continue to suffer from the vast disparities which exist among us, deceiving ourselves about our progress which, in fact, is only fictitious. The unrestricted veto, besides putting an end to the inter-American system, would have converted Latin America into a battlefield for military experimentation in the manner of Spain prior to the Second World War.

Was the United States completely convinced of the virtue and necessity of the unlimited veto? Judging from the behavior of its delegates, and the encouragement Latin Americans received from Nelson Rockefeller, I think that its position stemmed from an agreement made to ensure Russian membership in the new world organization.

Some memorable, informal meetings to resolve this issue took place in Secretary Stettinius's penthouse on the top floor of the Mark Hopkins Hotel. We chairmen of eight Latin American delegations attended in order to decide upon continental policy. Bolivia, Brazil, Chile, Colombia, Cuba, Mexico, Peru, and Uruguay joined with the United States to discuss how to integrate the inter-American system into the new world organization, preserving its independence and avoiding the crippling effects of the veto. I consider it an honor to have participated in this group of the principal American nations. This time the Bolivian delegate did not remain in the background, nor was he manipulated like a puppet from behind the scenes. I participated in these arrangements knowing that my contribution was needed.

The most delicate question was how the American states could resolve internal conflicts and protect themselves against external aggression without interference from outside the continent. What was to become of the Act of Chapultepec, approved a few weeks earlier, in which foundations were laid for a treaty of continental defense? Theoretically, the creation of the United Nations would make regional treaties for joint military action in the event of aggression unnecessary. Presumably, the Security Council would act swiftly to stop an aggressor. However, it was difficult to foresee how effective the new organization would be, and the veto hung like a sword of Damocles over any action of the majority. Prudence counseled the development of another mechanism as a second line of defense.

There were only two alternatives: to reject the veto completely or find a way to reconcile the two extremes. It was obvious that total rejection would have diminshed the prospects for approval of the Yalta provisions and for ratification of the charter by the great powers. Acceptance of the unlimited veto, however, could have been the death of the inter-American system.

Since the veto was introduced in San Francisco in an amendment sponsored by the great powers, an affirmative vote of two-thirds of the conference was necessary for its inclusion in the charter. A joint action by the twenty Latin American republics, with the support of other European, Africa, and Asian nations, would have killed the veto. But it would also have defeated the purpose of the conference. Thus our meetings were extremely delicate.

Many drafts were presented. Some were prepared by the Latin American group and others by the U.S. delegation. These were then discussed with the Russians who, predictably, forwarded them to Moscow. We discussed each draft word by word. There were moments in which the failure of the conference seemed inevitable, because if a formula satisfactory to the Latin Americans were not found, they were determined to vote against the veto.

As this drama unfolded, I came to admire the skill and persuasive powers of the Stettinius-Rockefeller team. The most important members of the U.S. delegation attended our meetings—Senators Arthur Vandenberg and Thomas Connally, Governor Harold Stassen, John Foster Dulles, Averell Harriman. The secretary of state's flexibility was demonstrated, not only with the Latin Americans but with members of his own delegation, many of whom did not believe that the survival of the inter-American system was so vital. There were some who maintained that this was a good opportunity to terminate the organization on the grounds that it was not very effective.

It took a long time to awaken the United States to the importance of the inter-American system. To this day the regional system has not fulfilled its highest goal, continental unification, but has provided a stage and microphone for speeches on freedom and democracy. Its positive contributions have benefited almost exclusively the United States, allowing that country to exercise its own power by peaceful and friendly means rather than by force, especially at times when that force was needed in other parts of the world.

The impasse over the veto was formally broken by an agreement containing three main provisions: (1) a new and clearer formulation of the article on regional arrangements; (2) the approval of a new version of Article 51, providing that nations can act jointly to repel an act of aggression without waiting for the secretary-general, the Security Council, or the General Assembly to act; (3) the United States' solemn promise to sign a continental defense treaty based on the Act of Chapultepec.

Latin America's struggle in San Francisco to limit the veto resulted in the following provisions of Article 51:

Nothing in the present Charter shall impair the inherent right of individual or collective self-defense if an armed attack occurs against a Member of the United Nations, until the Security Council has taken measures necessary to maintain international peace and security. Measures taken by Members in the exercise of this right of self-defense shall be immediately reported to the Security Council and shall not in any way affect the authority and responsibility of the Security Council under the present Charter to take at any time such action as it deems necessary in order to maintain or restore international peace and security.

Article 51 was considered then as a concession made by the United States and Great Britain to Latin America. They obtained its acceptance by the Soviet Union, arguing that its approval was the only way to ensure the necessary support for incorporating the veto into the charter. We never dreamed that this article would be the foundation of a system of collective defense organized by democracies all over the world. The North Atlantic Treaty, conceived in the same terms as the Treaty of Rio de Janeiro and other regional arrangements, today constitute the defensive bulwark of the democratic countries.

At a meeting in Stettinius's penthouse, I expressed my views on a continental defense treaty. The defense of the continent and, in particular, of Latin America, is a problem which cannot be resolved by distributing arms or by organizing armies. Each Latin American country must individually and jointly, develop a competency to defend itself and its allies. But in order to do this, it is essential to increase the economic and human potential of these countries. It is much more important for the future defense of the continent to develop and utilize its potential riches than to supply weapons which eventually will be obsolete. The last war has shown us that the accumulation of armaments is not the key to victory. Victory results from the industrial capacity to produce arms at a given moment. In other words, continental defense will be nothing more than a theoretical expression as long as it is not closely linked to industrial development.

The positions of the parties on the issue of continental defense were paradoxical. The United States had developed positive values which could be lost by defeat in war. The treasures it had to protect were its way of life, its liberty, its developed resources, and its status as a world power. On the other hand, the position of the Latin American countries was based more on a dream than on reality, on the hope of developing their wealth and becoming economically and socially strong. If both sides were interested in defending the continent—as we were—then the party with the most to lose had the greatest interest in continental defense. Yet it was the Latin American countries who pressed the United States to agree to measures which would make collective defense possible. The United States left the impression that these agreements were concessions to historical loyalties and tradition rather than a means of coping with the realities of contemporary world politics. We were engaged in strange discussions: the North American delegates were dedicated to opening the doors to a political or military attack from any one of the continent's unprotected flanks; the Latin American delegates sought to protect those flanks, knowing that an attack by an extracontinental power would not stop at the Rio Grande or the Gulf of Mexico.

In spite of the fact that the compromise offered the possibility of maintaining the inter-American system, several American countries refused on principle to vote in favor of the veto. Two countries, Colombia and Cuba, went further and voted against the amendment. Fourteen countries, Bolivia among them, abstained to allow the great powers the two-thirds majority that they needed. Thus the veto power which has since caused so many problems was ratified.

As long as there are areas where human labor and natural resources are exploited, there will be rivalries between the powers for control of those zones. While there is imperfect coexistence within the United Nations, the veto will constitute a weapon in the cold war. Therefore, the next step should be to find a way to restrict or eliminate the veto without giving way to anarchy. The functioning of the organizations affiliated with the United Nations, upon which its effectiveness depends, will only be possible in a world in which the exercise of sovereignty has limits, even for the most powerful nations. Otherwise, international peace-keeping forces, committees for the control of armaments, and international economic organizations, will function in a vacuum or events will convert them into instruments unilaterally serving the interests of certain powers.

The Second World War and the conference at San Francisco have demonstrated that small nations are practically nonexistent as far as the major decisions which affect the destiny of humanity are concerned. The twenty Latin American nations, with their 150 million inhabitants and a continent full of promises for humanity, had the same amount of influence as Belgium, Holland, or Yugoslavia. While we spend ourselves in petty domestic rivalries or in international conferences, other countries with less ability pull ahead of us. United for a moment, Latin America was able to produce Article 51 of the charter. Permanently united in its objectives and interests, it can occupy the position it rightly deserves in the leadership of mankind.

The Uruguayan Foreign Minister and Russia

An episode which created a sensation at the conference and which foretold the future occurred at the time final agreement was being reached on Article 51. Secretary Stettinius invited all the chairmen of American delegations to his apartment to inform them about the latest developments and to request their support in the coming vote. Stettinius made a brief speech that was received favorably by all the delegates. Upon conclusion of his statement he asked if anyone else wished to speak. The only one who wished the floor was Foreign Minister Serrato of Uruguay. He made a long speech praising the efforts of the democratic world and especially of the United States, concluding with a phrase shocking for those times: "Russia is the world's number one enemy."

Since Russia was one of the sponsoring powers with whom several countries maintained diplomatic relations, an air of suspense settled over the room. Avra Warren then began to translate the speech into English. I do not know whether he did so deliberately or accidentally, but his translation did not include Serrato's drastic assertion, the only really important part of the speech. Stettinius and the other American delegates present applauded courteously. However, I could not pass up the opportunity of seeing these gentlemen's reaction to the Uruguayan's charge, and so I spoke up.

"Mr. Secretary, I regret that my esteemed friend Avra has forgotten the most important sentence uttered by the distinguished foreign minister from Uruguay. Begging your pardon, I will complete the translation. The omitted sentence was 'Russia is the world's number one enemy.' "

Almost all of the members of the North American delegation blanched. Serrato thanked me for the clarification and then came a deathly silence.

Stettinius recovered, exclaiming, "Well, my dear colleagues, here we have a table with sandwiches and drinks. Please join me." Then in an aside he said, "Thank you, Víctor. That was certainly hot and I would not have missed it for anything in the world."

The incident could not remain secret because almost forty persons had heard the statement. It reached the press and was published. Apparently the Kremlin was able to counter the attack for Serrato ultimately resigned.

Internees of Axis Origin

Although not a United Nations matter, another problem that required settlement at the end of World War II involved internees of German and Japanese origin. As a preventive measure against the Axis powers, the United States established controls over businesses owned by Germans and Japanese in the Latin American republics. Blacklists were prepared and accounts were blocked. In the countries that had declared war against the Axis, arrests of individuals of German and Japanese origin were made. Many of the Germans singled out by U.S. intelligence agencies for arrest were Bolivian citizens who had long years of residence in the country, were married to Bolivian women, and had every right as citizens to the state's protection. This problem arose not only in Bolivia but in the majority of the American republics.

The United States demanded not only the seizure of Germans and Japanese thought to be dangerous, but also their encarceration in specially organized camps in the United States. About fifteen hundred persons from Latin America, primarily of German origin, were confined in these camps. With the end of the war, the destruction of Germany, and the occupation of Japan, their families pressed for their return. The Department of State adopted a strange position: the internees would be deported—to Germany!

The great majority of the internees had completely broken ties with their native countries. In a sense they were foreigners, who, if returned to the devastated lands of Europe, would only be a burden on the already suffering population. At the same time, their families in America missed them greatly and they were being denied their legal rights.

About a dozen countries had turned over Axis subjects to the United States. All the ambassadors of these countries received instructions from their respective governments to demand their return when the war was over. In two or three of our joint efforts, we were refused, and the majority of our colleagues had given up. Only Ecuador and Bolivia remained firm in their demands. Then a powerful ally, Senator William Langer of North Dakota, came unexpectedly to our assistance. One day he invited me to his office on Capitol Hill and asked me if it was true that we were working for the return of Axis subjects to our respective countries. My first reaction was to telephone my friend, the Ambassador of Ecuador, Galo Plaza, who came immediately to Senator Langer's office.

There the senator told us that on a visit to some concentration camps he had seen an old man behind the wires who reminded him of his father. He could not allow people belonging to his own culture to live under conditions which contradicted democratic principles and the constitutional process of the United States. As U.S. senator, he was prepared to take every action possible to stop their deportation. Since the war was over, he believed that they should be returned to their home countries.

We informed him of our efforts, but to our great surprise the senator had already arranged an interview with Attorney General Thomas Clark. I remember exchanging glances with Ambassador Plaza, who was thinking the same thing as I: The correct diplomatic reply would have been that, given our position as ambassadors, the prescribed channel for dealing with the U.S. government was the Department of State and that to deal with other agencies concerned with internal affairs would be improper. We were both thinking, however, that this, perhaps, was our best opportunity to serve a humanitarian cause. If, to conform with diplomatic usage, we passed up such an opportunity, we would be neglecting our duty as human beings. Conscious of the danger this course held, we accepted the interview for that evening. What I did not know was that the ship with its cargo of deported persons was to sail from Ellis Island for Germany the very next day.

Our interview with the attorney general, who has the rank and power of a minister of state in the United States, had an unexpected beginning which increased our risks. Senator Langer, who had accompanied us to the interview, said more or less the following. "May I introduce the distinguished ambassadors of Bolivia and Ecuador who come to lodge a protest against the Department of State for failing to recognize the rights of German subjects who were in their custody by refusing to turn them over."

We quickly explained that we were not registering complaints against the State Department but merely exploring another avenue to see whether the U.S. government would accept our reasoning. Our legal arguments were based on principles accepted in international law in the Americas. We pointed out that the internees had been turned over to the United States in trust and that any offenses committed against continental security should be judged and punished in the countries where the offenses had taken place. The United States lacked the jurisdiction to try crimes committed on the sovereign territory of another nation. There were also a number of political reasons for returning these citizens to their home jurisdiction, not the least being the problems each government faced regarding their nationality and the actions taken by their families. Moreover, these persons had been hurriedly arrested and many errors might have occurred in their identification as dangerous Axis subjects.

Attorney General Clark heard us out patiently for nearly an hour and a half. Then he withdrew momentarily to confer, I suppose, with one of his advisors. A few minutes later he reappeared to tell us that that very night there would be a meeting at the White House to decide the matter. It was clear that he was fully convinced of the justice and solidarity of our reasoning. On leaving the imposing building of the U.S. Department of Justice, I said to Ambassador Plaza, "Have you considered that the State Department would be within its rights to request our immediate recall?"

"I have thought about it, and I know it," he replied. "However, I believe that these men have a sense of fairness and justice."

The next day we were informed that the deportation order had been revoked. On several subsequent occasions I have recalled this affair as a demonstration of the spirit which inspires the actions of our powerful northern neighbor. Would another nation with so much freedom of choice, power, and pride have acted in the same manner? After witnessing the spread of dictatorships and the conversion of men into machines by totalitarian methods, I attribute special significance to the attitude of the U.S. Department of Justice on this occasion.

When I went to the Department of State a few days later, I was received as cordially as ever by those officials whose decision had been reversed. One of them, who had most strongly defended the sanctions against the Axis subjects, made a sporting comment. "You certainly carried the ball across the goal line. We have to admit that you won the game."

The upshot of this affair was that Senator Langer arranged for the U.S. government to pay for the prisoners' passage home.

8

Postwar Tin Negotiations

Once the Second World War had ended, the real situation in Malaya came to light in spite of attempts to keep it secret. The destruction of the tin mines by retreating Japanese troops was more serious than had been imagined. Moreover, political unrest had followed the liberation of Southeast Asia. The Asian workers of the postwar period were different from those who had worked docilely for their bowl of rice under the domination of the British and Dutch. Nationalistic ideas were spreading throughout the colonial nations as the desire to enjoy the benefits of their countries natural wealth was awakening in the people. The prestige and authority of the colonizer were rapidly diminishing under the impact of mass media which allowed an unprecedented dispersion of news and revelations. The production of tin in that region could not be resumed under the same conditions as existed during the colonial regime before the war. We had foreseen this development in our negotiations, but the North Americans refused to admit it in their discussions with us.

Those of us who assumed control of the Bolivian government in the revolution did so with the intention of using mining as a tool to develop the productivity of our land. If we have not yet developed our agriculture and industry when the mines no longer produce tin, Bolivia will become a nation of ghosts haunting abandoned pits. Our policy should be to obtain the best possible price for our minerals and to invest our earnings in plows, tractors, dams for irrigation, aqueducts, bridges, and roads. Mining production must be carefully protected to extend the benefit of this mineral wealth over as many generations as possible; intensive production is no solution in itself.

The fundamental concern of the North American negotiators was how to force us to produce the greatest amount of high quality ore. The negotiations were characterized by penalties for impurities in the ore and premiums for volume production. In the negotiations for the third contract we were asking for $0.67 per pound of tin, while the buyer insisted on maintaining the price at $0.635, always with the charge of $0.065 to defray smelting costs. The discussions about this difference of $0.035 illuminated not only the difficulties of the negotiations but the drama of the Bolivian people.

Hochschild's Plan

One day Mauricio Hochschild, owner of the mines that produced the majority of the ore sold to the United States, appeared at the Bolivian Embassy in Washington. He maintained that we would not be able to gain any advantage in the negotiations if the Bolivian government did not demonstrate its desire to cooperate by lowering production costs while maintaining the volume of exports. He said that he had studied the current situation in the United States and was aware of our painful experience with the previous spokesmen of the U.S. government. His solution to the problem was that the governments meet one another halfway, each conceding $0.035. The United States would increase the price by that amount while Bolivia would decrease taxes and devalue the Bolivian peso by about 10 percent.

Hochschild was extremely skillful in presenting his arguments. He had a strong personality and cultivated mind and was driven by audacity and a courage which was, at times, reckless. I found these traits attractive, although we were adversaries. He was the mortal enemy of my government and had made a careful study of its weaknesses and of the kind of blow which would be most damaging to us. My duty was to parry these blows and return them if possible. In fighting a man like Hochschild, however, it was a mistake to use violence.

In reply, I said that the United States, which was well acquainted with our economic and social situation, would not seriously believe that any government of Bolivia was in a position to make such concessions. The North American negotiator knew of our needs: roads, bridges, irrigation dams, agricultural machinery, light industry, schools, teachers, judges, hospitals; in a word, everything. How could anyone imagine that we could squeeze the already limited budget of Bolivia to "collaborate" with the United States, which in one hour of war spends enough money to eliminate the poverty of more than three million Bolivians? We had a government budget of approximately eight dollars per capita. Why should we reduce that tiny amount to contribute to the revenues of the richest country in the world?

To lower taxes would mean a reduction in teachers, schools, judges, and social security, not to mention weakening the very foundations of the government. Altering the exchange rate meant an automatic reduction in salaries. Was it just in any way that three million people suffer reduction in their income to protect the profits of a few, including Mr. Hochschild? I declared that it would be better to close the marginal mines and run the risk involved in reducing the profits of the large mining interests. In the end, it was preferable to exhaust every recourse in trying to convince the North Americans that they would gain nothing from our desperate situation. If they wanted our tin, they should be willing to pay for it.

It was already clear that Hochschild had another purpose. The conspiracy to overthrow Villarroel's revolutionary government had three centers of activity. The first, within the country, was taking advantage of the venality of some military officers and of the political ambition of the Communist party, the PIR. The second was operating from a neighboring country, using the press, professional international agitators, and the underhanded activities of diplomats accredited to La Paz. The third center, in Washington, sought to weaken the government economically in order to create conditions favorable to its plans, sowing seeds of discontent among the military, the police, and the people in general. The last objective could be achieved by forcing the government to lower taxes and devalue the currency. On this third front every weapon was employed, including psychological pressures and intimidations. For the tin barons, the contract negotiations were only one aspect of a comprehensive plan. They tried to use the negotiations to strike a blow at the Villarroel government.

For two months Hochschild had been telling me that I should adopt a conciliatory attitude toward the tin barons, accepting a tax reduction and devaluation. His words speak for themselves. "Mr. Ambassador, the Bolivian government should read the handwriting on the wall!" This reference to the Book of Daniel carried a terrible threat:

Mene, mene, tekel, upharsin. . . . God hath numbered thy kingdom, and finished it. . . . Thou art weighed in the balances, and art found wanting. . . . Thy kingdom is divided, and given to the Medes and Persians. . . . In that night was Belshazzar the king of the Chaldeans slain.

Mauricio, like the Prophet Daniel, made a prediction, two aspects of which came true. The days of the government of Villarroel were numbered, and at its end, this good man was murdered and his body profaned by men and women paid to hate their brothers.

During the administration of President Busch, the mining companies had reduced tin production to less than nineteen thousand tons annually on the pretext that the reserves were being exhausted. In doing so, they had strangled his government, the forerunner of the revolution. They could no longer use the same tactics because the United States would not have allowed it; full production was necessary for the war effort. This time they devised a new plan: they would take advantage of the United States' unwillingness to increase prices in order to force a reduction in the fiscal resources of Bolivia at a time when price inflation would make the crisis even more serious. While punishing the Bolivian people for daring to want freedom, they would establish as an indisputable principle the mine owners' right to international protection.

Braden's Support for Hochschild

The unbelievable came to pass: in a formal meeting with the Bolivian delegation about the tin contract, an official spokesman of the Department of State revealed himself also as the spokesman for the interests of the tin barons.

Assistant Secretary of State Spruille Braden convened a formal meeting in his office. Those present were Mauricio Hochschild; Claude Kemper, representing the Aramayo Company; Arturo Grunebaum and Jorge Zalles, representing medium-sized mine owners; René Quiroga Rico, representing the Mining Bank and small mine owners; engineers Jorge Sánchez Peña and Raúl Canedo Reyes, as technical advisors; and myself, ambassador and chief of the delegation. From the United States there were two officials from the FEA; James Espy, the Bolivian desk officer; James Wright, a senior official in the Department of State; and Spruille Braden, who presided.

The floor was given to me and I made a detailed exposition of our position, supported by statistical evidence. We asked for a readjustment, retroactive to July 1, 1945, fixing tin prices at $0.67 cents per pound. After listening to my arguments, Braden said that Mr. Wright would speak for the Department of State. Wright's statements duplicated Hochschild's proposals to lower Bolivia's fiscal revenues. He criticized the Bolivian tax system and referred to the inconvenience of maintaining current official exchange rates, concluding that the only possible solution was for Bolivia to modify its tax schedules and exchange rates in specified amounts. All this made up the "contribution" of the Bolivian government. Added to the $0.635 which the United States was prepared to pay, the Bolivian government's adjustments would bring the yield to the mine owners to $0.67, the amount they sought to maintain the volume of output.

I had to call on all my powers of restraint to avoid expressing an angry protest which would only have made things worse. I must confess that I was unprepared for such a situation. For the first time the Department of State had openly sided with the mine owners in the internal Bolivian struggle. Was this to mean the definitive victory of the tin barons over the rights of the Bolivian people? Would we have to surrender in this confrontation where our forces were simply too weak? Our adversary could see that the economic policies of the Villarroel government were beginning to yield fruit. If that progress were allowed to continue, it might mean the consolidation of the regime. The government had demonstrated irrefutably to the people that the way pointed out by the new leaders was the only one which would lead to liberation. The peso was growing stronger, fiscal controls had stopped inflation, and gold reserves were accumulating in spite of the drain caused by importers associated with the tin barons. The mining oligarcy was seeking to overturn these gains, this time openly aided by the State Department.

The situation was too grave to be discussed in an impromptu debate which would probably weaken our position. The other Bolivian representatives looked at me in anguish, having perceived the well-aimed blow of the mining interests. I forced myself to appear unperturbed. After a brief silence I said: "I am neither prepared nor authorized to discuss this new phase of the negotiations, that is, the stipulation that Bolivia adopt certain measures in its domestic affairs. I request that the meeting be adjourned so that I may consult my government."

"With great pleasure, Mr. Ambassador," responded Braden. "The meeting is adjourned until the ambassador suggests a date for its resumption."

Hochschild could not disguise his satisfaction. His eyes shone with joy and his usually reserved and calm manner became effusive. We left the State Department together and he accompanied me to the embassy offices. There he told me, as if it were taken for granted, that the matter was settled. "Mr. Ambassador, regarding the statement which we have heard this afternoon, I urge you to recommend immediate acceptance in your report. I am convinced that the government will accept your advice, and I imagine that you also see no other solution to the matter."

"I am going to think about it, Mauricio, and I will let you know as soon as possible," I responded.

I retreated rapidly to the embassy residence, wishing to be alone to weigh the problem. I was convinced that this was part of a plan to overthrow the Villarroel government. Some groups of opportunists had been trying to influence certain military leaders who headed the government. They argued that it was "necessary to broaden the civilian base," admitting the collaboration of "experienced" people. They hoped to gain control of leadership positions at points where the conspiracy was aimed, thus weakening the revolutionary activity of the government. What was happening in Washington was coordinated with the intimidation of the armed forces; it was a way of informing them that the only solution, in the end, would be for the government to commit economic suicide by knowingly diminishing the resources which it needed to support itself. Consequently, my recommendations on the proposal made by the Department of State could play a decisive role with respect to the success of the conspiracy.

I had to find a way to continue the negotiations without consulting my government, without even communicating the proposal made by Wright in the name of the Department of State. It seemed impossible, but when one pursues an objective with sufficient zeal and faith, it is always possible to find a way to achieve it. So it was in this case.

When Secretary of State Byrnes named Spruille Braden to replace Nelson Rockefeller as assistant secretary in charge of inter-American relations, the U.S. Senate was reluctant to confirm him, considering the openly interventionist position he had taken while ambassador to Argentina. Braden had spent some difficult and embarrassing moments in hearings before the Senate Foreign Relations Committee. He was severely scrutinized by the committee's leaders, Tom Connally and Arthur Vandenberg, who had returned from the San Francisco conference strengthened in their position as undisputed leaders of U.S. foreign policy. They also had remained strong in their conviction that the respect and sovereignty of other nations were essential to peace and to U.S. prestige in the world.

After a long delay, Braden had been approved, but only after listening to severe reprimands and advice about his new position. He was deflated and began his appointment under the watchful eye of the Senate. In these circumstances, I found the lever that I needed.

My Successful Counterattack

The two leaders of the powerful Senate Foreign Relations Committee honored me with their warm friendship. On more than one occasion these eminent gentlemen had listened to my ideas about the international relations of the American continent. Spruille Braden knew this very well. Before taking any action, I thought it wise to visit the senators and ask them if the nonintervention policy, which they had so insistently recommended, had recently suffered any change. They emphatically assured me not only that there had been no change in that policy, but that the committee was prepared to exercise particular caution, given Braden's past record. They asked me if I had some special information, but I responded that as of the moment, I had nothing. I added that if I found anything concrete I would return to them, and then make a public statement. They were somewhat intrigued, but did not yet insist on a further reply.

Armed and shielded by their assurances, I requested an immediate interview with Assistant Secretary Braden. Believing that I brought some reply from my government, he asked me if we needed to speak together before the meeting. I told him that I considered a preliminary conversation urgent. He received me with his customary effusion. At that time we were already speaking to one another in the familiar form of *tu* when speaking Spanish. "It is always a pleasure to see you here," he said. "Have you sent your report?"

"That is precisely what I wanted to discuss with you, Spruille. Frankly I am afraid to send it. . . ."

"Afraid?"

"Yes, afraid, Spruille, and that is what I want to explain to you. You know of my personal friendship with Senators Connally and Vandenberg. Yesterday I was with them and we talked about things of general interest, including the topic of intervention. They told me that they were prepared to watch your activities very closely, because they are not sure that you have abandoned your ideas about intervention. They asked me if I had some doubt about your position in this respect. The matter proposed by James Wright in the name of the Department of State came to my mind immediately. I believe it amounts to an attempt at intervention, possibly in good faith, but, inevitably, intervention."

"But a friendly suggestion cannot be intervention."

"There is no need to quibble over words, Spruille. Modification of our laws according to your specifications is required as a condition for signing a contract on which our life depends. This can only be interpreted as an act of intervention, since the Department of State is in an indirect, but imposing manner, laying down the law in my country. It can be deduced from the Senate speeches that intervention is not understood only as landing troops or financing revolutions. It is possible to intervene by dictating a country's internal legislation, as in this case. But my intention is not to discuss the true meaning of intervention. What I want to tell you is a fact. If I communicate Wright's proposal in the name of the State Department, I am making this matter public. I cannot request secrecy over a question of such public importance in my country. Once the matter becomes public, I must give it the interpretation which, according to my way of thinking, it merits: this is an attempt to intervene in a completely domestic matter. I assure you, Spruille, that I will so interpret it and afterward I will return home, since I imagine that under such circumstances my presence will not be viewed as desirable by the Department of State. If we did not know of the position and authority of the leaders of the Senate Foreign Relations Committee, perhaps the incident would not be so serious. I fear, though, that there will be trouble between the committee and the State Department. My experience tells me that if such a conflict arises, we will lose in the end, in the one thing that concerns us: the price of our minerals. For this reason I said that I was afraid to transmit the proposal to Bolivia without speaking once again with you."

Braden's expression had been changing as I developed my thesis. Ordinarily expansive and confident, he became unsure and fearful. His anxiety was real when he asked, "Have you told the senators about our last meeting?"

"I have not said a word, Spruille, for the same reasons that I have not consulted my government. The last thing I want is for sensationalism to surround this matter."

"I am grateful to you, Víctor," Braden said with a sigh of relief. "If you do not plan to leave the city, can I call you in about two hours?"

He called me in less than two hours. We convened a new meeting for all those who had attended the previous session. Hochschild responded to the summons in a baffled manner because, through his sources in Bolivia, he knew that the government had not received any word from me. He asked me, intrigued, if I knew the reason for the meeting. I told him that I had no idea.

Braden opened the meeting with special solemnity, and gave the floor to James Wright, who said, "In the last meeting held in this very room, I expressed certain ideas. With the permission of the secretary, I wish to retract each and every one of my words and ideas. I request that the secretary order the destruction of the minutes that were taken in that meeting."

After a deliberate pause, Braden spoke, giving his words the clarity and authority which the occasion called for. "You gentlemen have heard the request of Mr. James Wright. To this I must add that any ideas that Mr. Wright might have expressed in the last meeting do not represent the thinking of the Department of State, nor of any official agency of the United States government. I wish to emphasize that the policy of the government of the United States is one of nonintervention in the domestic affairs of other countries. Therefore, the discussions about the new contract for the purchase of tin will be treated simply on the merits of the proposals, without considering matters which are in the province of the Bolivian government. If the Bolivian ambassador is in agreement with these statements and does not wish to speak, then the meeting is adjourned."

Hochschild's consternation was an eloquent expression of the hope he had placed in these maneuvers, which he believed had sealed the fate of the revolutionary government. As he left the State Department, he managed to regain control of himself, but was no longer full of confidence. He seemed to be perplexed because he could not explain the change in position, nor the reasons for his sudden defeat.

The negotiations dragged painfully on. I pulled every possible lever, taking advantage of my personal friendship with Charles Henderson, now president of the RFC and John Snyder, who at the time was the man closest to President Truman. Mauricio Hochschild recovered from his surprise, persisted in his arguments, and even proposed that we accept $0.65. I remained unmoved. Finally, on July 18, 1946, we closed the deal with the representative of the RFC, signing a contract that awarded us $0.675, taking as a reference point the volume of production of the year before. We had won a total victory on this front and I planned to take a rest for the first time in many long months.

Villarroel's Assassination and Its Aftermath

Three days later, on July 21, 1946, President Gualberto Villarroel was assassinated. As a result of a painful paradox, the fruit of all our efforts served, in the end, to benefit our enemies.

Several questions arise with respect to the U.S. decision to enter into a new tin contract on the basis of terms we had proposed several months earlier. Was it because the U.S. government had been informed in advance of the conspiracy against Villarroel? Was the purpose of the delay in concluding these arduous negotiations to give the conspiracy time to mature? Or, on the contrary, was the acceptance of the terms we had requested a tardy effort to bolster the government? These questions may remain forever open and can only be answered by those who were directing U.S. policy towards Bolivia at that time. In my own mind there has remained a still more painful doubt since I am convinced that much of the suffering which my country has since experienced began with this episode.

My position on the tin question and the United States was based on several fundamental premises. As was demonstrated in World War II, tin is an irreplaceable metal for uses of a strategic nature. The only tin deposits on the American continent are found in Bolivia, naturally protected by the isolated geography of the region. Those located elsewhere have proved vulnerable to occupation and control by foreign powers. Even the location of tin smelters for Bolivian ores outside the continent places the supply of tin in a dangerous position in case of a world conflict, and the smelting of tin ores in the United States has proved to be uneconomical. On the basis of these premises, I reached the following conclusions:

1. Bolivian tin should be considered a strategic resource of the

American continent, and as such, it should receive special treatment outside the current world market.

2. Bolivian tin production should be maintained at the levels and prices established by the economy of the country, without risking exhaustion of the reserves. Stockpiles of refined tin should be maintained in peacetime, for an indefinite period.

3. So that Bolivia's progress does not depend on an intensive production of tin which might accelerate the exhaustion of the reserves, new tin and other mineral deposits should be developed in Bolivia, by means of continental effort.

4. The refining of tin should take place in Bolivia, as should that of other minerals such as lead, zinc, copper, wolfram, antimony, bismuth, etc.

5. Scientific prospecting in the Bolivian Andes and the application of economic methods for the recovery of the metal should be considered as strategic operations of the American continent.

Reviewing these points after many years, I see that they are still applicable. It is essential to adopt an international policy which will not be affected by military coups in our country.

On July 21, the bullet-riddled body of Gualberto Villarroel was hung from a lamp post in the Plaza Murillo in La Paz. Augusto Céspedes, in his extraordinary book, *El Presidente Colgado*, relates, as only he can, what happened on that fatal Sunday. "In the bloodstained bundle hurled from the balcony to Ayacucho Street, the crowd recognized a human form, barely identifiable because of its wounds and disfigurations. According to Díaz Arguedas, 'they had to open the eyelids to verify its green eyes' and thus recognize Villarroel."[1] Thus ended the first act of the national revolution, as once more the mining oligarchy attempted to tighten the chains of oppression around the Bolivian people.

For those of us who had followed Villarroel, six years of suffering began. The tin-mining oligarchy set an example by publicly hanging the bodies of Villarroel, Waldo Ballivián, Luis Uria, Max Toledo, and Roberto Hinojosa on that infamous day. The persecution continued with a manhunt through the streets of La Paz in the midst of an orgy, sustained by money and liquor, taking place in front of the embassies where the followers of Villarroel had taken refuge. This was followed by a smear campaign which attempted to bury the true objectives of the revolution and the ideals of the Chaco generation under a mountain of lies.

Early in the morning of July 22, I sent a cable from Washington resigning as ambassador. I was instructed to turn over the files immediate-

1. Augusto Céspedes, *El presidente colgado: historia boliviana* (Buenos Aires: Editorial J. Alvarez, 1966), p. 249.

ly to Raúl Díaz de Medina, a man who had collaborated in writing the Hull memorandum of January 1944. A few days later, *Life* published a photograph of the body of President Villarroel hanging from the historic lamp post in the Plaza Murillo. I was informed that this photograph had been submitted by Raúl Díaz de Medina and a journalist, Montaño Daza. The paradox is that years later both served governments which attempted to base their prestige and policies on the cry, "Glory to Villarroel."

The bloodbath which was meant to extinguish the people's revolution culminated in the hanging on September 27, 1946, of Majors Jorge Eguino and José Escobar, who were handed over by the guards of the La Paz prison to a group of drunken thugs. They were led, amidst every kind of abuse, in a spectacular parade, to the Plaza Murillo. There, as a sacrifice to Tomás Monje Gutiérrez, who had made himself president and who impassively witnessed the bloody scene from behind the curtains of the Palace of Government, they were hanged on the same lamp posts. Since that time, those posts have become symbols of the people's revolution.

In the middle of August, I set off from New York harbor heading for South America. After a brief stay in Arequipa, Peru, I decided to return to Bolivia, disregarding the advice of my family and friends. Within twenty-four hours of my arrival in La Paz I was seized, and the minister of government summoned "the people" by radio to witness a repetition of the crime committed against Escobar and Equino. I was held incommunicado at the La Paz police station, on the corner of the Plaza Murillo. A police officer who was probably disgusted by the government's cowardly actions, informed me that a group of gangsters was being used to continue the bloody retaliation. This officer provided me with a soldier's uniform and so, with the rest of the troops, I listened to the harangue of Roberto Bilbao, the heroic minister of government behind the lynchings. My people were not fooled, and not even the paid criminals showed up for the event.

That very night I was taken to the concentration camp on the island of Coati. On this romantic island, according to the chroniclers, the *ñustas*, the mothers, wives, and sisters of the Inca aristocracy, were raised. Now it sheltered a score of politicians, victims of the insanity of the police of the mining oligarchy. Here the reality of our struggle was presented to me with dazzling clarity; the enemy would not hesitate to use any force to destroy us and to excise, as Dr. Hertzog said, the renovating impulses of those who dared to challenge the authority of the tin barons in Bolivia. My imprisonment in Coati lasted for three months; I was then exiled to the city of Arica.

It was in this city in northern Chile that I received the invitation of

Bryn Hovde, president of the New School for Social Research, to give some courses in the graduate faculty of political and social sciences as visiting professor. I gratefully accepted this invitation and honor. During the academic years 1947–48 and 1948–49, I taught two courses and one seminar on themes related to the inter-American system and its relations with the new world organization.

After several years in politics and diplomacy, nothing could have been more refreshing than that contact with academic life in the United States. I found the atmosphere of the New School of New York especially stimulating because it is a university founded by intellectuals expelled from Europe during the Nazi domination. Professors and students work in a democratic environment which promotes study and thought in an atmosphere of understanding and freedom rarely found in human relations. My contact with people of all ages who were passing through the last stages of their academic preparation opened a new world for me. I was able to combine my practical experience in government, politics, and international affairs with the search of eager minds, anxious to find answers to the difficult questions raised amid the uncertainty of the early postwar years. These two years filled me with optimism and strengthened the convictions that had led me to side with the forces of reform in my country.

From 1950 to 1952 I worked with the International Basic Economy Corporation (IBEC) in its early promotional efforts in South America. I was especially involved in new trends in the North American strategy of direct foreign investment. Up to that time, capital investment in Latin America had been primarily in industrial activities involving the extraction of raw materials or other primary commodities to meet the needs of foreign markets. In other words, these activities were limited to producing minerals, petroleum, meat, coffee, sugar, wheat, wood, etc., to be used in more sophisticated industries or in overseas markets. There was almost no investment which might increase the domestic supply of consumer goods or which encouraged the opening of new fields to strengthen the domestic economy of Latin American countries. The International Basic Economy Corporation was organized with these goals in mind. Its founder, Nelson Rockefeller, risked large sums of money in yet unexplored fields as well as his personal prestige in the eyes of U.S. businessmen who viewed this new kind of enterprise with skepticism.

In 1951, the Bolivian government, then headed by Mamerto Urriolagoitia, called elections, after taking all the precautions recommended by the experts for winning elections against the will of the voters. The plan was that the new government would be the winner of a rigged contest between Gabriel Gonzalves and Luis Fernando Guachalla. Both of these men were dominant figures in the tin-mining oligarchy which had been restored to power after the death of Villarroel. This time, however, not even the prisons overflowing with MNR militants nor the neighboring countries filled with Bolivian exiles could prevent the outcome of the election. Efforts to conceal the defeat by controlling the voting in outlying areas of the republic were to no avail. The huge majority of the votes went to the candidates who had been almost surreptitiously nominated by the MNR. Víctor Paz Estenssoro and Hernán Siles Zuazo were elected president and vice-president respectively.

The coup d'etat which followed was another maneuver by the tin-mining oligarchy designed to frustrate the will of the people. Urriolagoitia nullified the elections which he himself had called and handed the presidency over to General Hugo Ballivián whom he had named commander in chief of the armed forces. Once again, the only alternative was a popular uprising to reestablish the process which had begun with Gualberto Villarroel.

9

The Second Mission Begins

On April 9, 1952, the MNR took over the Bolivian government, thereby assuming the popular mandate it had won in the elections of May 1951. The MNR had been prevented from assuming office by the coup d'etat of mid-May 1951, known to the public as the *Mamertazo*. The popular uprising of April 9 which defeated the oligarchy's army was the first step in the second phase of the revolutionary process begun by Villarroel. With respect to recognition by other governments, especially within the inter-American system, the MNR coup had the characteristics of a democratic movement. The temporary seizure of power by Vice-President-elect Hernán Siles Zuazo and the handing over of that power to President-elect Víctor Paz Estenssoro amounted, in form and essence, to the elimination of a spurious regime and the reestablishment of a legal government, democratically elected according to the constitutional practices in force at that time. Nevertheless, recognition was delayed many weeks, suggesting that once again a campaign of slander was in the making with the purpose of distorting the motivating forces of the national revolution.

At this time I was abroad in a high position in IBEC. I had just finished a special mission in Ecuador to transfer a mechanized agricultural enterprise to the Development Bank of that country, and was preparing to take a well-earned vacation at the end of which I intended to resume the same type of activity.

In the middle of May 1952, I returned to Bolivia to enjoy the atmosphere of freedom which had been denied to us for more than six years. I was ready to help by offering advice to the revolutionary government, but always with the intention of continuing my private business. When I arrived in La Paz, however, I realized that there was a serious menace threatening this second stage of the revolution. The first statements by the leaders of the movement of April 9 were a firm reiteration of the revolutionary platform which had been pronounced from exile and prison.

This platform consisted of nationalization of the tin and wolfram mines belonging to the three great mining interests; agrarian reform, including redistribution of land and the return to Indian groups of what had been illegally taken from them; and universal suffrage, without discrimination on grounds of sex, education, or economic position.

The decision to carry out such reforms was bound to alarm not only the tin barons and the creole landowners, but also other reactionary forces in the Western Hemisphere who immediately put themselves on the alert in order to cooperate in a new slander campaign. Their strategy was to identify the Bolivian movement with international communism, arousing U.S. public opinion concerning the danger involved in establishing a beachhead in the heart of South America. Once again their aim was to drown the revolution and our hopes for social justice in blood and lies.

This new plan to deceive Americans led me to decide to work wholeheartedly with the revolutionary government in whatever position would be assigned to me. When, at the beginning of June 1952, President Paz asked me to take charge once again of the Bolivian Embassy in Washington, I resigned my position with IBEC.

Truman in the Oval Office

I arrived in Washington in the middle of July 1952 and presented my credentials to President Truman on August 11. Once again I made the trip from the embassy on Massachusetts Avenue to 1600 Pennsylvania Avenue in one of the White House limousines. Once again I waited briefly in a room full of cushioned armchairs and passed again through the solemn corridors of the White House. Thus I entered the Oval Office on which each president impresses his personality with new pictures on the walls and curios on his broad desk.

We had met before and so when he stood up to acknowledge my greeting, he did so familiarly, addressing me by my first name.

"We are happy to have you here again with us."

"I'm even happier to be here again and to see that you are still in the White House."

After the ritual exchange of envelopes containing the speeches which are read, but never aloud, and the formal delivery of my credentials, he asked me what I had been doing during my absence from Washington. I told him that I had spent part of that period in New York, as visiting professor in an American university and in private activities. I informed him that I considered myself indebted to him for a certain sum of money. I explained that I had bet on him in the last election when someone offered me odds of ten to one. He laughed in his usual very frank manner and said that he imagined there was nothing left to spend, even belatedly, in a toast to the victory.

Truman left his chair and walked to a large globe at the far end of the room. He looked for Bolivia and with some difficulty found the small blue spot of Lake Titicaca. Then he told me the following. "When the president of Chile, Mr. Gabriel González Videla, was here in Washington to see me, I had the opportunity of saying to him that I considered it imperative for Bolivia to be given access to the sea. I am convinced that this is a problem which we cannot ignore and which we must try to solve by peaceful means. President González Videla was enthusiastic about my proposition and told me that the first step was to consider the matter of compensation. He pointed out that, as a basis for negotiations, the use of the waters of Lake Titicaca to irrigate the north of Chile could be studied."

After a brief pause he continued vehemently, resting his hand on my shoulder: "Víctor, I'm really enthusiastic about this project! I wish you could use these waters to create soil as rich as California's in the north of Chile and at the same time give Bolivia free access to the sea and reestablish goodwill between two nations who should confront their destinies together. What do you say?"

I was sincerely moved by the goodwill and enthusiasm shown by the president, but I could not fail to recognize the shrewdness with which the Chilean dignitary had avoided the central issue by proposing a solution which presented almost insurmountable physical and political obstacles. My answer was more or less the following. "Not only as ambassador from my country but also as an ordinary Bolivian citizen, I am deeply grateful for your interest in solving the problem of our landlocked position. I appreciate your having brought this problem to the attention of the president of the country which, in another era of our history, seized from us in a war of conquest that which legitimately was ours. I cannot help admiring the skill and cordiality with which the Chilean president approached this delicate matter. Deflecting the waters of Lake Titicaca, besides being an engineering project of exceptional proportions, has international complications because Bolivia and Peru have joint ownership of the lake's waters. On the other hand, providing Bolivia with its own sea coast would be a political decision for the nations that participated in the tragic war of 1879. I believe that making Bolivia's access to the sea depend on a hypothetical solution such as the deflection of the waters of Lake Titicaca would only postpone indefinitely such an act of justice. However, Mr. President, I thank you wholeheartedly for your kindness and I hope that someday, with the help and influence of the United States, we will be able to solve this matter which represents such a shameful blot on our hemisphere."

President Truman realized the complexities of the problem upon which he had touched, and he closed this part of the conversation by saying, "Well, we'll keep working on this matter."

Goals of My New Mission

My second mission to Washington, like the first, faced serious international problems. Although World War II was over, the United States, much to its regret, was deeply involved in the Korean War. This war did not arouse any enthusiasm among U.S. citizens; on the contrary, it created an atmosphere of mistrust toward everything connected with or influenced by the Communist countries. Americans slowly but surely came to the realization that the war could not be ended easily. This knowledge brought with it not only a flood of opposition to the American intervention but also the exacerbation of anti-Communist sentiment, symbolized by the trials and sentencing of the leaders of the U.S. Communist party and of Alger Hiss, a former high official in the Department of State. The Soviet colossus loomed on the world horizon, backed by a sea of humanity in China. All these dangers were viewed as posing once again a threat to the democratic way of life and to the very existence of free nations. For these reasons it is easy to understand why the Bolivian tin barons concentrated their efforts on labeling the new government as a regime influenced and directed by international communism. This was an attempt to duplicate the results achieved with the earlier slander campaign against the Villarroel government. The mission in Washington was, therefore, exceptionally delicate and important to the future of Bolivia, involving the charges of communism against my government, the sale of our tin and wolfram, the Bolivian agrarian reform, and our plans to develop the country. My most urgent task was counteracting the mine owners' efforts to distort with false charges of communism the true political, economic, and social processes at work in Bolivia.

The preliminaries of the struggle were ended by a decree ordering state intervention in the great mining companies as a first step towards full nationalization. In retaliation, the propaganda machinery organized by the agents of the tin-mining oligarchy, with the cooperation of displaced politicians, was ready to present the reforms of the revolutionaries as Communist inspired. The United States at that time was fighting Communist forces in Korea and, in order to strengthen the home front, had started a campaign to eradicate any symptoms of Communism within its own boundaries. Obviously, the United States could not look with favor upon a regime which, according to the propaganda, was the product of Communist maneuvering in South America.

As always, the minerals that occupied a predominant place in our economy were another major concern. The Korean War had produced a considerable increase in the prices of minerals, especially of tin and wolfram. Tin had reached a price of nearly $2.00 per pound, but the Bolivian producers had signed contracts with the U.S. government for $1.215 per pound of refined tin. The U.S. at this time considered it extremely important to increase its tin stockpiles. The Bolivian producers were demanding an increase in tin prices because they believed that their production costs had increased considerably due to the Korean conflict. A special commission sent by the Bolivian government and entrepreneurs was negotiating in Washington when the uprising of April 9, 1952, took place.

Concerning tungsten, the main producer of this mineral was China, who now belonged to the ranks of adversary nations and could no longer be relied on to meet U.S. needs for immediate consumption or for reserve supplies. This situation caused alarm among policy makers, and a plan was adopted to promote increases in wolfram production in other regions of the world. The United States offered long-term contracts with artificially inflated prices of as high as sixty dollars per sales unit, although the market price had been about twenty dollars.

The large companies involved in mining in Bolivia hastened to increase their capacity for wolfram production and signed contracts with the United States, which, after the nationalization, became the responsibility of the Bolivian Mining Corporation. The U.S. agencies dealing in the purchase of minerals, such as the General Services Administration and the Bureau of Mines, were totally opposed to the Bolivian government taking over the contracts; they argued that the original seller had disappeared, thus annulling the agreement.

There were two principle motives for this attitude. First, the panic due to the wolfram shortage had passed, because intensive production in many regions of the world had sufficiently compensated for the loss of Chinese production. Second, many of the technical officers of the specialized agencies, especially of the Bureau of Mines, were engineers who had worked in the Bolivian mines. The same organizations held that the nationalization of the mines meant, in fact, a confiscation of property. It was therefore possible to place an embargo on Bolivian minerals shipped to the United States. All this had serious political and legal implications which had to be treated with extreme caution in view of their direct bearing not only on the course of the national revolution but also on the capacity of the government to meet the most basic needs of its people, especially with respect to food and health.

The Bolivian government had acted in a way which further complicated the situation. The nationalization of the mining companies was made with the understanding that the state would discharge and rehire all the workers and employees exactly as if the transfer had been made in a normal way between private parties. Government officials arranged severance pay and rehiring, without having exact information on the seniority of the workers and without possessing the necessary resources for expenditures of such magnitude. No other revolution, no matter how leftist, has acted in this fashion because a basic preoccupation of cautious leaders is to avoid weakening the structure of the revolutionary government. In our case, in order to make payments to thousands of workers and employees, a large part of the country's monetary reserves were used up. The government was left practically defenseless, not only in very difficult international negotiations, but in its efforts to acquire machinery, spare parts, explosives, and other items which were absolutely necessary to maintain production. We had almost killed the goose that laid the golden egg.

Another of my major responsibilities was furthering understanding of the Bolivian agrarian reform in the United States. Although the reform did not directly affect U.S. interests, most American leaders were suspicious because they knew nothing of the agrarian system which had prevailed in Bolivia up to that moment. Under the influence of reactionary propaganda, these leaders were inclined to oppose the reform, believing that it violated the democratic principles of the hemisphere. At that time, a great deal of talk about agrarian reform originated in Communist China. This intensified the dangers of the situation because it could easily be used by the propaganda machinery of the tin barons and of their allies the landowners.

Frank Lausche, the conservative Democratic senator from Ohio, was typical of those who were suspicious of our agrarian reform. One day he asked me, "Víctor, isn't this really a Communist-type measure?" I replied by describing my relations with the agricultural laborers on our family properties before and after the revolution.

As a young man, I used to visit the several thousand acres of land that my family had held for many generations. I would sit on a chair in an open space, and the peasants would come up to me, kneel on the ground, kiss my hand, and leave some kind of tribute, like a chicken or some handicraft object. I would pat them on the head and offer friendly words of reassurance to old and young alike. After everyone had completed this formality, and there might have been over one hundred persons involved, I would order large containers of alcohol, mixed with some sweet liquid, to be opened and served. After several drinks, frequently too many, the peasants would begin their native dances and after a while go home.

After the 1952 revolution, most of my family's properties were re-distributed among these peasants, but, under the terms of the reform, I was able to purchase from some of my relatives the central house and some surrounding land. It so happened that my first return visit after the redistribution occurred while I was foreign minister. On my arrival, several hundred peasants gathered to meet me, headed by the leader of the local peasant union who insisted on reading a formal speech as I stood before the large group. I was then asked to take the arm of the leader's wife, and my wife his arm, and walk together to our family residence. The ministry officials who accompanied me, sometimes doubling as a kind of bodyguard, were concerned, but I asked them to follow quietly behind.

On arrival at the house, it appeared that there was to be a party, but I, of course, had made no provision for refreshments. The peasant leaders said that made no difference since they had brought the food and beverages themselves. We all ate, drank, and danced together. As the party was drawing to a close, the union leader, surrounded by his companions, approached me, shook hands, and said he hoped that from now on we would live and work together as friends.

I concluded by telling Senator Lausche that I could provide him with lots of statistics, but they would be insignificant by American standards. What it all boiled down to was that about 70 percent of all Bolivians were serfs before the reform and afterwards they were men. The issue was more important than politics or economics; it was a question of human dignity. After I had finished, Lausche said he had no more objections to the agrarian reform.

One of the great deficiencies of U.S. interpretation of events in Latin America, such as the agrarian reform, is its unreliable and shallow information concerning social problems and cultural values in each of our countries. At least until that time, a large segment of the American public tended to generalize about Latin American society on the basis of stereotypes disseminated by the mass media. One depicted the peoples of Central America subject to exploitation by the fruit companies; another, glorified by cheap movies, showed adventurers and revolutionaries of the Pancho Villa type. The American public, therefore, had serious doubts about the sincerity and the urgency of profound reforms in the agrarian system and believed that it was much more important to keep intact the principle of man's unquestioned right to private property. Thus, the key issue was to convince the public that the reform was actually designed to implement that right more efficiently. The purpose of forming a large class of rural property owners was twofold: to achieve social justice, and to promote orderly economic progress.

Finally, the diversification and development of the Bolivian economy was another of my long-range tasks. Villarroel's brief regime, his heroic death, and our six years of prison and exile had convinced us beyond all doubt that our people could be raised from poverty only through heroic measures. Specifically, we needed the powerful backing of a stable and autonomous economy which would not be totally dependent upon the tyranny of export markets. The mining economy had created an anomalous situation in which a large part of the revenue obtained from mineral exports was used to import items that we could easily have produced ourselves: sugar, rice, lumber, meat, and, in certain years, even potatoes from Holland. This caused the Bolivian people indescribable suffering. It was essential to develop our own internal resources, and the first step would be to feed our people with the products of our own land.

With regard to fuel, the Bolivian Petroleum Corporation (YPFB) had been organized in 1937 to continue the work of exploration and exploitation of concessions which had belonged to the Standard Oil Company of New Jersey and had reverted to the state. The corporation had not been able to produce even 30 percent of the gasoline and kerosine required for internal consumption, and of course, no airplane fuel at all. The foreign exchange obtained through the exportation of minerals was invested in these commodities for current consumption so that very little remained to invest in capital goods and development projects.

The brief era of Villarroel's government had provided enough experience to convince us that these problems were not to be confronted with mere decrees or revolutionary verbosity. It was necessary to start a policy of investments which, beginning with the essential infrastructure, could lay the foundations for integral development of the country. As a first step, it was vitally important to obtain capital for road construction and hydroelectric projects. This capital was in the United States, and only through a deft policy building an atmosphere of rapprochement and confidence could conditions be created to attract both private and public capital.

These issues should have been the main concern of all the Bolivian missions accredited in Washington, London, and Paris. The main interest of previous governments had been in other spheres, however, and the diplomatic machinery had been used by them to back up the individual interests of the mining companies. This explains why diplomatic functions in the United States, England, and France had been systematically entrusted to members of the Patiño and Aramayo families, or to certain employees of their companies. The main responsibility for having perpetuated the concept of a semicolonial Bolivia falls directly on the men who, with passports and diplomatic appointments, served as high employees of those mining companies, as delegates to international confer-

ences, or as officers of the internal administrative apparatus of the Bolivian
government. They were constantly and totally subjected to the directives
issuing from the offices of lawyers and administrators of the mining companies. The rest of the world was used to our voluntary submission.
We now had to plan the new foundations on which we wanted to build
our international relations.

In short, the panorama which confronted us could be described in the
following way: the State Department was mistrustful of a regime which
had been accused six years earlier of collaboration with German Nazism
and which now seemed to have acquired contacts with international communism. In view of its present involvement in Korea, the State Department seemed unwilling to deal with us in an understanding fashion, at
least not before an exhaustive analysis had been made.

The reforms announced in Bolivia lent themselves to misrepresenta-
tion by reactionary interests which depicted them as part of Communist
strategy to create problems for the United States in South America. The
great propaganda machinery of the tin barons concentrated on this objective; the revolutionary euphoria of the first few months favored the
purposes of that machinery. Under these circumstances it would have
been sufficient for the success of a mission to obtain the neutrality of
the United States. Therefore, the main events leading not only to the
neutrality of the U.S. government toward the Bolivian internal struggle,
but to its economic and fincancial support for the national revolution,
deserve to be told to new generations who live in a world different from
our own.

Opening Skirmishes in Washington

My first contacts in Washington proved that the former owners of
the Bolivian mines had initiated an active and well-directed effort to
discredit the Bolivian revolution and its leaders, as well as to misrepresent
its motives. The decree prepared by the Commission for the Nationalization of the Mines, which provided for government intervention, had
already been the object of wide-spread publicity representing it as the first
step towards confiscation. Similarly, the presence of certain labor leaders
inside the government was depicted as clear proof of the new government's Communist leanings. It was imperative to act quickly, and I therefore hastened to interview representatives of important news media. My
analysis of the workers' movement in Bolivia, a movement which now
wholeheartedly supported the national revolution, was the basis for the
argument which I presented to the nation's leading columnists, reporters,
editors, and other newsmen who specialized in Latin American affairs.

In New York my first step was to get in touch with old friends from *Time*. I had lunch with two of its Latin American editors, and in this interview they specifically mentioned that the magazine believed Juan Lechín to be a Communist agent. My answer was categorical, and because it was based on facts, it made a strong impression on them. I reminded them that during the final stages of World War II, when the United States and Russia were close allies, one of the most valued spokesmen for the Latin American workers was Vicente Lombardo Toledano of Mexico. I pointed out that Lombardo Toledano was considered an enemy of the United States and an agent of Russia in the early 1950s and was believed to have played the same role during the war. On the basis of this premise, I reminded them how he had opposed the admission of the Bolivian labor delegate to the Philadelphia Labor Conference of April 1944, on the grounds that he was under Nazi influence. Later on Juan Lechín, who at the time was secretary-general of the Bolivian Miners Trade Union, tried to obtain a visa to enter the United States. The visa was denied because the current spokesmen for the workers, who were influential with the Allies, persisted in their accusation that Lechín was linked to Nazi activities in Bolivia. My personal intervention as ambassador to the United States was necessary to obtain a visa permitting Lechín to stop in the United States on his way to Europe. Was it fair that this same Lechín who had been accused of Nazi connections in 1944 would now be classified as a Communist agent? Although I personally had nothing to do with Lechín's election as leader of the mine workers and did not share many of his ideas, nor favor his current methods, I could not accept this contradiction. Lechín was simply a mining leader who drew his strength from the trade unions in Bolivia.

A few days after my arrival in Washington I was informed that the former mining entrepreneurs, Patiño, Hochschild, and Aramayo, had enlisted the services of the public relations firm, Nathanson Brothers of New York, through a contract involving more than half a million dollars a year. This firm was entrusted with the task of portraying the new Bolivian government and the MNR as instruments of the Communist efforts in the Western Hemisphere. To this end, the firm had flooded every publication in the United States, all the offices of senators, representatives, governors, and influential figures, with literature following the views expressed in Carlos Víctor Aramayo's newspaper, *La Razón*, from 1946 to 1952. This colossal propaganda campaign succeeded in creating an atmosphere which was neither reassuring, nor propitious.

They could not, however, misrepresent or destroy my personal reputation. The U.S. leaders reading this propaganda knew that during the last six years I had been working first as a professor in an American university and afterwards in confidential missions for a large corporation well known to U.S. businessmen. It was obvious that an individual who had merited such trust could not be a Communist, nor could he willingly defend a Communist regime. Besides opening the doors to institutions and persons, doors which otherwise would have remained locked, this fact automatically cast doubt on the allegations of our adversaries.

One of the propaganda devices used by Nathanson Brothers were periodic "reports" on the background and objectives of the Bolivian revolution. Of these, perhaps the most important and picturesque was prepared by a little-known newsman, Stanley Ross. He had been asked to write a pamphlet "revealing" to the American public the behind-the-scenes story of Communist penetration in Bolivia. Duly advised by some of Aramayo's newsmen, he produced some three hundred pages. My personal impression is that Nathanson was not satisfied with the work and that the author himself had doubts about its possible impact. The fact is that Stanley Ross sent intermediaries to the embassy offering to sell the work to us so that we might avoid its publication. Judging from a copy given to me by some friends in the press who had been consulted in the matter, I knew it was only a recapitulation of everything that had already been said and did not add anything to the pack of lies already published in some Latin American newspapers, at the instigation of the mining oligarchy. Accordingly, I flatly refused to consider even the possibility of negotiating with Ross. Unfortunately, I did not know that he had shrewdly made the same proposition directly to the Bolivian foreign office. The minister of foreign affairs, thinking he had found the source of the poison that was tormenting us, ordered the purchase of the document for $500!

Later Nathanson Brothers circulated other publications, such as the translation, certainly vastly improved, of *Un Pueblo en la Cruz* by Alberto Ostria Gutiérrez.[1] This book, elegantly printed and bound, was widely distributed at no charge. They also transcribed hundreds of thousands of editorials and articles which had appeared in Spanish-language newspapers, written by journalists hired by the tin barons. Naturally, each of these was accompanied by an English translation with brief and skillful explanations. During the first part of my second mission, I concentrated on neutralizing this propaganda and making known the truth about the socioeconomic process in Bolivia.

The Public Relations Arena

Those who visit the United States for the first time sometimes find it difficult to understand the role of public relations offices and their impact

1. Santiago de Chile: Editorial del Pacífico, 1953.

on business, politics, and society in general. In the United States all the great industrial corporations, the important politicians, the universities, the foundations, the trade unions, the civic associations, the important figures in business, theatre, sports, etc., hire the services of these specialized offices. They are frequently mistaken for offices of publicity, but in the United States, in the world of business and the promotion of human endeavors, the two activities are only complementary. The one is like a physician who diagnoses an illness; the other is the specialist who brings about the cure through adequate treatment. Public relations offices are composed of professionals who are knowledgeable about the reactions of the public and give advice on ways of popularizing a concept or promoting a personal image. They evaluate the reactions of the press and publicity organs in order to give advice about selling a product or a personality.

The English verb *to sell* is translated in Spanish as *vender*, but the two are not always equivalent in meaning. In English, *to sell* may not involve the transfer of an object from one person to another for payment; it also means to convince an individual or a group about an idea, a personality, or a piece of merchandise. In English, besides its materialistic meaning, this verb also means trying to obtain victory in a battle in which shrewdness and know-how come into play. Thus, for example, one can *sell* a country to the U.S. public, that is, facilitate recognition of its prestige, its cultural values, and its interests.

Nathanson Brothers was supposed to sell the idea that the Bolivian revolution had Communist origins and was, therefore, a threat to peace in the hemisphere. They tried to develop this central idea by using great sums of money, going so far as to buy newsmen and to woo other influential persons. The final objective was to create a wave of aversion which would force cancellation of the Bolivian reforms. Nathanson Brothers explicitly admitted to the Department of Justice that it received a retainer of more than two hundred thousand dollars a year from the tin barons. To this one would have to add the expenditures not included in the formal declaration. Although the real sum has never been revealed, I am convinced that from 1952 to 1955 it was well over two million dollars, exclusive of expenditures made in other countries of the hemisphere. The irony of this is that these financial resources came from the famous retained shares (*retenciones*) from tin ores, and from the twenty dollars per unit of wolfram which the pressure exerted by U.S. mineral purchasing agencies, had forced us to pay to the tin barons. In other words, they were trying again to reimpose the oppressive bonds which had subjugated Bolivian miners, using the very product of the men's work and sacrifice.

The public relations expert acts on the assumption that there is always a vulnerable spot in human nature. He may appeal, for example, to the inherent sense of justice and truth or, in other cases, to the fear of losing positions of privilege, status, or convenience. Once he has carried out a study of the subject, the expert advises his client about the form and content of communications with the target public, whether individuals, groups, or news media. He often functions as a link between his customer and the news media, preparing for the latter, in an accessible and clear format, the points or concepts which he wishes to communicate.

The weakness of the propaganda campaign launched by the tin barons was that their position was negative. They were trying to play up the fear of the Bolivian revolution without offering a positive alternative such as a leader who might inspire confidence, a viable new order or new organization; in other words, something which would attract public support. Moreover, none of the tin barons wanted to appear in person to champion their cause. They believed that they could achieve their objectives by giving prominence to secondary figures, most of whom were displaced politicians whose authority was diminished by their loss of control of the government. Their accusations of foreign interference could not substitute for their own incompetence.

We, on the other hand, could present ourselves as victors in a revolution, offering to build a new order on the ruins of one which had generated only internal discord. We had the enthusiasm and faith of idealists who inspired respect even if we were considered unrealistic. We were defending something concrete, and all of us, from the government to the most humble elements of our society, were working together toward a common goal. They could classify us as fanatics, dreamers, or madmen, but never as mercenaries.

The only possibility of justifying this last label would have been to prove that the revolution was following Communist directives and had been launched with the help of funds from this source. Since they were never able to substantiate this charge, their statements began to be regarded as words enunciated only for effect; in the end, they did not impress anybody. In our struggle we found a concrete objective stemming from a need to solve real problems—the social and economic backwardness of Bolivia and the insultingly extravagant life of those who had in the past usurped the production of minerals in our country.

Our Appeal for Justice

In a democratic country, representative institutions are constantly at work checking the pulse of public opinion which eventually will manifest itself in elections. The first step in obtaining any advantage in dealing with such a government is to win over public opinion. In our case, we had first to counteract the activities of the tin barons and then take the offensive by presenting their true nature to the American public.

We based our campaign for public understanding on several fundamental points. We maintained that in nationalizing its mines, Bolivia had merely exercised her sovereign rights; the economic repercussions, both positive and negative, affected only the Bolivians. Throughout our entire campaign, we made no attempt to apologize for the step we had taken, asking only for understanding of the reasons behind our actions. We had a similar approach to other reforms made during the course of the revolution—agrarian reform, electoral reform, etc. The more we emphasized our right to sovereignty, the more we could avoid the possibility of new battlefronts being opened to our adversaries.

It was also important not to exaggerate the claims we had against the former owners of the nationalized enterprises, so as to avoid detracting from the seriousness and integrity of our position. Regrettably, this policy was not uniformly implemented in the first few months of nationalization. We contradicted the statements made by the minister of mines that the companies not only had no right to any type of compensation, but that they owed more than five hundred million dollars to the state. These statements were interpreted as arguments aimed at avoiding legal procedures, thus weakening our position concerning the true sums which the former entrepreneurs should either pay or collect.

We consistently denied any affiliation with extranational or extracontinental political forces. This strategy was especially designed to destroy the rumor that the Bolivian revolution was inspired and financed by international communism and to oppose all attempts to convert it into one more pawn in the cold war. The Bolivian revolution, radical, extremist, and profound, only obeyed the radicalism, the extremism, and the profound objectives of our people, exclusively Bolivian.

The best defense against the publicity campaign financed by the tin-mining oligarchy was to direct our blows at its most vulnerable spots. We tried not to mention the names of the tin barons; they had little or no significance for the American public. Rather, we attempted to unveil the truth about their methods and policies which had led the desperate Bolivian people to seek liberation through violence, thus perhaps endangering an important stage of their growth and development. Obviously, the true record of these mining companies facilitated the presentation of a moving and convincing picture of Bolivian reality.

Once we agreed upon these basic strategies, we started our campaign through personal contacts with the owners, the directors, the editors, and the columnists of the most important publications in the United States.

My observations have convinced me that the majority of American news-men are well-intentioned individuals. They do not have strong prejudices except on domestic issues where they have had to develop a clearly de-fined personal position. Concerning the affairs of other nations, they are objective and willing to listen to and appreciate reason, especially when dealing with a high official such as an ambassador whose record inspires their confidence In my many personal interviews I indicated specifically that one objective of my mission was to prevent the U.S. press from again becoming an instrument of certain international financial interests for perpetrating tremendous injustices against an entire country. These inter-ests were using public relations and propaganda to turn men of goodwill into their accomplices.

The propaganda of the former mine owners was thus examined with a more critical eye, and, as a result, more than 90 percent of it ended up in the wastebasket. One of my contacts summed up the situation by saying, "When I receive all this literature and then compare it with notes taken during my interviews with you, the whole affair seems so confusing and contradictory to me that I end up ignoring it completely." This was precisely the effect I wanted to achieve in this first stage of the con-frontation: to have the international press forget us momentarily and allow us to erect the first few guideposts of our revolutionary march.

Our adversaries were and still are unable to understand how we could make so many friends in the U.S. press and in other important sectors of public opinion. They could not comprehend the attitude assumed by men such as Arthur Sulzberger, Herbert Matthews, and Bill Lawrence of the *New York Times*; the director of the *Washington Post*; Sam Kauffman, director and owner of the *Washington Evening Star*; and columnists of the stature of the Alsop brothers, Marquis Childs, Arthur Krock, Drew Pearson, and Walter Lippmann. These parties, as well as traditionally conservative papers such as the *Christian Science Monitor*, not only began to show a favorable neutrality, but eventually became defenders of the Bo-livian revolutionary cause, within the limited space that these newsmen and publications give to Latin American affairs. On the other hand, the millions spent by the tin barons resulted only in coverage in newspapers specializing in metals, such as the *American Metal Market*, distributed among businessmen and entrepreneurs who deal in minerals, and a few articles in financial newspapers such as the *Wall Street Journal* and *Barron's Weekly*. Because of the limited circulation of these publications, all of this was not enough to impress those responsible for policy with regard to Bolivia.

It was important for us to convince the United States of the advan-tages of continued negotiations with a country that had nationalized its mining industry, thus preventing a policy of repression in fear that Bolivia had set a precedent which could affect U.S. investment in other Latin American countries. This issue is still being debated today, for there are people in the United States who maintain stubbornly that if that country had adopted a policy of economic strangulation of the Bolivian revolution, it would have avoided what has since happened with American investments in other countries. During our campaign we convinced the American public and those persons occupying leading positions that in Latin America a widespread social upheaval was in the making and that the Bolivian revolution was one of its first manifestations.

One of the most impressive facts about the United States is the eagerness of the people to know the truth. The American citizen is aware of the limitations of the mass media, which is in many cases controlled by large corporations and often obliged to filter the news through the screen of their interests and responsibilities. This seems, in my opinion, to be the reason why the average American citizen belongs to various civic or religious groups which try to inform their members of the truth through direct contact with actors in current events. The citizen can then write to his senator or representative, who will give careful consideration to this correspondence, especially when it represents a trend. Another source of political influence lies in the centers of higher learning which maintain permanent liaison with Congress. Through contacts remaining from my previous university appointment, I made known to universities, and civic and religious groups, my desire to explain in person the reasons for the Bolivian revolution. There were weeks in which I received up to six invitations. Only physical limitations prevented me from utilizing this opportunity more than about once a week, and this involved travel to most of the states of the nation. The results of this effort surpassed my expectations and gave me new reasons to admire American democracy.

10

Nationalization of the Tin Mines

In order to understand the nationalization of the large tin mines in Bolivia, it is necessary to consider certain peculiarities of their origin and ownership. These companies were not originally multinational corporations financed by American, English, or European capital. Early development of the mines was in the hands of Bolivians, and only when they had grown larger did they receive extensive international financing; foreign capital was virtually nonexistent in the development of the Bolivian mining industry. The explanation may be Bolivia's geographic isolation which makes direct contact with the outside world more difficult, or the continuous political upheavals in Bolivia for more than a century after independence.

During colonial times, Bolivia's most important economic asset was the forced labor of the indigenous *mitayos*, men taken from the Indian communities to search for rich veins of silver in the Andean mines under the whip of Spanish overseers. The Creoles who replaced the Spaniards during the republic of the nineteenth century continued the system of exploitation. Coups d'etat were financed by this silver, often provided by a few families from Chuquisaca who constituted a kind of mestizo aristocracy, their wealth based on the labor of the descendants of the *mitayos*. In the meantime the republic languished between internal conflict and wars with neighboring countries. The government was unable to lead the nation out of its backwardness, and rich areas of the national patrimony suffered from the voracity of neighboring countries.

With the arrival of the twentieth century, tin and rubber became essential raw materials for manufacturing. At that time new political currents were appearing in Bolivia, mainly due to the development of the city of La Paz. The so-called federal revolution involved the reorganization of the country's ruling families as well as an attempt to organize the armed forces along the lines of modern European military technology. French and German officers were hired to assist in the formation of a professional and technical officer corps. Unfortunately, this revolution proved to be just one more of the many illusions which deceived the people, a people who were gradually becoming aware of the injustice of their traditional servitude.

At this time, the exploitation of tin was undertaken in several mines which had originally produced silver. This was followed by the incursion of Chilean financial adventurers who had acquired the necessary technology in mining nitrates and copper and now formed companies whose shares were traded on the stock market in Santiago. Mining operations controlled from outside the country proved to be virtuallly impossible, however, because of geographical and human conditions in Bolivia. Less than thirty years after their initiation by Chilean capitalists, the mining operations were returned to native Bolivians through skillful financial maneuvering. Several corporations arose, first Aramayo, then Patiño, and later that of Mauricio Hochschild, a fascinating personality of Austrian origin, a naturalized citizen of Argentina, and a multimillionaire in Boliva.

These three mining enterprises determined the course of Bolivia's history in the first half of the twentieth century. In order to guarantee the exploitation of both minerals and men, they gained control of the government through a favored group of agents and carefully selected and well-paid military officers. They distorted the original objectives of the armed forces, turning the officers into simple mercenaries unconditionally committed to their interests. Governments had a fundamental duty: to protect the immense earnings of the companies, keeping the people ignorant. If a government official dared to deviate from the directives sent out by the mining companies, the government was overthrown by military officers on the companies' payroll. The companies were also high-handed in their dealings with the people: they allowed no criticism or opposition. Besides the periodic repression exercised by the government in power, they cruelly employed economic and social strangulation against any citizen who dared to question their tremendous power. As soon as the owners became millionaires, they emigrated, moving their companies to other countries. Patiño Mines moved to Delaware in the United States; Aramayo Mines went to Switzerland; and Hochschild divided its offices among the United States, Switzerland, and Chile.

Several months before the revolution began the large mining companies initiated a campaign to obtain a price increase after the old contracts expired at the end of 1952. The price in the old contracts was $1.215 per pound of refined ore. The mine owners had informed the buyers that they could not keep up the work for less than $1.30 per pound

without losing money. Ricardo Martínez Vargas, Bolivian ambassador
to Washington, backed by Luis Fernando Guachalla, an ex-ambassador,
failed to obtain this increase, which would have benefited the mine
owners and only indirectly the government. During the last few months
of 1951 and in early 1952, Senator Manuel Carrasco, prominent attorney
for the mining interests and, at the time, president of the Bolivian Senate,
was in Washington. Together with Miguel Etchenique, another high official of the mining interests, he tried unsuccessfully to obtain the increase.

Stuart Symington, then president of the RFC, the organization authorized by the U.S. government to purchase minerals, peremptorily
opposed any increase in the price of tin. Senator Lyndon Johnson, having
arrived at the same conclusions as Mr. Symington, began a Senate investigation of tin mining. Both men believed that while the increased
production costs in Bolivian mines were a fact, the higher prices would
have to be universal and would, therefore, result in excessive earnings for
tin producers of other regions.

Since the Patiño enterprise had important investments in tin production on other continents, its owners were interested only in a general
price increase and not in arrangements which would benefit Bolivian
mining exclusively. They were less concerned about the tin produced in
Bolivia than about the immense profits they would receive from other
areas, especially from Malaya and the Belgian Congo. It became clear later
that the United States was even then prepared to try to compensate
Bolivia for its higher production costs and did so a few months later.
However, since special prices for Bolivian tin would have been arranged
between the two governments, the agreement would have afforded Bolivian politicians, no matter how servile they may have been, some independence and thus threatened the mining interests' complete hegemony
in the country. Therefore, the Bolivian negotiators who obeyed the instructions of the mining industry before the revolution never bothered
to explore other types of compensation.

It is difficult to fit Hochschild and Aramayo, the other two members of
the oligarchical triumvirate, into this scheme. I have the impression that
both believed that the combined interests of Patiño, the British, and the
Dutch would suffice to overcome the resistance offered by Stuart Symington, even though he had the complete confidence of President Truman.

Subsequent events show that the Bolivian revolution would have
taken place with or without an increase in tin prices. This increase would
have benefited the government only superficially and the people not at all.
Yet the Bolivian mine owners charged that Symington's opposition to
the price increase was responsible for "Communist" subversion in Bo-

livia. They said that if the increase had been immediately forthcoming, both they and the government would have been in a position to defeat the subversion. This strange and unjust accusation had the virtue of bringing Stuart Symington, a powerful ally, to my side in defense of the revolution.

The Campaign Against Nationalization

On October 31, 1952, the MNR government nationalized the three large mining companies. The decree, affirming the principle of compensation for the expropriated companies and listing the government's counter-claims against them, symbolized the defeat of the tin-mining oligarchy in Bolivia. They proceeded to campaign abroad for the recovery of their properties and their political position in Bolivia. In order to understand their campaign, it is important to place in proper perspective the reception of the decree in the United States.

In the United States, respect for private property is viewed almost as a religious principle. Only in rare cases may private property be nationalized in the public interest, and seizure must be preceded by prompt and adequate compensation. Thus, the United States permits the expropriation of land or other types of property for public works such as irrigation, roads, or urban development, but the expropriation of industry is inconceivable. Even during the war, when all industrial activities were theoretically under the state control, the government worked through private ownership and only intervened directly when a strike or lockout threatened the war effort. Many of the so-called public services in the United States are in the hands of private enterprise—electric power, telegraph and telephone communications—and even where government participation has been of such magnitude as to show truly positive results, as in the case of the Tennessee Valley Authority, proposals are made periodically to explore the transfer of these projects to private organizations.

The general reaction in the United States to the nationalization of the large mining corporations in Bolivia was unfavorable. The public simply could not understand how the state could take on the activities of private enterprise. It tends to believe that nationalization reflects the opportunism of politicians who want to make a quick fortune at the expense of the state, or that the expropriation is the result of Communist influence. This is why explaining the nationalization of the Bolivian mines was more difficult and complex than it might seem at first glance and why the tin barons found such fertile ground in the United States for sowing confusion during the first months of the National Revolution.

One of the first major steps of the public relations firm contracted by the tin barons was to convene in New York City all the mining engineers who had left the Bolivian mines immediately following nationalization. In a well-planned publicity campaign involving news dispatches from La Paz, they scheduled a sensational news conference when the technicians and their families arrived in New York. They tried to make three main points. First, the "confiscation of the mines" was a brutal measure which endangered the lives of the engineers and their families. Wives and children were brought forward to attest to the charge, citing imaginary threats. Second, tin mining in Bolivia was such a complex process that in the hands of the state, and especially in the hands of the labor unions, state control would not last more than six months. The technicians predicted that the workers would take over the stores and distribute the food and goods; they would limit themselves to selling the minerals already extracted, and then with no plans for the future, the work would come to a halt when the reserves were gone. Finally, since tin was such an indispensable strategic element for the West, extreme measures must be taken to avoid complete destruction of the mines.

Since these statements came from technicians who had worked in the Bolivian mines for several years, they had a great impact on American public opinion. The organization which showed the most partiality was the U.S. Bureau of Mines, some of whose employees had worked in the now nationalized companies. The weekly reports of the bureau were completely opposed to nationalization.

Our major problem was to convince the RFC to sign a long-term contract, for a period of two or three years, at a fixed price. The RFC gave the impression that the dispute over nationalization could not be resolved without the express acceptance of the former owners, arguing that the tin coming from Bolivia could be attached under court orders, thereby involving the RFC in litigation. At the same time the State Department, assuming that the interests of many U.S. citizens were involved in the nationalization, presented a memorandum whose central thesis was that while the United States recognized Bolivia's sovereign right to nationalize the companies, fair, prompt, and effective compensation would have to be paid the former owners before bilateral negotiations could be resumed.

Confronted by the fact that U.S. government institutions were supporting the demands of the former mine owners, I took energetic action on two fronts: one was directed toward public opinion in the United States, and the other toward the U.S. government. On the first front every means at our command was used to make known the record of the mining companies in Bolivia. After about six months of intense campaigning, the first results were reflected in the attitudes of the Department of State and the RFC. Both agencies, which at first seemed impermeable, began to demonstrate a more open attitude.

Convincing the government itself proved more laborious work, but we tirelessly attempted to find friends who understood Bolivia's revolutionary process. By March 1, 1953, I believed we were ready to sign the first long-term contract with the RFC. Before this, I had arranged as a temporary measure for U.S. purchases of mineral shipments as they arrived at embarcation ports on the Pacific. However, in order to guarantee the security of the government as well as the industry, it was absolutely necessary to conclude a long-term contract.

Bolivia Victimized by Promoters

The Bolivian government recognized the principle of compensation for the nationalized mines, and direct negotiations were begun between the government's Bolivian Mining Corporation and the former owners over the amount and the form of compensation. This opened up possibilities for a new contract for a reasonable period of time and at an acceptable price. Unfortunately the first difficulties came from our side, resulting from our inexperience and from provincial rivalry among our politicians and leaders who think that a prominent position suddenly gives them the know-how that is only acquired by experience.

The Bolivian Mining Corporation and the Mining Bank signed a contract conceding the monopoly for the sale of Bolivian minerals to a small U.S. company, the Mercantile Metal and Ore Corporation. In a country like the United States, there is an abundance of organizations formed by adventurers who profit from abnormal situations and take advantage of the credulity and inexperience of the weak. The Mercantile Metal and Ore Corporation perceived our weak points: the virtual prohibition on the sale of minerals produced in Bolivia, and the ingenuousness of some Bolivian leaders. The company sent a very skillful and audacious attorney, Milton Gould, to Bolivia. With the argument that while the United States could refuse to buy tin directly from Bolivia, it could not refuse an offer made by an American company, he soon had the personnel of the Mining Corporation and the Mining Bank in his pocket. He impressed them with eloquent arguments, claiming to have influential friends in the U.S. Senate and on the board of directors of the RFC.

All this is conceivable in a country where businessmen do not always play their cards openly, but I have never been able to understand why the Bolivian embassy in Washington was not consulted first, nor why reports were not requested about the solvency and veracity of such skillful negotiators. I was greatly surprised when Mr. Gould appeared at the embassy accompanied by a person of Russian origin. Gould was holding an option, dated September 1, 1952, and signed by official agencies of the Bolivian government, which gave his firm a commission of nearly four million dollars without it having to guarantee anything nor risk one cent of capital, except for the cost of plane tickets and expenses in La Paz. With the audacity typical of the promoters of imaginary businesses and, possibly, as a result of the treatment he had received in Bolivia, he tried to give orders about Bolivia's international policy and the conduct of the Bolivian government.

Our first step was to investigate the company which had succeeded in negotiating such a lucrative contract. New York bankers I consulted, as well as the reports of Dunn and Bradstreet, agreed that the company was a tiny business which operated from one room, had very little capital, and was virtually unknown in the business world. It was an extraordinary arrangement. These people were going to earn four million dollars each year through the efforts of the Bolivian ambassador in Washington!

Just to be sure, I asked some of my friends in Congress and in the government if the United States would more readily buy the nationalized minerals through an intermediary firm instead of through direct government-to-government negotiations. At all levels the answer was the same: If the United States decided not to buy the minerals, it would not do so even if we were to hire the most powerful company in the nation as intermediary. In fact they were not pleased to see an American company trying to profit from an unusual situation in which the refusal or resistance of the U.S. government might appear linked to an act of extortion. I concluded that the contract was disadvantageous, not only because of the astronomical commission to be awarded, but because the participation of these businessmen would be harmful.

I refused to deal with these businessmen and decided not to sign any contract during the period of the option. I was not informed, however, of one very important detail, although the company's representatives took care to let me know about it later: the option had been extended for a longer period than stipulated in the original contract. Unknowingly I signed an agreement for the sale of 5,000 tons before this additional period had expired, and the storm broke loose.

Mr. Gould presented a complaint in a New York court demanding the sum of $1,400,000 as a judgment for breach of contract. He obtained the seizure of the bank accounts of the Mining Bank, the Mining Corporation, and even of the Central Bank of Bolivia. Apparently the judicial process in New York State allowed this type of action. We would have thought that the judge's first act would be to notify the accused party of the content of the complaint. For this judge, however, the demand of one of the interested parties was enough to order the immediate seizure of substantial resources belonging to the Bolivian government, national companies, and private individuals. Here the procedures for collection were unusually severe, above all against a country which was known to have few reserves.

I protested vociferously at the Department of State where I went to request recognition of the sovereign immunity of the funds of the Central Bank and of official organs like the Mining Corporation and the Mining Bank. After a rather long discussion, the State Department decided to recommend immunity for the accounts of the Central Bank, but it refused to extend that recommendation in favor of the Mining Corporation and the Mining Bank, reasoning that while these institutions might belong to the Bolivian government, they functioned as private enterprises in fulfilling commercial contracts. As a consequence, they declared them subject to judicial actions.

In my note to the foreign office of March 20, 1953, I expressed the opinion that, once the account was blocked, and before taking further steps, the Mining Bank should have consulted the embassy in order to devise the most expedient measures for its defense. The Mining Bank ignored the embassy once again and engaged a group of defense lawyers. I had no objection to that action, but it merely confirmed what the embassy already knew: the first step should have been an attempt to gain legal immunity for the Mining Bank through diplomatic channels. I proceeded quickly in the case of the seizure of the Central Bank's funds, fearing that the bank might also try to hand over its defense to a law firm or send a special agent who could defeat the embassy's effort. I hastened to write a note demanding the intervention of the Department of State, an action which succeeded, as I reported by cable. In this affair, which was decided in favor of the Central Bank, lawyers from the United States and Bolivia did not take part.

The Mercantile Corporation claim for $1,400,000 for commissions in the contract for the sale of tin was relegated to the slow process of judicial review. The attorneys for the Mining Bank, as is customary for American attorneys, advised an out-of-court settlement. After long negotiations, an agreement was reached in which Mercantile was paid $250,000. While the embassy's efforts had saved a considerable sum of money for the Bolivian government, the damage to our reputation remained. The prestige and methods of the authors of the nationalization of Bolivian mines was brought into question in a country where business skill is highly valued. This could affect future negotiations.

Moreover, it created an obstacle in the sale of tin to the official agencies of the U.S. government.

Proposal for Arbitration

On January 31, 1953, I sent a note to the Bolivian foreign office transmitting a proposal formulated by Thomas Mann who was then chief of the division of American republics in the State Department, and who was later assistant secretary of state for Latin America and undersecretary of state for economic affairs. Mann's proposal was as follows: If the Bolivian government agreed to submit the compensation claims of the former owners of the nationalized mines to international arbitration, the United States would sign a three-year contract to buy tin for $1.215 per refined pound.

To appreciate the importance of this proposal, it is necessary to look at some previous events. Even before the nationalization of the mines, there had been rumors that the United States was on the point of completing its stockpile of tin. I suspected that these rumors were part of the campaign of intimidation initiated by the tin barons, and for this reason they were not given the importance that they deserved. Upon my arrival in Washington I confirmed that suspicion, but I also sensed that this could be a weapon in the hands of the former mine owners. Mann's proposal renewed these fears, as I explained in a letter to Foreign Minister Walter Guevara.

In my meetings in La Paz with the president and his aides before assuming my post in Washington, I had advised them to proceed with caution in the nationalization of the mines. I foresaw the possibility of becoming embroiled in serious problems regarding prices and the maintenance of production. In Washington, my fears were confirmed when I saw the impression made by the propaganda of the tin barons upon high American officials and upon the conduct of the special agencies of the American government. There was talk not only of a legal embargo on Bolivian exports, but of a loss of interest in continued purchases now that the stockpile was near completion.

On February 12, 1953, the Department of State officially informed me that the United States had completed its stockpile of tin and would make further purchases only at current market prices, not at a fixed price, and added: "The Department of State is aware of the gravity of this situation for Bolivia and does not wish that this decision be viewed as an 'ultimatum,' nor as a catastrophe. It is simply the presence of a new factor which complicates even more the continuation of tin purchases and the arrangement of existing problems as a consequence of the nationalization of the mines in Bolivia." The spokesman for the Department of State referred to the possibilities which had been discussed in Bolivia about the sale of tin to Russia, commenting, "This fact is not sufficient to modify the decision already made, nor is the threat that the Bolivian government become Communist." In this respect, it is interesting to remember that in a memo sent to the Bolivian foreign office, December 28, 1953, I refer to a dinner which the Russian ambassador to the United States, Georgi Zarubin, gave for me. We discussed there the possibility of Russia buying 25,000 tons of Bolivian tin. The sale never materialized and in fact, in January 1958, the U.S.S.R. dumped large quantities of tin on the market.

With the official announcement in March 1953 that the American government would make future tin purchases only at world market prices, which had been steady at $1.215 per pound, the price suddenly fell to only $0.70 per pound. This meant the loss of more than one-third of Bolivia's foreign exchange revenues and placed almost all the tin industry in a marginal situation. The State Department's recommendation not to view this as a "catastrophe" was merely rhetoric. Along with the problems accompanying the profound changes brought about by the revolution, the Bolivian economy suddenly found itself on the verge of bankruptcy. It is only fair to recognize that the situation could not have been foreseen in January when I communicated the Department of State's proposition to prolong the fixed prices for three more years if we would submit to international arbitration. Clearly this matter was not international, but entirely domestic.

The fall in price meant a difference of almost $0.50 per pound of tin, amounting to nearly $1,000 per ton. Since annual production was at 30,000 tons the total would be $30 million for one year and $90 million for the three years. If we take the proposal transmitted by Mann seriously, it meant that the United States was giving extraordinary value to the precedent of submitting the question of indemnity for nationalized property to international arbitration. Moreover, the annual consumption of tin in the United States is approximately 200,000 tons. Should it be understood that the American government was willing to pay that higher price for three years? If this were so, we would arrive at really high figures, supposing that the world market price remained at its current low level. Although this was not very probable because of the disturbing situation in Korea and the rest of Asia, the swift decline in world prices after the American announcement was an indication of depression in the international tin market.

Settlement with the Mine Owners

The Bolivian government's decree of October 31, 1952, fixed the amount that should be paid to the former tin-mining companies, based upon their accounting records, as $16,774,194.103 and 304,544,288.14 bolivian pesos, a total of approximately $18,200,000. This compensation was paid despite the fact that the tin companies still owed the state large sums. The new government instructed the treasury to report the amounts of foreign currency that those companies had not returned or presented for settlement in accordance with the decrees of June 7 and July 7, 1939. According to the report compiled by the general comptroller's office on July 4, 1957, Patiño Mines and Enterprises had the following unpaid balances:

U.S. dollars	99,867,843.38
British pounds	29,721,005.17
Bolivian pesos	48,416,739.92

On July 12, 1957, the Central Bank of Bolivia informed the Ministry of Mines and Petroleum that certain sums, arising from the legal obligations of Patiño Mines and Enterprises since January, 1939, remained outstanding. Sums in foreign currency for which no account had been made totaled $218,474,368.83 and £47,716,841.08; sums reported but not deposited were $543,060.00 and £647,956.05. The mining companies never made a serious effort to explain why they did not account for such large sums of money.

The companies also misled the public by their frequent charge that the Bolivian government never made a formal offer to negotiate compensation. This statement is false. On November 10, 1955, a representative of Patiño Mines proposed to extend the percentage of their continued participation in a share of sales (*retenciones*) for a period of ten years. This proposal was accepted by the government in a letter dated May 18, 1956, in which it was stated that such *retenciones* for a period of ten years would constitute the final and definitive payment for the value of the expropriated properties. The government's counterproposal was justified because:

1. The *retenciones* are proportionate to the price of tin on the world market; consequently, a higher price will be accompanied by a larger payment.
2. In the case that, for reasons beyond the control of the producers of tin, the price falls to such levels that production becomes uneconomical, it is clear that these properties and their installations would decrease in value proportionately.
3. In the four years between 1953 and 1957, more than $12 million was paid to the former owners; within a period of ten years that sum would have been more than tripled as long as prices were maintained at a proportionate level.

Nevertheless, Patiño rejected the proposal.

The government also had a just protest with respect to the Patiño company's conduct. In most of the meetings held until 1957, the Patiño representatives refused to recognize the government's right to expropriate. It is true that that right is not clearly recognized in the Bolivian constitution. However, a commission whose task is to negotiate the amount of indemnity is not the place to resolve a constitutional issue. The companies had at their disposal the processes prescribed by law through which they could oppose the nationalization of the mines. The natural course would have been to make an appeal to the Supreme Court claiming the unconstitutionality of the nationalization decree.

·Another element of the controversy was the unrealistic evaluation the companies placed on their properties, using figures based either on cost of replacement or on the value of future profits. Patiño, for example, calculated the value of their expropriated property using the former method at $70,383,035.00. To arrive at this figure they tripled the value of their investments prior to 1941, according to a memorandum of November 20, 1954. By the second method, the value of future earnings, they estimated a sum of $50,669,277.00. With respect to this last figure, it is necessary to observe that the tin companies had repeatedly declared that they could not make a profit at a price less than $1.25 per refined pound.

A property such as a mine has a value in relation to its current sale value, calculated not by future profits, but by current profits. The prices of tin and tungsten, then and in the foreseeable future, were such that there was virtually no margin for profit except in a small fraction of the expropriated mines. If proposals were made to buy these properties, and if the proposals were presented under existing profit margins, it is extremely doubtful that such proposals would equal even the values mentioned in the companies' books or recognized by the nationalization decree.

The companies producing tungsten received larger indemnities than those that produced tin. Because of the price of tungsten in existing contracts with the General Services Administration, the Bolivian Mining Corporation authorized payment to former owners of $20 per unit of wolfram sold. In the Patiño group, for example, a small mine like the Bolivian Tin and Tungsten Corporation received indemnities by June 1957 totaling $3,113,833.03, while Patiño Mines and Enterprises, which produced only tin and was the largest mine nationalized, received $1,707,615.55. For the same reason the Hochschild group, which included many properties that produced tungsten, received an indemnity prior to June 1957, of $5,534,494.19.

The former owners continued their campaign to obtain a reconsideration of the nationalization until 1957 as a result of pressure exerted by the United States. Finally they were forced to realize that they could not continue to deceive the American public indefinitely. As will be seen later, the United States not only abandoned its pressure tactics on behalf of the tin barons, but decided to give financial and economic assistance to the reconstruction plans of the MNR regime.

Balance Sheet of Nationalization

It is difficult to determine who came out ahead in the nationalization of the tin mines. More time must pass before this matter can be judged dispassionately, away from the political and emotional pressures endured by those of us who participated actively in these events. Nonetheless, I will attempt to present a foundation for an objective analysis.

The principal objective in the nationalization of the mines was political. If anyone thought nationalization would have positive economic effects, the years and events have since proved him wrong. The political situation was such that drastic action could not be postponed; the arrogance of the mine owners and the flattery of their supporters had cut them off completely from the social and political reality of the country. Certain spectacular events strengthened their belief that their grip on the nation was so strong that a few intellectuals and romantic politicians could not break it: first, the suicide of Germán Busch soon after having dictated the law of June 7, 1939, requiring the complete surrender of foreign exchange from sales abroad; second, the hanging of Gualberto Villarroel for having dared to adopt a policy favorable to the working class and to guarantee the organization of the labor movement in the mines. The impunity with which a mercenary minority acted against Villarroel made the tin barons optimistic and arrogant. Their cruel persecution in the following six years, however, only served to fortify the spirit of resistance of new generations. It became clear that the people could move forward only when the agents of oppression and stagnation had been eliminated. The results of nationalization must be analyzed in human terms which are not easily measured by exclusively quantitative economic values.

Let us examine the other side of the coin. If the mines had not been nationalized, what would the tin barons have done when the United States announced the end of the purchases at a fixed price, forcing a sharp drop in prices on the world market? The companies' statement that they needed a price of at least $1.25 per pound to continue production without losses was close to the truth. Would they have been able to sustain the loss of $0.50 per pound only to maintain their property rights? The most probable outcome would have been mass dismissals, generating one of the largest social conflicts in the history of the republic. In the end, they would have proceeded just as the railroads did: acknowledging the deficits caused by the competition of truck and plane transport and the obsolescence of their equipment, they simply handed their installations over to the state.

If these premises contain something of the truth, then we must conclude that the nationalization of the mines saved the companies from bankruptcy. It guaranteed them an income during one of the most critical periods for producers of raw materials in underdeveloped countries. Yet they chose to assume the role of both victim and judge of the policies which the Bolivian government was forced to adopt in order to obtain financial and economic aid to overcome the crisis.

Mining has been and continues to be the most important industrial activity in the republic. In this field technicians, geologists, metallurgists, and economists play dominant roles. More than fifty years ago the Liberal party tried to foster economic and technical independence by creating the School of Mines as one of the most important institutes of the University of Oruro. Since that time hundreds of Bolivians have passed through its programs; while it can be criticized, that training is more valuable than improvisation or routinely acquired knowledge based on work in the mines. If we recall that Bolivia has traditionally been a mining country, it is reasonable to conclude that the administration of the new state enterprise should have been the responsibility mainly of Bolivian mining engineers. They had studied locally or had been fortunate enough to acquire knowledge in foreign universities. Reality, however, has been different.

Friction between the technicians and workers has become more acute, endangering the industry. On the one hand, the engineer, who always holds subordinate positions, has found his authority decreasing; he almost always lacks the backing of the boss, the state, which, for political reasons, prefers to side with the workers. On the other hand, the workers have suddenly found themselves to have powerful influence which they often use in trivial matters, frequently undermining the engineers' authority. In this tense atmosphere between the two most important elements of mining production, labor leaders and military officers have found a vacuum that is easy to fill. This is especially true of retired officers who, lacking professional responsibilities, can easily adapt themselves to anarchic situations. The Bolivian Mining Corporation, instead of being managed by Bolivians who are best qualified for the task, has become the refuge of retired military officers and second class politicians, skillful in surviving political changes through flattery and mimicry. Under these circumstances the state enterprise is not exactly a model for those who

believe that underdeveloped countries will achieve economic independence through the expulsion of private companies.

It is premature to reach conclusions regarding what the country
might have gained with political stability. It is evident that the imposition of private interests by a privileged group in control of the state has
been completely eliminated. What has replaced it is still a question mark.

11

The Twilight of the Tin Barons

By the end of 1952, the tin-mining oligarchy had lost control of Bolivia, politically and economically. The former owners of the mines then shifted the theater of their main attack against the revolution to the United States, trying to hamper our sales of minerals and siphon off for themselves a large share of the profits by influencing foreign governments and mineral refining operations. The almost total absence of refining capacity in Bolivia made us especially dependent on those who controlled tin smelters. Only through exceptional efforts and intimate knowledge of U.S. domestic politics were we able after many years to defeat their shrewdly devised and well-financed strategies.

Conflict with Ex-Senator Tydings

In their attempts to defend their interests and attack the MNR government, the tin barons secured the services of Millard Tydings, an ex-senator from Maryland. His assistance gave them a great advantage and posed a serious threat for us. He was a politician of considerable influence in the Democratic party, having been Senate majority leader. He was married to one of the daughters of multimillionaire Joseph Davies, the first U.S. ambassador to Soviet Russia, whose wife was the famous Marjorie Merriweather Post, heiress to the huge breakfast cereal fortune. Tydings was also associated with a group of attorneys who had close connections with both political parties. As a former senator he had access to congressional chambers, a privilege which was extremely valuable for influencing decisions of these branches of government. The tin barons did not hesitate to pay this gentleman a fat fee.

Tydings carried out activities parallel to those of the Nathanson Brothers public relations firm. Both cooperated in reporting alarming news about the Bolivian revolution to legislators, members of the executive branch, and journalists. They also called for the use of all kinds of pressure to force the Bolivian government to return the nationalized industries, or to pay astronomical compensation.

Only intense, sustained, and personally dedicated action could neutralize the tremendous influence of the ex-senator from Maryland. Much of this was provided by the fervent dedication of Gardner Jackson, one of the best friends we had, who worked in favor of the Bolivian revolution. He was an intellectual who had emerged from the worker and union movement immediately following the First World War. His personal wealth was sufficient so that his actions were generally dictated by conviction. He did not hesitate to place his person or his wealth in support of his ideals. One action, which characterizes him eloquently, was his serving as secretary-general of the movement in Massachusetts to prevent the execution of Sacco and Vanzetti. For this, and other reasons, he was a man who had the respect of both conservative and liberal American politicians. No one ever questioned his integrity, nor his sincerity.

When I first met him, Jackson's efforts were focused on the defense of labor union interests, he visited the Congress frequently and had close contacts with legislators. Thus he could learn about Tydings's movements and the names of the senators and representatives he visited. Once I possessed that information, I could present myself before those same senators and representatives in such a way that my visit would be meaningful. In doing this, the help of several of my friends in the Washington community was invaluable. I called on the congressmen soon after Tydings did, presenting the other side of the story. They received me in a spirit of understanding and equanimity which does them honor.

The congressmen often told me that the United States had been built on the principles of absolute respect for private property, repudiation of any form of confiscation, and the conviction that law alone maintains order in society. Accordingly, they considered violent changes of government to be the antithesis of order. When they understood the motives behind the Bolivian revolution, however, they could not help but see that justice was on our side and that domination of the Bolivian people had been so complete that rebellion was the only alternative.

My first talk with Millard Tydings took place in the residence of the Bolivian Embassy in an interview requested by him. A cultured and intelligent man, he began by expressing his admiration and affection for the Bolivian people. He added that this was not the first time that he had so expressed his affection for a foreign people. Only a short time before, he had participated in litigation between a people's government of the Middle East and certain capitalist interests in the United States. His dedication to and defense of the just demands of that nation had resulted in a favorable decision. Our dialogue continued roughly as follows.

Andrade: I must explain to you, Mr. Tydings, that the position of the Bolivian government is final concerning the forum and the authority for settling any complaint regarding the decree to nationalize the mines. If the former owners are not satisfied with the amount of compensation established by the law, if they are not in agreement with other aspects of this arrangement, and if, finally, they believe that the government did not have the right to nationalize an industry, the Bolivian judicial system is open to them. Our constitution, legal codes, and judicial procedures are broad and provide means for dealing with controversial administrative decisions. If Messrs. Patiño, Hochschild, and Aramayo still had any respect left for the country in which they made their fortunes, they would have adopted the remedies provided by our laws and would have made the appropriate appeals in our courts. Therefore, Mr. Tydings, I must tell you that I do not have jurisdiction to recognize an appeal here in the United States, nor can you, nor should you, as an attorney, pursue this course.

Tydings: Mr. Ambassador, I believe that you do not understand my role. I am not attempting to secure a judgment against Bolivian authorities or against a decision by your government. I am simply here as the representative of those firms to see if I can reason with the authorized representative of the Bolivian government and thereby find a solution which is favorable to the interests of both my clients and the Bolivian government. You well know that in this country there is a strong reaction against the confiscation of private property. The action that you have taken must have an effect on the opinion of the people who must negotiate with you for the purchase of Bolivian products. Therefore, this problem does not belong to the judicial process.

Andrade: Mr. Tydings, I regret having to say that I disagree with you. Bolivia is a sovereign nation and the United States has subscribed to pacts recognizing that sovereignty and the juridical equality of all states. The ownership of Bolivian products is established in Bolivia and no authority in this country, or any other, no matter how high, has the power to know or judge whether that ownership is properly established. If we were not to accept this principle, we would create legal confusion in relations among friendly countries. I do not believe that the United States government, nor any other serious body in this country can sustain the contrary.

Tydings: Allow me to ask you, Mr. Ambassador, if up until this moment you have been able to sign a contract for the sale of nationalized minerals.

Andrade: Your question is rhetorical because you know very well that I have not signed any such contract. You are insinuating that the United States will refuse to buy Bolivian tin as long as the tin is nationalized or while the demands of the ex-property owners are unsatisfied. For your information, Mr. Tydings, I must tell you that although it would seem that this may happen, I, who am not an American citizen, have much more faith than you in the judicial integrity of this country and in its spirit of justice. If the United States needs tin, it must buy it. I do not believe that it will use our economic weakness as a lever to make us accept something immoral and illegal.

Tydings, standing abruptly: Mr. Ambassador, if you do not accept the demand for compensation of Messrs. Patiño, Hochschild, and Aramayo, I give you my word that you will not be able to sell a pound of tin in this country.

With cold courtesy I showed him the door, and so ended this historic interview.

This was only the first intercession of ex-Senator Tydings who continued his intensive efforts to prevent the United States from buying tin from the nationalized mines. The change in government brought about by the electoral victory of General Dwight D. Eisenhower, who took office on January 20, 1953, was favorable to us. In the new Republican administration, Tydings's personal influence as a leading Democrat was considerably diminished. Nevertheless, using his contacts with former colleagues in Congress, he carried out many activities which might have led to catastrophe without extraordinary efforts on our part. Tydings, in the main, did not obtain what he wanted, but he was responsible in part for the pressure which made future tin purchases contingent on provisional arrangements for the payment of compensation. I believe that this was the origin of the policy which forced the Bolivian government to pay the retenciones to the former owners in addition to twenty dollars per unit of wolfram on contracts still recognized by the GSA.

The RFC, representing the American government, continued to buy shipments of tin, and in 1953 the United States initiated a policy of direct economic assistance to the MNR regime. Meanwhile, Tydings publicly announced that he would seek reelection as senator from Maryland in November 1954. He was counting on the support of the Democratic party machine in Maryland, and his election was possible. It was under these circumstances that the second offensive against the Bolivian government began.

Taking advantage of his friendship with the senator from Rhode Island, Theodore Francis Green, who at that time was chairman of the Senate Foreign Relations Committee, Tydings requested a special hearing of that committee. He opened his statement by greeting the committee's members and expressing the hope that in a few months he would take his seat with them instead of being simply a private witness. With this crude introduction, flaunting his political influence, he began a violent attack against the Bolivian revolution. He demanded an investigation of the decision of the Eisenhower administration to extend economic and technical cooperation, which although limited, was sufficient to prevent a tragic collapse in Bolivia. His speech lasted more than an hour and was widely publicized by Nathanson Brothers. The impact of these statements was serious and delayed the work of the more timorous members of the State Department and the economic and technical assistance agencies. However, I must admit that the principle actors in this new U.S. policy toward Bolivia remained firm, prepared to respond to the charges or to an investigation.

Meanwhile, in addition to the sharp drop in the price of tin, production had fallen off because of the workers' lack of discipline and because of the deterioration of equipment which had not been maintained nor modernized by the former owners. This produced such a grave economic situation in Bolivia that only the assistance of the United States could avoid a repetition of the famine which had occurred in our country during the War of the Pacific. The tin barons and their lawyer and lobbyist attempted to cut off that aid and subject a nation to hunger, blood, and tears.

What could be done to counteract Tydings's testimony? The fear of the weak is always that in an encounter with the strong, in this case the Republican administration and the Democratic-controlled Senate, their interests will be sacrificed. The Bolivian people had no choice but to appeal to the democratic principles and the spirit of justice in American society.

I sent a letter to the chairman of the Senate Foreign Relations Committee although this was not in accord with diplomatic practice. The letter was brief and simply stated that before the committee took any action which might affect my country's interests, and in keeping with American democratic practice, it should hear the views of the Bolivian government which had been so harshly attacked by ex-Senator Tydings. I then offered to appear before the committee. Visiting the members of the committee individually, I gave each a copy of the letter and pointed out that Mr. Tydings had used an advantage that contradicted the tradition of fair play which is respected as a religious precept in both public and private life in the United States.

My objective was to halt the investigation which Senator Green had already accepted in principle. If the investigation were to be carried out, my goal would then be to convert the hearing granted to me into a sounding board so that the entire country would hear the truth about Bolivia's plight. This would have been the first time that a foreign envoy had appeared before the Senate, an event that would have created great interest and drawn an extraordinarily large audience. The Bolivian point of view would have been sustained, defeating once and for all the reactionary forces who were using foreign soil to try to mortally wound the revolutionary government.

The request to be heard publicly in the Senate committee caused a stir. On the one hand, there were some members who were inclined to grant me the opportunity; on the other, there arose the danger of establishing a precedent which could be extremely embarrassing for the government in the later conduct of international relations. Although the State Department did not do so publicly, I have been informed that it exerted influence to prevent establishing this precedent. The outcome was that the committee tabled the proposal to carry out an investigation of aid to the Bolivian government, and a movement of sympathy and support for our cause became apparent.

As might be expected, this episode aroused much interest in the press. I was interviewed by several journalists who referred to my fears about the attitude that the Senate would assume and asked what I thought would be the result of an investigation. They also asked me if I was prepared for the possibility that Tydings would be elected senator. I answered: "The American Senate is composed of ninety-six members. My faith lies in respect for the integrity of that institution and of its members. In any case, even if Mr. Tydings is elected, I am firmly convinced that the other ninety-five senators have never been on the payroll of the former owners of the Bolivian mines." This statement created quite a sensation in spite of the fact that Tydings was a powerful man who might increase his power in the coming elections.

This episode had a dramatic finale. Some weeks later I ran into Tydings in the Chevy Chase Club. Wanting to display his tolerance and wit, he referred to what had happened in a superficial and joking manner. When his arrogance became intolerable, I told him simply: "Mr. Tydings, I regret that you may be using your political power to attack a weak, defenseless nation. Do not forget that pride is a poor counselor and that life sometimes holds surprises for those who forget that we are all mere mortals." I had been thinking of unexpected results in the election, but I could not have foreseen what actually happened. Less than two weeks later, Tydings suffered a stroke which left him paralyzed. One of his relatives had to withdraw his candidacy for him, and some months later, in spite of all the efforts of modern science, Tydings died. His death marked the disappearance of one of the strongest supports of the Bolivian mining companies in the United States.

The Wolfram Contracts

When Generalissimo Chiang Kai-shek was finally expelled from continental China by the Red Army of Mao Tse-tung, the situation of the tungsten supply for the Western world became exceedingly precarious. Production and consumption of wolfram has always been closely tied to war and peace. Tungsten is used to temper steel in the armaments industry; therefore its value rises in time of war. When China, the largest producer and supplier of tungsten ore, suddenly entered the Communist orbit, not only was the West left without this strategic material, but the Communist bloc gained an important resource. The United States had no alternative but to raise its prices with the result that one unit of wolfram which in 1950 was valued at $28.25, rose to $61.02 in 1951 and in 1952 reached its maximum price of $64.04. Based on these extraordinarily lucrative prices, the companies of Patiño, Hochschild, and Aramayo had each signed contracts which ran to the beginning of 1956.

Wolframite and scheelite, the two best known tungsten ores, are not rare, nor are they deposits concentrated exclusively in certain areas of the world. Production is possible on almost every continent. The result of the U.S. policy of incentives was decisive. By the middle of 1952, the production of these minerals outside the Soviet sphere had more than offset the shortage caused by the stoppage of shipments from Red China, and prices on the free market had fallen. Then a policy which I have been unable to explain to this day brought about the unexpected.

The GSA, the official U.S. agency in charge of the purchase of tungsten minerals, suddenly announced the refusal of shipments from Bolivia. The logical explanation suggested deceit. The contracts signed by the GSA had been with the Patiño, Hochschild, and Aramayo Companies, not with the Bolivian Mining Corporation. Consequently, it had grounds for refusing shipments covered by contracts signed by the three companies. If the Bolivian Mining Corporation, or any other company, wished to negotiate the sale of tungsten minerals, it would have to do so according to current market prices of under $20.00 per unit. This was less than one-third the amount agreed upon with the companies.

We vehemently protested this unfriendly attitude, since such an injustice was incomprehensible. The United States had had access to Bolivian wolfram during the war, thanks to the efforts of the mine workers and not to the commercial activities of businessmen who lived comfortably in New York, London, or Paris. We argued that the GSA's position damaged the prestige of the United States and went against the ideals proclaimed in the struggle against the totalitarian powers. Unfortunately, the officials in charge of the administration of these contracts turned a deaf ear to our arguments. They wanted to establish precedents that would discourage future nationalizations, to punish the nation that had dared rebel against its oppressors. The irony of the affair was that this policy had been carried out by a Democratic administration which had been strengthened politically in the twentieth century by raising the banner of social justice.

Once again our weakness forced us to accept any condition which would assure the flow of foreign exchange so vital to feed our people. The GSA informed us that it would continue to accept shipments of wolfram as long as they came with the label of the former owners of the companies. The companies demanded twenty dollars per unit, which was applicable to the amount of compensation required, in order to sign the shipment documents. In this way, our revenue, which would have eased the grave impact of the fall in the price of tin, was cut by one-third.

Periodically the United States has employed the inducement of high prices to encourage the production of some essential raw material without considering the grave social and economic consequences which price increases produce in the long run. No one can oppose a country's offering an attractive price or other advantage in a time of international strife. However, when the destiny, the happiness, and the social and economic security of their allies is involved, this policy should be adopted only after a careful study of the likely repercussions when prices return to normal. Experience has shown that this frequently produces a much more serious crisis. The law of the jungle, survival of the fittest, cannot be reconciled with a modern society based upon the principle of human solidarity, adopted after centuries of conflict and individual and collective sacrifices. In this case, the brutality of the measure was even more evident because it was adopted on the principle that liberty, self-determination, and the rights of all nations were being defended. Such measures were thought to be in defense of the weak, since the strong have the means to defend themselves.

When a commodity suddenly increases in price, two results follow: some individuals can amass a personal fortune overnight; others benefit from an automatic increase in salaries and services. This, however, creates a standard of living which cannot be maintained unless the temporary situation becomes permanent. The resulting political and social problems are in no way the same as those which characterize a society already making systematic social progress. Instead, they impede orderly advance, making the society move in fits and starts, involving setbacks injurious to the best development plans. A nation must create services proportional to its income; when these are substantially increased, the government is unable to return to the original levels without generating tremendous political convulsions, riots, coups d'etat, and other violent upheavals. Considering these facts, it is odd that North Americans frequently wonder why we cannot stabilize our politics and the succession of our governments.

In Bolivia, the mining of wolfram has been limited to the small companies because the large corporations have found prices and consumption levels too unstable, and because the processing of this mineral is simpler than that of tin and requires less investment in machinery and treatment plants. At times the discovery of some deposits has led to exceptional good luck. The story is told of a resident of Oruro at the time of World War I who went on a hunting trip in the mountains and discovered that the miserable house of a peasant and the walls of his animal pens were made of stones containing more than 50 percent tungsten. For a modest sum he obtained the right to take the stones with him and then sold them in Oruro to the mineral buyers. The profit from this sale yielded a fortune exceeding one million pounds sterling.

One of the most profitable businesses for certain foreign firms, in which the industrialist Hochschild was a major investor, was the purchase of minerals. The small mining companies possessed very little capital and so obtained loans from the large commercial houses which they afterward repaid in minerals, naturally yielding to the requirements of these businessmen with respect to interest, mineral yields, and prices. In this way Hochschild, Phillips Brothers, Tennant and Sons, and other businessmen of lesser importance made huge fortunes.

With the purpose of limiting the excessive profits made by these large corporations at the expense of the efforts and needs of smaller mining interests, the government founded the Mining Bank of Bolivia soon after the Chaco War. This state agency was to serve a double function: first, it was to replace the large mineral buyers; second, it would assist small companies lacking the capital to carry out geological or metallurgical studies. The creation of the Mining Bank would thus mean the end of private middlemen and speculators, and concentrate sales, distribution, credits, and exportation in a government agency. Theoretically the basis upon which the bank was conceived was beyond reproach and was supposed to favor the small mining industry. Unfortunately, the results were otherwise. Small mining interests have had difficulty in obtaining credit because they lacked the capacity to influence public agencies just as they lacked industrial capacity. Prices paid by the new public agencies for minerals have been generally less than those paid by the businessmen. The maintenance of a gigantic bureaucracy has required greater and greater revenue, which the producers have been forced to supply. The plans for promotion and prospecting were never put into effect. In addition, the large companies adapted to the new situation with equal or even greater profits, operating in conjunction with the Mining Bank and acting as its agents in the sale of products abroad. The purchase of minerals simply changed hands and increased the burden on the small producer.

Principally for technical reasons, the major smelter for tungsten in the United States has been that of Wah Chang in Glen Cove, Long Island. The president of the corporation and its virtual owner was K. C. Li, a man of Chinese origin, now a naturalized citizen of the United States. When I met him Li was about sixty-five years old; what he lacked in size—he was less than five feet tall—he made up in intelligence, cleverness, and good will. He was one of the most respected experts in metallurgy, a specialist in rare metals. He had invented several systems for processing these metals and employed them in his smelters, still holding the patents. Because Bolivia was the principal supplier of wolfram, Li processed all the minerals of tungsten coming from Bolivian mines.

Li was extremely fond of playing golf and was a member of the best clubs in the New York area, one of them being the Piping Rock Club. One day while we were waiting our turn to continue our game, enjoying the magnificent view of Long Island Sound, he suddenly said, as though giving free rein to a spontaneous thought, "Víctor, why is it that we [Wah Chang], who refine all Bolivian tungsten, have to buy it from intermediaries like Grace, Phillips Brothers, or Tennant and Sons? Why do we not buy it directly from the Mining Bank of Bolivia or from the Mining Corporation, and let these organizations benefit from the commissions that I now pay to the middlemen?"

The proposition seemed so forceful that I reported it to my government by cable and then confirmed it by letter. This could mean hundreds of thousands of dollars for the Bolivian government with no additional effort or modification in the methods of production or marketing. It would also initiate a connection between production and processing which could be extremely profitable if extended to other minerals. The strange thing is that several weeks passed and I received no answer, not even a confirmation of the receipt of my insistent inquiries. This forced me to travel to Bolivia.

Then I discovered something unknown to me before: several of the high officials of the purchasing houses had been managers or high-level personnel of the Mining Bank. Little insight was needed to realize that a web of interests had been woven about the minerals. Part of the web was formed by the connections of state employees, responsible for the sale of the minerals, with the old commercial houses. In spite of all my efforts I could not overcome this obstacle and returned to Washington with the intention of shortening my stay abroad and returning as soon as

possible to Bolivia. There I hoped to fight more effectively from within
against the vested interests which undermined our principal institutions.

The Texas City Smelter

Britain's leadership in the production of coal and steel had long since
passed to the United States by the time of World War II. Although tin
ores were no longer being mined in the British Isles, England, for peculiar
and artificial reasons, continued to control the smelting and marketing of
tin. This was possible because one of her colonies, Malaya, turned out to
be the largest producer of tin ores. The United States never expressed
interest in establishing a tin smelting industry, in spite of the fact that it
consumed, then and now, more than 60 percent of the tin produced in
the world. Nor did the emergence of Bolivia as the second largest producer of tin in the world, during and after World War I, inspire the
United States to smelt tin, although shipments from Bolivia would have
had easier and safer access to all U.S. ports. On the contrary, it seemed
that the smelters were encouraged to stay in Europe, especially in England and Holland. Moreover, England, with its traditional commercial
and political skill completely absorbed the principal Bolivian producers,
incorporating them into the international system of the tin industry.

The Second World War drastically altered this situation, demonstrating unmistakably the danger of depending upon either a European source,
subject to the uncertainties of navigation in seas unprotected from sub-
marine attacks, or an Asian source, subject to blockade by the Japanese
navy and infantry. During a critical period, Bolivian minerals were the
only ones which could meet the military and civilian needs of the West.
As a result, the United States government had decided to build a tin
smelter in Texas City, Texas.

When the war was over and tin production resumed in Asia and Africa,
the government smelter at Texas City was to be turned over to private
interests. If this did not prove feasible, the smelter was to be closed and
deliveries resumed once again from Europe. However, the conflicts in
China and in Korea forced the United States to continue smelting operations in order to build the stockpile back up to a high level. When negotiations were terminated in Korea and Eisenhower had fulfilled his
promise to end hostilities, the administration again planned to close the
smelter.

The closing of the smelter could have brought an economic collapse
for Bolivia which sent half of its concentrated tin to Texas to earn the
dollars that Bolivia needed to buy food and other essential articles. Once
again we would be subject to British control of prices and smelting costs.

Consequently, we tried to keep the smelter in operation. Purchases of tin for the stockpile would continue to require at least twenty thousand tons from international markets. This would be very important in avoiding an even greater fall in prices. In July 1953 the Department of State informed us that the American government would be prepared to sign a new contract for the purchase of tin concentrates for an additional period of one year. This announcement came as a corollary to a decision by Congress to maintain the operation of the Texas City smelter.

Why did the government reverse its decision to close the smelter? The weekly news magazine, *Time*, which is so conservative in its appraisal of men and events in Latin America, published an editorial on June 20, 1955, commenting on the U.S. smelter and my work as Bolivian ambassador. It pointed out that the Texas City smelter, built by the U.S. government, was losing more than a million dollars annually in producing Bolivian tin for the U.S. stockpile. Texas City was the only large tin smelter, and Bolivia the only important source of tin in the Western Hemisphere. Without them the Americas would be at the mercy of the British-Dutch cartel's fixing of prices and would be vulnerable to loss of its source of tin in wartime. For these reasons, Congress had extended the operation of the smelter for one more year. In its issue of June 20, 1955, *Time* published a flattering article about my role in the Congress's decision. With what was perhaps exaggerated praise, they explained how persuasive I had been in making Bolivia's case, mentioning my small salary, limited expense account, and my entertaining songs in Aymara to which I sometimes provided accompaniment on the guitar.

For an envoy from a small country, Washington is a labyrinth through which it is difficult to find the right paths to negotiation. The Department of State is a cumbersome mechanism and its principal officials are continually weighed down by problems arising all over the world. The official in charge of relations with a specific country is a subordinate whose mission is to compile data for decisions by his superiors. These decisions are not made by a specific office, nor by an individual, but rather with the participation of several agencies or semiautonomous bodies which differ in their authority and jurisdiction. In addition to this, the relations maintained between the executive offices and the respective committees of the Senate and the House of Representatives are extremely important.

In the midst of this gigantic administrative apparatus, the most important task is to discover who possesses the authority and the influence necessary at that moment and in that matter, and to influence his decision. An ambassador can go around in circles for years, wasting his time in fruitless negotiations, if he has not been able to determine who has authority regarding a certain matter. Thus, the point is not to apply pressure to everyone, only to the key people. In this way one's arguments should be made not only to those who can understand, but to those who can act effectively in one's favor.

In the case of the Texas City smelter, the authority lay with Congress since the executive had already expressed the desire to close the smelter. Fortunately, the representative of the district where the smelter was located was a good friend, Clark Thompson, who, in turn, had close ties with Senator Lyndon Johnson, the Senate majority leader. The data which I submitted, together with the great influence of both legislators, persuaded Congress to keep the smelter in operation under government auspices until the end of 1956. Afterward it was transferred to the Wah Chang Corporation, which continued to process tin ore from Bolivia and Indonesia.

On February 25, 1960, K. C. Li sent me a very interesting proposal which I immediately transmitted to my government. Wah Chang offered to smelt all Bolivian tin ores in an electrolytic plant to be installed next to the Texas City smelter. In addition to making the U.S. market more competitive with the London market, it would provide profits from the by-products which, under the contracts with the Williams Harvey and Capper Pass smelters, would be subject to special charges.

The reopening of European trade routes after 1945 and the decline of mineral purchases by the United States favored the revival of the English and Dutch smelters. These smelters were able to survive thanks to contracts with the Bolivian Mining Bank and Mining Corporation. The European companies in which Patiño had substantial investments continued to make profits from Bolivian minerals. For these reasons, healthy competition between the different smelters would benefit Bolivian producers.

On July 20, 1960, I submitted a memorandum outlining all of these points. Although this proposal could have constituted the first step toward freeing ourselves from the yoke of the English smelters, I never received a reply and nothing ever came of it. Mystery continued to envelop negotiations and the contracts for the sale of minerals.

The Defeat of the Tin Barons in Washington

Bolivia's dependence upon mineral exports had produced a doubly dangerous situation. On the one hand there was, before the revolution, a concentration of wealth in the hands of an elite who used its money and power to dominate the country, establishing special privileges for the few which contrasted sharply with the poverty and ignorance of the many. Secondly, the importation of essential consumer goods depended on foreign currency earned in the exportation of minerals, a dependence encouraged by the tin barons because it strengthened their grip on the people and on their governments. The political vulnerability of the government was a consequence of its economic weakness. The government had to submit to the dictates of the tin barons in order to maintain itself in power and to survive economically.

The goals of nationalization of the mines were to eliminate the political and economic power of the wealthy minority and to develop alternate sources of wealth. To achieve this, the earnings of the mines had to be reinvested in other sectors of the economy. After the revolution, many formerly imported commodities were produced locally, some even exported; imports of others were reduced.

Our struggle abroad was intense and became unusually violent because the former mining interests tried to defeat our policies by tendentious and slanderous propaganda. In this battle I occupied the most critical position of my career, a position often misunderstood by my compatriots. I was forced to make personal sacrifices and participate in a conflict I had not sought. I lost friends and personal advantages. In the end I had to close my eyes to the painful sight of some members of my group who looked for personal gain, negotiating with their former masters under the table while I resisted the implacable war of words and intrigue. Our resistance was not equally strong on every front, a fact that, more than anything else, may have encouraged our adversaries to continue their attacks in a battle which ultimately proved so costly to both sides.

The tin barons were trying to defend a weak position. True, they were favored by the ideology of the Eisenhower administration which respected private property and repudiated any kind of government intervention in production. However, Eisenhower's spirit of justice was against them. Guided by his pragmatic and utilitarian philosophy, Eisenhower made a definitive statement about the tin stockpile which quieted our critics. Using the direct language he learned at West Point, Eisenhower said, on June 21, 1953: "It is preferable to accumulate tin than . . . gold in Fort Knox."

12

Aid for the Revolution

Convincing U.S. leaders that the tin barons' charges about the Bolivian revolution were false was one thing; persuading them that the economic assistance needed for the revolution to survive and flourish was in the U.S. national interest and a worthy humanitarian cause was quite another. Since the Republican administration with which we dealt during the fifties was especially predisposed against government ownership and operation of industrial activities, our success in persuading that administration to come to the aid of the Bolivian revolution was noteworthy. We had to persuade the Eisenhower administration that nationalization of the tin mines and agrarian reform were not obstacles to economic collaboration. Another related issue was the development of Bolivia's oil resources for which the Bolivian government had enlisted U.S. private capital. Economic assistance would involve more than simple authorization for the expenditure of specific sums of money; it required intimate collaboration between the two governments in identifying and implementing economic activities which would promote Bolivia's development. In the late fifties and early sixties, Bolivia received more U.S. economic assistance per capita than almost any other country in the world. How this came about constitutes a unique chapter in U.S. relations with Latin America.

Milton Eisenhower

Dr. Milton Eisenhower, brother and advisor to the president, was one of the valuable contacts to whom I had been introduced by my friend, Gardner Jackson. Since he was in the field of higher education, his keen mind had access to new and daring ideas, yet he could maintain an independent position. He had just been named president of Pennsylvania State University, but since his brother had great respect for his judgment and integrity, he spent most of his time in Washington, working in an exceptionally discrete fashion so as not to awaken the jealousy of the Department of State or other agencies of the government.

At a family party in Jackson's house I had the opportunity to describe to Milton Eisenhower the process of change and reform taking place in Bolivia. As an intellectual he was fascinated by the story of men who were struggling to emerge from a semifeudal state and to form a community which would participate in the social progress already begun in the rest of the world. I have reason to believe that our conversation suggested to him the idea of a visit to Latin America in order to study at first hand the delicate issues involved in our relations with the United States and the possibilities for mutual cooperation.

In mid-June, 1953, the U.S. government announced officially that the president had asked his brother, Dr. Milton Eisenhower, to make a goodwill tour to all the American nations as his personal representative. At the same time Milton made it known that he would not hold interviews with the accredited representatives in Washington nor accept social engagements. It was clear that he intended to maintain the most objective position possible before departing on such an important trip. However, I could not refrain from trying to speak with him before his trip to caution him about the efforts that some Bolivian citizens would make, aided by government officials opposed to the revolution, to confuse him and influence his evaluation. Once again I turned to the indefatigable Jackson, and with his help, obtained an interview on June 17, 1953.

When one dedicates oneself totally to a cause, convinced that it is just and true, one's spirit generates powers to overtake adversaries. I expressed to Milton Eisenhower my fears that the tin barons and the displaced politicians in their service would use contacts with high officials in other South American countries to interview him. I enumerated the arguments that they would use against our cause, especially those about our supposed ties with international Communism, based on selected statements of euphoric elements of my government. I also predicted he would hear alarming descriptions of the nation's economy, especially of mining, labor anarchy, and impending bankruptcy. Presenting the arguments that they would make against the agrarian reform, I advised him about the tension and disorder in labor relations in both industry and agriculture. I was like a doctor explaining to the family of a patient the dramatic side effects produced by a medication before it worked a complete cure.

Milton Eisenhower was not a revolutionary, nor a radical, nor even interested in the possibility of radical changes in the structure of American society. While he was not a conservative, he was cautious and analytical in making decisions or in recommending a course of action. But Milton is typical of many Americans, forged in the healthy atmosphere of a society which lives by work and faith. He also had the traditional characteristic of the U.S. citizen whose human dignity is based on pure respect for liberty, and who exercises and defends that liberty for himself and for others. The spectacle of the oppression of an entire nation by a bold, privileged minority, repelled him and made him one of the most important friends that we have had. On July 29, 1953, he returned from his trip through Latin America. Washington's views began to change slowly thereafter in favor of Bolivia.

In the United States, dramatic announcements of changes in foreign policy are infrequent even after a change of government. On the contrary, care is taken to preserve continuity. It is extremely rare for an official to venture a statement radically altering an established position. Such changes are effected with care in order to maintain appearances and save face for the politicians who have upheld and still uphold the opposing view. Therefore, these changes are difficult to perceive initially. They can be noted early only when one has experience interpreting attitudes and reading new directions between the lines.

The only concrete information which I could obtain immediately following Milton Eisenhower's return was a chance remark in an interview which we had. He asked, "How were you able to guess the things that your countrymen outside of Bolivia were going to say to me?" Soon other indicators began to appear. On July 5, I had told my government that the United States was prepared to purchase Bolivian tin at market price for one additional year and to send a commission to Bolivia to study the possibility of granting technical assistance. On September 29 I informed my government that I had obtained the promise that the United States would provide us food subsidies at an annual cost of between $8 and $11 million. On October 29 I cabled La Paz that the Export-Import Bank had decided to grant an additional credit of $23 million for continued construction of the Cochabamba–Santa Cruz highway. On January 11, 1954, I reported that Milton Eisenhower had proposed credit up to $3.5 million for oil exploration by the Bolivian Petroleum Corporation. Unlike the other measures, this loan was not granted despite the support of Milton Eisenhower and Vice-President Nixon. It was impossible to change rigid U.S. policy against conceding credit to a state agency competing with private oil companies.

By the beginning of 1954, we had counteracted the propaganda and influence of our enemies on the Washington front. These enemies, and their lobbyists, public relations agencies, and attorneys, continued their attacks. Since no sane person could accuse President Eisenhower of communist tendencies or doubt his commitment to the national interests of the United States, his administration's decision to give us economic assistance conferred great prestige on the Bolivian revolution. It also facilitated friendly relations with the governments of other countries where displaced Bolivian politicians in exile were stirring up suspicion and opposition. An additional and decisive factor was that our old friend, Nelson Rockefeller, had become undersecretary in the Department of Health, Education, and Welfare and was later a special advisor to the president on international affairs. The outcome of our efforts was that Bolivia became the first country in the Americas to receive technical and economic aid from the United States during the Eisenhower administration.

Our relations with the U.S. government were the subject of a cover story in the Spanish-language magazine, *Visión*, of September 27, 1957. The article described the importance I have always placed on developing personal relationships based on faith and goodwill. As an ambassador, for example, I went out of my way to meet informally with important individuals, playing golf, shooting on Chesapeake Bay, making music. In the course of such recreations, I was able occasionally to discuss the misfortunes of my country and gain a sympathetic friend for our cause. The article also brought out some of my convictions about diplomacy. I disagree that diplomacy is the art of hiding the truth elegantly. With modern means of communication, the truth can't be withheld for long. To introduce that point, *Visión* retold an anecdote which won a contest at the Burning Tree Golf Club. One day while I was researching a topic at the New York Public Library, I suddenly realized that I was late for a luncheon appointment and hurried to the telephone to explain to my hosts. I rushed into a booth which appeared vacant and was about to deposit a coin when a man who apparently had been waiting for the booth pushed me from behind and, not hiding his irritation, said, "Why did you push ahead of me that way? Didn't you see that I was waiting?"

As I turned to express my apologies, he saw me, and giving his temper free rein said, "Oh, you foreigners. . . . You should learn that in this country no matter who you are, you wait your turn."

I paused for a moment to decide whether to reply with equal vehemence but decided instead to say, imitating as best I could the accent of a redskin, "I, a foreigner? No sir. You are the foreigner! I am an American Indian." I apologized and the incident was closed.

In the United States, ignorance is pardoned, but never bad faith. In my lectures throughout the country, admitting an error awakens much more sympathy than strong assertions of opinion. The United States is a country which always favors the weak, the underdog. To take advantage of this trait for one's cause is the wisest course.

Victory Over Hunger

When the MNR took over in 1952, internal savings were almost non-existent in Bolivia. Low per capita production provided only bare subsistence for most of the population, and the fortunate few who had surpluses sent their savings abroad. Consequently, little capital was accumulated then, nor is it today. Foreign capital was essential for realization of our economic goals, but we were unable to provide conditions to attract it. Our only alternative was to build an infrastructure from public sources of foreign capital. To attract even public funds, however, we needed preliminary economic assistance in commodities.

The deficits produced after 1952 by decreases in the price of tin and the increase in production costs for both minerals and food exhausted the Central Bank's reserves. Inflation soared as currency was printed to cover domestic debts, but this method did not provide a means to pay for essential imports—wheat, sugar, rice, meat, oil, fuel, and lumber. The president of the Central Bank, Franklin Antezana Paz, went to Washington at the beginning of 1953 to negotiate an advance of $12 million from the International Monetary Fund, the amount the government had requested on November 12, 1952. The advance was to be used to pay for imports, not to support the Bolivian peso. As was to be expected, the request was refused since it greatly exceeded Bolivia's contribution of $2.5 million to the Fund. Within a few days Antezana became convinced that we would not to be given credit because of the mistrust created by the nationalization of the mines and the damaging propaganda of the former owners. The rapid decline in productivity due to political and labor agitation on the job also worked against us. The outlook was dark, and we had no more resources to pay for the importation of foodstuffs. If desperate measures were not taken, starvation, which had not been present in Bolivia since the War of the Pacific, would once again grip our people with all of its serious social and political consequences.

Given this situation, I sought aid in food, especially from the gigantic stores of surplus agricultural production. Senator George Aiken, chairman of the Senate Committee on Agriculture, helped me with such generosity and understanding that I cannot adequately describe it nor repay him. His decision in our favor ended doubts among officials of the departments of state and agriculture. We obtained our first grant in foodstuffs, wheat, flour, oil, lard, and cotton on September 29, 1953. This aid was a fresh breeze which carried away dark storm clouds on the horizon. The specter of hunger disappeared, and the supply of food for the people was guaranteed. With this support, the revolutionary movement was infused with optimism and, gathering momentum, prepared for the future.

The grants of surplus food continued for some time. As with all human activities, they were a source of new difficulties and suspicion, not so much during the distribution, but because of the funds they generated. The surpluses were not distributed free but were sold to the public for Bolivian pesos. These funds accumulated in a counterpart funds account to be used for projects undertaken jointly by the governments of Bolivia and the United States. In order to facilitate distribution, the food and other articles were made available to merchants on credit. Many did not pay their bills, planning to use their political influence to retain the proceeds. Projects which could have been completed thus had to be postponed, arousing the mistrust of those American officials who saw that opportunities had been established to enrich certain of the administration's favorites.

It is human nature to discredit the generosity of others. Skeptics believed that America's attempt to prevent suffering and hunger in Bolivia had selfish motives, namely, to get rid of burdensome surpluses at home. But their belief does not negate the great humanitarian impact of this measure.

The Cochabamba–Santa Cruz Highway

The Rio de Janeiro conference in January 1942 abounded with heroic rhetoric about sacrifices in defense of freedom and the self-determination of nations. It also dealt with economic matters and the hopes of Latin American countries to develop beyond the point of producing only primary products. For the first time the United States had been receptive to the assertion of the rights and demands of underdeveloped nations. Along with agreements for stabilizing prices and lowering the costs of the war effort, the United States had had to promise assistance for the economic development of other countries.

Unfortunately for Bolivia, we were not prepared then to state our aspirations in terms of specific plans. For some of our statesmen, the construction of the Cochabamba-Corumba railroad was an obsession, as if that would be the touchstone for development. They did not consider other sectors which were just as important, such as communications between different regions of the country, access to markets, and the development of our sources of energy. Upon noting our confusion, the United States decided to send a mission to study the problem, headed by the well-known economist Merwin Bohan. Bohan was apparently instructed to keep his recommendations within the probable level of credit that the United States was prepared to allocate to Bolivia. The principal recommendation resulting from the study was to initiate immediately the Cochabamba–Santa Cruz highway.

Because of the favorable attitude toward Bolivia which we succeeded in creating in Washington after 1952, we were able to obtain additional credit for the completion of the project. Its economic impact demonstrated that Bohan was right in assigning the work first priority. True, some complementary projects were required, but this road transformed the entire region and altered the bases of the national economy. During the close of the colonial period and the first years of the republic, sugar was transported on mules from the tropical region of Santa Cruz where it was refined by primitive methods. The rich who bought sugar could pay prices which covered the high cost of transportation. When the mines began to yield foreign exchange and the workers also demanded sugar, it was necessary to import sugar from refineries in Peru; rice was brought from Siam, meat from Argentina, flour from Chile and Argentina, lumber for construction from the pine forests of Oregon, and cloth came from England made of Egyptian and Indian cotton and Australian wool. Imports from the four corners of the earth penetrated the small world of the Bolivian *altiplano*, leaving little in the budget for opening new roads, building schools, paying teachers, or maintaining hospitals. Living to middle age was, however, a luxury which only the wealthy with access to the profits of the mines could afford. The peasant of the *altiplano* lived in a self-contained subsistence economy for years, producing meager food on the sterile wasteland, and weaving his own clothes from the wool of his faithful friend, the llama. The inhabitant of the tropics barely subsisted, lulled by tropical fevers. His growth and horizons were limited by forest and river barriers unconquered by man. The entire country stagnated. Communications established with Santa Cruz were the first step toward liberation.

Ten years after the completion of this project, Bolivia produced all its sugar, rice, meat, lumber, and cotton. The cultivation of corn, which until then had been limited to the small valleys of the Andean range, expanded to the plains of Santa Cruz. Tractors and mechanized planting liberated the peasant from the uncertainties of weather in the *antiplano* and placed their products within reach of the people. They did not have to worry about foreign exchange from minerals to buy bread. The road which linked the mountains with the plains of Santa Cruz meant a great deal for the individual rights of the Bolivian citizen, not simply because it suddenly generated a great flow of wealth, but because it increased his independence.

Hickenlooper's Trout

The official opening of the Cochabamba–Santa Cruz highway on August 25, 1954, was attended by a U.S. delegation which included Senator Bourke Hickenlooper, Representative Clifford McIntire, Lyn Stanbaugh and Robert Mormor, executives of the Export-Import Bank, and the well-known columnist, Drew Pearson. The inauguration proceeded as planned, and we took advantage of the occasion to point out the possibilities of development in surrounding areas and the complementary projects which should be realized with the continuation of the road to the north and the opening of regions to colonization. The ceremony was to conclude with a business meeting at government headquarters in La Paz, but was climaxed instead by a delightful episode involving Senator Hickenlooper.

Those of us who have worked on plans for economic cooperation in Washington know the importance of the opinions of legislators, especially of those who must review such plans. Hickenlooper was chairman of the Senate subcommittee for Latin America. His opinion carried weight not only in the Senate and House of Representatives, but also with the executives of the Department of State, the Export-Import Bank, and other special agencies with which we had to deal. A native of a midwestern state, a Republican of conservative family, he was as cautious and rigid as most American statesmen of the Midwest. Therefore it was very important to win his favorable opinion.

Once the visit to Santa Cruz and the northern provinces was concluded, the large retinue accompanying the president and his foreign guests decided to return to La Paz where a special program had been prepared. Due to bad weather, part of the return trip had to be made by automobile to the village of Comarapa where we boarded planes for La Paz. Because Cochabamba had prepared a large demonstration in honor of the president and his guests, we landed briefly at the Cochabamba airport where a huge crowd had gathered. Suddenly we were surrounded by an enthusiastically cheering multitude. A few minutes later we had to reboard the planes because only a few minutes remained for the takeoff under the security requirements established by the airport authorities. In the confusion, no one realized that Senator Hickenlooper had been left behind at the Cochabamba airport!

To my consternation, consultations during the flight with the pilots of each of the planes revealed that the senator had not boarded any of them. It was impossible to return because it was late, and there were no facilities for night landings. From the plane we attempted to communicate with the Cochabamba airport but were unsuccessful. We succeeded in establishing contact only after arriving at La Paz.

I spoke with the mayor and informed him of the unfortunate incident, describing Hickenlooper as best I could. I asked him to take care of the senator and to try to make his forced stay in the city as pleasant as possible. A few hours later, I received word that they had found Hickenlooper sitting on a bench in the plaza with an expression of complete disgust, muttering oaths in English. With the aid of an interpreter they were able to exchange a few words. However, Hickenlooper went straight to the lodgings that had been prepared for him without accepting the mayor's invitation, nor his excuses. Undoubtedly we were faced with a man who was cursing his luck for having the bad idea of accepting an invitation to come to Bolivia.

Very early the following day we sent a plane to fetch Hickenlooper. In the meantime I saw all of my hopes for the senator's help collapse. It seemed now that he had become our enemy. Then the unexpected happened. That night in La Paz I encountered William Dodge, an American resident, who managed an agricultural property on the shores of Lake Titicaca and who was an expert trout fisherman. Moreover, he had a fine yacht for fishing. Without knowing for sure whether the senator liked to fish, I asked Dodge to get his equipment together and make the necessary plans for a trout-fishing expedition on picturesque Lake Titicaca. Then I contacted the U.S. ambassador in La Paz, and together we planned the remaining details for the projected expedition.

When Hickenlooper stepped off the plane from Cochabamba, I was alarmed to see that my fears were confirmed. He had taken the mishap personally, as an affront to his rank and his pride. Nevertheless, I attempted to make him see the episode as a story to tell his grandchildren and then suggested that he change his plans to visit La Paz immediately in favor of going to fish for the colossal trout of the lake.

It was a beautiful day, clear as only a sunny day in the high Andean plateau can be, and a fresh breeze beckoned us to a rest in the country. Whether due to my persuasive tone or his love of fishing, the senator softened momentarily and, glancing at the natural beauty around him, agreed. In the short trip by car, I perceived the risk that we faced. Nothing seemed to excite him—not the colorful costumes of the peasants, nor the beauty of the plateau, nor the clarity of the sunny day which turned the lake deep blue, nor the luminosity of the mountain ranges beyond. The American ambassador observed my attempts to make Hickenlooper forget the unpleasant experience of the previous day with friendliness and compassion.

A few hours after setting out in Dodge's yacht a miracle occurred. Hickenlooper hooked a trout weighing thirty-four pounds, four ounces! From that moment there was no country more beautiful, more hospitable, nor more worthy of friendship and aid than Bolivia. A few months later, the trout, duly stuffed and mounted on native Bolivian wood in the Tihuanaco style, was presented to Hickenlooper in the drawing room of the Bolivian Embassy in Washington. For many years the trophy embellished his private office in the U.S. Senate. The famous author of the Hickenlooper amendment was a powerful and loyal friend of Bolivia.

Budget Subsidies

There is one category of aid about which I have serious reservations — the grants begun in 1957 to cover deficits in the Bolivian budget. In that year, the deficit amounted to almost 30 percent, although it declined in subsequent years.

The comedian and movie star, Bob Hope, told a story, later published in the *Saturday Evening Post*, that described an incident illustrating the predicament in which we found ourselves. One time when Hope went with President Eisenhower to the Burning Tree Club near Washington, Eisenhower's golfing party approached the crowded first tee and were waved through as a courtesy to the chief of state. Greeting them and expressing his appreciation for this gesture, the president paused in front of a gentleman who appeared to be foreign and greeted him with evident fondness and familiarity. They exchanged a few words, and Eisenhower, leaning on the arm of his friend, walked into a nearby grove of trees and remained there talking for several minutes. All those present stood waiting for the president to return. When he appeared, still accompanied by his friend, the game began. Before teeing off, Hope asked Eisenhower what the amount of the bet would be. The president quickly replied, "I can only bet one dollar for I have just lost two million dollars to the Bolivian ambassador."

The scene occurred just as Bob Hope told it, and it was the culmination of one of the most difficult negotiations I had to carry out in Washington. It involved a budget subsidy for the Bolivian government, that is, a gift from a friend to pay the salaries of public officials. The measure had passed through many clearances and was, naturally, a most controversial issue. There were officials in both the State Department and the Treasury who vehemently resisted granting this type of assistance, for it not only would establish a dangerous precedent, but could become an indefinite obligation injurious to both sides. A fiscal commitment to officials is awkward since their employment is difficult to eliminate or reduce later. Moreover, such a measure runs the risk of producing dubious results because the society or the individual accepting a gift from others, no matter how intimate and friendly the relationship, may incur a moral obligation difficult for both the giver and the receiver to bear.

Deep down I was, and still am, in agreement with these reservations, but I had to consider that our alarming fiscal position and the threat of bankruptcy facing our national treasury were the greatest allies of the counterrevolution. I therefore utilized all my influence and arguments to obtain a favorable response to my government's request. So, the much discussed matter arrived at the president's desk for a final decision. As luck would have it, the problem had been brought up with Eisenhower a few hours before his game with Bob Hope. I happened to be at the golf course, about to play a game with some acquaintances. Upon seeing me, Eisenhower remembered the matter and, with his usual spontaneity and straightforwardness, gave me the opportunity to repeat my arguments directly to him. His decision in our favor is now widely known in both countries.

History will judge this matter objectively when those of us who participated are gone. No one can deny that this was one of the most generous acts of our powerful friend because he did it without expecting anything in return. In fact, there was nothing for him to request. Because of its landlocked position, our country is dependent on others. Our voracious neighbors not only isolated us from the rest of the world but, when important sources of wealth appeared, kept large portions of our territory for themselves. President Eisenhower's decision to assist us in meeting our operating expenses was an expression of genuine solidarity. If we have failed sometimes to recognize this, it may be that having to resort to such a measure has made us disguise our shame in this way.

I am still not convinced that the government had no other choice and that we were forced to resort to this extreme measure. We had dissipated our gold reserves, the nationalization of the mines proved expensive, and the costs of production and imports had increased sharply. The deficit was tremendous and the national budget reflected all of these misfortunes. The alternatives were to cut back on government jobs, thus increasing unemployment in the middle class, or to secure this outside help. If we had decided to tighten our belts, temporarily reducing further our meager diet and working doubly hard, we might have emerged happier from this crisis.

A New Petroleum Policy

Although there had long been reports of seepage of oily substances in some gorges in southeastern Bolivia, it was not until after World War I that explorations were carried out to determine the presence of petroleum deposits in Bolivian territory. In 1922, the Standard Oil Corporation of New Jersey obtained a concession of 1 million hectares (about 2.5 million acres) for the exploration and production of petroleum. In those days, the limited means of communication made this work very difficult. While the territory explored was extensive, only three fields, with a limited capacity for production, were established after several years' work. These were at Camiri, Sanandita, and Bermejo. Although the small refinery operated in Camiri a few years before and during the Chaco War, the bulk of the fuel for motor vehicles and airplanes still had to be met by importing gasoline from Argentina and Brazil. Standard Oil took special care not to be identified with the Bolivian war effort, and simply handed over the operation of the small Camiri refinery to some Bolivian technicians. For Bolivians, burdened by a war so costly in lives and money, this action signaled total indifference to the Bolivian tragedy.

A review of parliamentary records from 1921 and 1922 involving the disputed concessions to Richmond Levering and Standard Oil of New Jersey leads us to some interesting conclusions. The attorneys of these companies deliberately raised exaggerated expectations, creating the false impression that the entire Bolivian southeast rested on a sea of petroleum. Their object was to assume an advantageous position by obtaining virtually unlimited tracts of land. In the October 3, 1927, session of the Bolivian Chamber of Deputies, Deputy Abel Iturralde made the following statements. "Before the opening of the regular session [of the Chamber in August], there were frequent meetings in the Government Palace, even on holidays. Such was the haste of Mr. Armstrong [representative of Standard Oil], that he sought to delude the Cabinet with grandiose prospects, none of which have been realized. At that time it was said that Standard Oil would spend $50 million and that within three years we would have a respectable budget because of the high profits to Bolivia from its 11 percent share in the exploitation of petroleum. . . ." At that session Deputy Iturralde opposed the granting of the concession to Standard Oil. The premise of his long speech was that this concession was monstrous because it meant handing over immense wealth for the benefit of foreign capitalism.[1]

The results obtained by Standard Oil after more than ten years of operation were disappointing for Bolivia. Rumors circulated about great discoveries which were being kept secret until reserves in other parts of the world were exhausted. Bolivia was supposed to remain with its arms crossed, chained to the interests of U.S. capital. These beliefs were not based upon a real understanding of the petroleum industry or of the needs for expansion of the large international corporations. They did, nevertheless, have a great impact on public opinion which was already in favor of expelling Standard Oil for its indifference to the country's problems in the Chaco War. Given this background, the concessions were vulnerable to criticism, easy targets for politicians whose platform was anti-imperialism.

The passage of many years and the experience of the development of this industry in the hands of the state make it possible to view the problem with greater objectivity. Was there some truth in the rumors that

1. Moises Alcazar, *Abel Iturralde, El Centinela del Petróleo* (La Paz: Editorial La Paz, 1944).

Standard Oil had discovered large deposits of petroleum, capriciously postponing their exploitation? The indemnity paid to Standard Oil in 1942 carried with it the condition that the company turn over all of the studies that it had carried out before the nationalization decree of 1937. In this way the government technicians were soon convinced that such discoveries were merely products of popular fantasy. In twenty-five years of operation, the Bolivian Petroleum Corporation (YPFB) found nothing spectacular in the fields explored by Standard Oil. The careful and extensive explorations after 1957 by more than ten other companies also show that the alleged discoveries were imaginary. All drilling begun under the new laws in 1956 had to be abandoned. Nor did the studies and explorations along the borders of Paraguay and Argentina produce the expected results.

The decree of 1937 to nationalize Standard Oil's property originated in Bolivian domestic politics. The public did not support the de facto government of General David Toro, but merely tolerated it out of weariness. The consensus of opinion was that much of the poor military leadership in the war was attributable to General Toro, whose attention was fixed on politics and not on the overwhelming problems of the battlefield. In order to win popular support, Toro attempted two dramatic steps. He proclaimed a socialist government, going so far as to invite some deserters from the Chaco War to form part of his government. He then revoked the concessions to Standard Oil in 1937, thus opening one of the most controversial chapters in the recent history of Bolivia.

The government of Enrique Peñaranda made a settlement with Standard Oil, paying them nearly $2 million after negotiations at the Rio de Janeiro conference in January 1942. This, however, resolved neither the problem of Bolivia's external credit nor of her domestic oil supply. The state agency which took over from Standard Oil made little progress, managing to produce only two to three thousand barrels per day at Camiri, Sanandita, and Bermejo. When the MNR took power once again in 1952, imports of approximately five thousand barrels daily were needed to meet the demands of transportation and industry. This cost us more than $5 million annually at a time when the fall in the market price of tin and the new fiscal obligations arising from the nationalization of the mines made this payment a great sacrifice on the part of the Bolivian people. Moreover, it meant the limitation of the availability of fuel, thereby halting all plans for economic diversification and the mechanization of agriculture.

Heroic efforts were required and they resulted in a reversal of our petroleum policy. Before discussing this, however, I must confirm here what I have stated publicly more than once. From my post in Washington

I did not participate directly in any of the decisions involving the new petroleum policy. I did not negotiate conditions for drilling, contract terms, incentives for investment, or other matters with any company. Nor did I participate in the selection or the employment of the attorneys who gave legal advice to the Bolivian government in drafting the new petroleum laws. Since I was not then a member of congress or of the cabinet, I had no part in the discussion, approval, or promulgation of the new petroleum code. If an explanation is to be made for the terms of the contracts made with corporations under the government's new policy, or for the drafting and enacting of the petroleum code, the legislators and members of the executive branch at that time must make it; I hope that they will do so in their own time. If I had disagreed with the new petroleum policy, however, I would have made my position known beforehand, and would have fought that policy both inside and outside the country. If I cooperated, it was because I was in agreement with the principles of the policy. What has happened since has not made me change my mind.

The country did not, nor does it yet, possess domestic capital for the development of industry. The pilgrimages made by representatives of the Bolivian Petroleum Corporation to nearly every capital of the world in search of loans or partners for the government in the exploration for and exploitation of petroleum were a complete failure. In order for the country to determine its prospects for self-sufficiency in fuel, and for joining the world petroleum market, it was necessary to resort once more to private enterprise. This was done at the beginning of 1956. After 1964, when the MNR was no longer in power, the fruits of the petroleum policy became, unfortunately, the spoils in disputes between rival military governments and, in some cases, their Communist collaborators.

In the past several years there have been efforts to explain Bolivia's petroleum problems by means of simple slogans. Those who naively believe that the small output of Bolivian petroleum can play a role in the international power struggle between capitalism and socialism attempt to quiet opposition with well-known clichés: "imperialist," "sold out to the Yankees," "reactionary," etc. In spite of this, I am convinced that the great majority of interested Bolivians appreciate this problem from a practical point of view, concerned exclusively with the interests of the Bolivian nation and its hopes for progress.

At the beginning of 1956 I received instructions from the government to invite the oil companies to apply for concessions for the exploration and exploitation of oil fields. The year before, arrangements had been attempted with the controversial Texan, Glen McCarthy, but he did not have the necessary capital to exploit the concessions. Apparently his objective was to trade them later to another organization which, in fact, he did.

The best way to carry out my government's instructions to invite foreign participation was to do so where petroleum operations in the United States were concentrated, namely, in Tulsa, Oklahoma. On February 16, 1956, I was invited by the Tulsa Chamber of Commerce to give a talk at its headquarters. There I described Bolivia's new petroleum policy and the guarantees which the government was offering to encourage capital investment in that industry. The audience consisted of representatives of most of the world's great oil consortiums. In the question and answer period, they openly expressed their doubts about the government guarantees, citing the abrogation of the contracts with Standard Oil of New Jersey. They pointed out that one of the few corporations not represented at the proceedings was, precisely, Standard Oil, in spite of the fact that it was the only company which had "experience" in Bolivia. As a result, everyone was awaiting that company's reaction to the Bolivian invitation.

Afterward, one of the large companies let me know that it was interested in going to Bolivia, but only if Standard Oil was not opposed. In this matter I called upon my friend, Nelson Rockefeller, and requested his aid in keeping Standard Oil from expressing its opposition to other oil companies making investments in Bolivia. Nelson helped me obtain an interview with one of Standard Oil's most important executives. I specifically requested that, if they did not wish to return to Bolivia, they at least refrain from expressing a negative attitude toward the possibility that other companies do so. This promise they made and subsequently kept.

On March 20, 1956, I received news from La Paz that an agreement had been made with Gulf Oil Corporation. Fourteen consortiums applied for concessions. The principal ones were Gulf Oil of Pittsburgh, Standard of California, Shell, and Tennessee Gas–Monsanto. Several of these companies drilled without success, although Chaco Petroleum found signs of natural gas. The only company which persisted and found some deposits of oil was Gulf, acting through one of its subsidiaries, Bolivian Gulf Oil. After a few years, its production reached forty thousand barrels of crude oil per day. It was then necessary to construct a pipeline from Santa Cruz to Cochabamba to connect with the pipelines built some years earlier between Sicasica and the port of Arica in Chile.

In 1958, Tennessee Gas Transmission Corporation of Houston employed construction engineers of the Bechtel Corporation to prepare a preliminary report for the construction of a pipeline for the possible exportation of Bolivian natural gas to Brazil. The report was produced with the aid of economists from Stanford Research Institute and the London *Economist* Intelligence Unit. The conclusions of this study were extremely favorable, discussing possible capital investments of between $229.5

million and $346.5 million for exportable quantities of 200 to 600 million cubic feet per day. Referring to the feasibility of the project, the report asserted: "An analysis of the project's operations indicates that, when the São Paulo market is developed for Bolivian gas, the profits will be sufficient to justify the investment and to pay the producers of gas approximately eighteen cents per thousand cubic feet. Although this may not be realized during the first stage, taking in, perhaps, the first several years, the earnings should reach satisfactory levels in subsequent stages of development."

Eventually the gas was exported to Argentina. I have cited this study to illustrate the amount of capital needed to develop this source of power, so important for the industry of South America. The pressure applied later by extremist groups created an atmosphere unfavorable to the continuation of this industry in private hands. The exportation of natural gas, however, was not the solution to Bolivia's economic problems, but rather a hopeful start indicating the possibility of diversification. In order for the earnings from natural gas to have a significant impact upon the national economy, producing a rise in per capita income, these figures would have to increase tenfold. To achieve this, huge capital risks, which were impossible to finance with the credit obtained by the state, were required.

An incident which occurred with the de facto government of General Alfredo Ovando appears to corroborate this thesis. On seizing power in 1969, Ovando nationalized the operations of Bolivian Gulf Oil and immediately sent an emissary to the U.S.S.R. to suggest that it assume responsibility for the development of the natural gas industry. The Kremlin showed no interest whatsoever in marketing natural gas, in exploration for new deposits, or in financing the completion of the pipeline to the Argentine border. In the end, the nationalization of Gulf's holdings in Bolivia boomeranged on the radical groups who soon lost all their influence, especially in the areas affected by the measure. Nationalization did not result in the greater availability of resources because the sales receipts did not cover the heavy operating expenses, and the government, in addition, was forced to pay compensation to the former owners.

13

The Second Mission Ends

United States economic assistance to Bolivia has had a long history, from the wartime aid of the early forties to the comprehensive programs of the Alliance for Progress in the sixties. In his second term, after the war, President Truman appointed a commission headed by Nelson Rockefeller to prepare a preliminary study of ways to make development plans in the Western Hemisphere more efficient. The commission proposed the creation of an Inter-American Development Bank with an initial capital of $500 million to be provided in its entirety by the U.S. government. In those times, the proposal seemed daring, and the sum mentioned was considered excessive in relation to the desired objectives. During the balance of Truman's term almost nothing further was done.

It remained for Eisenhower's administration to broaden the concept of reconstruction which until that time was considered applicable only to countries physically destroyed during World War II. Now it was being recognized that many countries which had not been within the zone of conflict had, nevertheless, suffered such great disturbances that their prewar social and economic equilibrium was completely destroyed. One of these countries was Bolivia: costs of production had risen, her needs had increased greatly, yet there had been no corresponding increase in resources. As a result, assistance was essential for developing Bolivia's internal resources.

Development Planning

Since many international conferences have been devoted to development planning, there was much anxiety about whether the United States would cooperate effectively in the development of other nations of the hemisphere. The cooperation took several forms, one of which was using economists employed by international organizations. The Economic Commission for Latin America was one entity which studied the Bolivian problem in detail and collaborated in preparing a plan of economic development which was presented in the early sixties to a technical committee within the inter-American system. This committee was created as a result of a speech made by President Kennedy on March 13, 1961, to Latin American ambassadors in Washington, marking the beginning of the Alliance for Progress. The committee of nine technicians, sometimes called "the wise men," did not play the role which had been expected, frittered away its time in academic discussions, and in the end lost its original authority.

The plan presented for Bolivia was probably less complex than those for other countries. The committee did not approve, nor criticize, the report in part or in its entirety. In other words, proposals for Bolivian development remained the same—a bilateral program to be worked out between Bolivia and the United States. Since that time, other plans have been proposed but all have been based without important deviations on the original proposals. The same issues were faced each time: What are the most critical needs? Where should priorities be placed? Where can help be obtained? Each time it was necessary to return to the beginning. Bolivia lacks everything and, therefore, the most important projects are those of infrastructure: building roads to cities within the country and to neighboring countries; developing our sources of energy; encouraging per capita productivity, thus improving conditions for the individual citizen; obtaining foreign capital while increasing internal savings for the funding of domestically-financed projects; improving the efficiency of our products and the internal market. None of these projects were implemented because, due to a strange process, many leaders changed their minds when faced with the responsibility of making the decisions. They expected to find the answer in theoretical discussions or in changes in the basic structure of Bolivian society.

The Cuban Revolution

My second mission to Washington was interrupted in August 1958 when I returned to La Paz to serve as foreign minister in the government of President Hernán Siles Zuazo, a position I held until December 31, 1960, when I returned to the Washington embassy. As minister, I headed the Bolivian deligation to the Thirteenth General Assembly of the United Nations in New York that fall of 1958. Several Latin American delegates, deeply concerned about the situation in Cuba, sought means of ending the civil war there. Clearly, the American nations had no authority to intervene in this internal struggle, either individually or collectively; the problem was to find a solution consistent with the principle of nonintervention. A proposal, which was quickly accepted, called for sending a group of former Latin American presidents to Havana. With the moral authority of their high positions, they would attempt mediation to avoid further bloodshed and encourage a political settlement. The ex-presidents were to meet in Caracas early in January 1959 on their way to Havana.

On December 31, 1958, the dictator Batista, seeing that he no longer had any support in the country, fled into exile. The rebel forces from the Sierra Maestra triumphantly occupied the entire island. The mediation plan was overtaken by events, and a great drama, for both Cuba and the other American nations, began. President Siles was infected by the general enthusiasm at the overthrow of the Batista dictatorship. He instructed me to go to Havana as Bolivian foreign minister to express not only our recognition of the new government organized by Fidel Castro, but our solidarity with the Cuban revolutionary movement.

Like President Siles, my first reaction to the Cuban revolution had been one of sympathy. When I heard of their first international difficulties, I still believed that they could be the victims, as we were, of the activities of exiled groups who were trying to win outside support for interests they could not defend through their own efforts. Then, however, the bloodshed began in Cuba. The victorious guerrillas disregarded Christian virtues of forgiveness and generosity so important in our Latin traditions. I realized that the original goals of the revolution were giving way to the influence of other systems which would create a regime of terror to serve foreign interests. I decided not to carry out the presidential order, maintaining a discreet silence. In fact, my silence was really a prayer by one who had experienced the futility of the hatred and fratricidal fury of our own internal struggles.

Although I was strongly critical of the Castro regime once its abuses became obvious, I must also express my concern about U.S. sponsorship of the exiles' landing at the Bay of Pigs. Nonintervention is a fundamental tenet of the inter-American system, and the Cubans alone should plot their course for the future. If an American nation decides to choose monarchy, theocracy, or communism as the basis of its government, that is its problem; other American nations must accept the decision. In the Bay of Pigs disaster, not only were the precious lives of many young Cubans lost, but the operation itself proved fruitless. This action cost the United States dearly. For the average Latin American, the United States was greatly diminished in stature after April 20, 1962. The courageous decision to confront the Soviet Union's effort to install guided missiles in Cuba did not alter their earlier opinion.

My views on this subject were not directly relevant to the interests of the Bolivian revolution, nor related to our negotiations with the United States. Just as an attorney must put his client's interests first, so must a diplomat put first those of his people and government. I attempted to avoid undermining the negotiations by ignoring the clamor over matters which did not concern us directly.

The revolutionary regimes of Bolivia and Cuba differ in their origins, methods, and objectives. The Bolivian revolution began with the Chaco War and had the objective of internal reforms and the removal of obstacles to the country's progress. The revolution's methods were not shaped by a dogmatic political philosophy, nor by commitments to similar movements in other parts of the world. The program was designed to benefit the people of Bolivia. To achieve this purpose, close relations with the United States were important for the sake of obtaining the financial and technical aid necessary to carry out the constructive programs of the revolution. The Cuban revolution, on the other hand, was anti-American from the beginning. It was not only a reaction against the excessive influence of the United States on the economic and social life of the island, but a result of the revolution's extracontinental ties.

I discovered that our foreign office was flirting with Cuba, a country which had openly declared itself in opposition to the inter-American system. This was during the critical years of tension caused by Cuban attitudes, not only toward the United States but toward other Caribbean countries. If Bolivia wished to demonstrate a leftist position, then we were confessing weakness or uncertainty about the goals of our own revolution. If the object was to force the United States to pay the highest price for our cooperation, then we were demonstrating an approach that would later cost us dearly. Or, if we assume that President Paz Estenssoro favored collaboration, why did his Minister of Foreign Affairs, at the meeting held in Washington at the beginning of October, 1962, voice his opposition to the policy of strengthening the political defense of the continent? This ambiguity, so dangerous for a country which confronted the grave problems resulting from revolution, could not be tolerated, and that was one of the causes for terminating my second mission in Washington.

Bolivian Politics

After I resumed the ambassadorship in 1961, my friends and I in the United States passionately followed developments in Bolivia, watching for any signs of weakness in our common front or deviation from our revolutionary objectives.

Paz Estenssoro, who returned to the presidency in August 1960, provided firm economic leadership in the expenditure of our limited funds for seed projects and infrastructure. Some day the country will recognize this. He insisted passionately on initiating projects which, even if they did have large objectives, could not be described even by his most entrenched foes as representing political opportunism.

So much could not be said, however, for his political leadership, particularly toward the end of his second term. We viewed with anguish the crumbling of the political forces which had carried forward the first phase of our revolution. This collapse was due partly to the suicidal attitude of the head of the party, Paz himself. Opposing groups appeared and multiplied within the party, symptoms of complete disintegration. During the first days of the revolution, Juan Lechín had organized the leftist sector of the party, consisting of a marxist wing and a labor wing. Walter Guevara, a former foreign minister, had led away part of the party in his struggle against *caudillismo* (personalistic leadership), forming first the MNR *Auténtico* and later a separate, opposition party. Day after day new groups appeared with the names "socialist," "intransigents," "advance guard," etc. The party appeared to be dissolving rapidly, a process seemingly unperceived by Paz. If he was aware of it, he must have believed that it would not affect him as the only undisputed leader. Our allies in the United States and I realized that his conduct was a serious threat to the revolution. The alternatives were disastrous: either *caudillisimo* was to be accepted as the only solution, or the party would disintegrate and the revolution would be handed over to upstarts. The latter course meant abandoning the objectives of the revolution, once more defrauding the people and losing this last opportunity for the nation to achieve progress and liberation.

None of my letters from Washington produced results. My personal trips to Bolivia had no effect whatsoever upon the president, his advisors, or his most influential friends. Consequently, in October 1962, as a final contribution to the work begun after the Chaco War, I decided to return to Bolivia and dedicate myself completely to the task of bringing the leadership of the party to its senses.

General elections were to be held in May 1964. It had been known since the end of 1962 that Paz intended to impose his reelection on the country, contrary to the constitution, and to good sense. As I declared in a report which was published in a La Paz newspaper in 1963, I was openly opposed to his reelection as likely to cause the fall of the MNR regime and the interruption of the revolution.

The arguments which I had used in the United States in defense of the Bolivian revolution had two major points: first, it was the only way to improve my country; second, it was the perfect opportunity for the United States to show the world that it was not opposed to radical movements which tried to liberate the people from misery and the tyranny of the privileged classes. I had asserted that the conditions were perfect for making cooperation with Bolivia a show case now that there was a strongly nationalist party, committed to achieve for its people what had not been accomplished in a century and a half of independent life. I suggested that in this task the United States could assume a unique role, demonstrating how a capitalist society can find a basis for cooperation with another society which, in the interests of its people, had departed from the orthodox capitalist mold. If we now used impressive rhetoric to build only a personalistic and provincial regime, we would be deceiving our partners and undermining the show case argument. Deception could not survive for long, and we would retrace our steps to the backwardness the revolution had tried to overcome.

In this connection, the conduct of the two U.S. ambassadors in La Paz from 1960 to 1964 was not only contrary to the traditions of the United States, but full of danger for relations between the two countries. It is very possible that both men were victims of Paz's ambition for reelection which led him to look for excuses to justify the unjustifiable, unnecessarily introducing foreign elements. During those years, the U.S. ambassadors seemed to be a part of the president's political family, attending mass meetings organized by fanatical friends or agents of the president. Paz was trying to use the presence of the ambassador to impress upon the people that his reelection was essential to continuation of U.S. economic cooperation. The Bolivian people are slow to detect foreign influence, but even so, it was difficult for them to overlook the presence of foreigners at political meetings. On the surface they acquiesced, but there was much resentment underneath.

Although it is hard to believe, U.S. ambassadors wished to appear before their Washington superiors as exceptional personalities enjoying the favor and the confidence of the Bolivian chief of state. They did not realize that, while this might represent a professional triumph for the representative of a small nation, it is insignificant for the representative of a powerful nation. The ambassador of the United States, the Soviet Union, Great Britain, China, or Japan carries great weight in international relations, proportional to his country's powers and prestige. Thus the persistence with which the American ambassadors accompanied the president in his political excursions was unnecessary. It constituted interference in wholly domestic matters. What were their objectives in compromising themselves and their country? Even if U.S. policy favored Paz's reelection, this was the least advisable way of assuring it. In every society, no matter how weak, it is natural to repudiate foreign influence.

In trying to explain the intense anti-American reaction in Bolivia during the administrations of Ovando and Torres, I have been unable to find a source other than the ambassadors' conduct, however well intentioned it was. From my position in Washington it had been impossible to change their attitudes, which I deemed threatening and dangerous. I could not express concern to high officials of the Department of State because they might have attributed my action to jealousy or personal ambition. The only alternative was to leave the embassy and attempt to reverse these distressing tendencies through discreet action as a private citizen. Unfortunately, but not unexpectedly, my presence in Bolivia did not change the situation. We persisted in following the path to destruction.

As I feared, Paz imposed his reelection and after three months was driven from power. The disappearance of the MNR as the leading political force in the country produced a void into which the nation rapidly descended. The revolution was transformed into meaningless slogans. Bolivia returned to a vicious circle of coups d'etat and once again lost the opportunity to conquer her destiny.

14

Facing the Future

As long as the people of the Americas are divided and our national sovereignties persist, each government should comply religiously with the policy of nonintervention. Only by complying in all aspects of our relations—political, economic, and cultural—can we create the mutual respect which is essential for moving toward greater integration, the best hope of the peoples of America. The experience of the United States shows that positive economic results can be achieved over large geographic areas and with large markets. If customs barriers had divided the member states, the United States could not possibly be what it is today. This example should persuade us to seek to fulfill Bolivar's dream. Traditional regionalism, petty rivalries, and the glorification of militarism have added historical barriers to the geographic barriers that already separate us. We ought to take the integration of the peoples of the Americas seriously, with all our cards on the table, and without using this great goal to achieve transitory local victories. In Bolivia, particularly with respect to integration plans in the Andean group, we must take note of our own shortcomings which, if not resolved promptly, may not only retard industrialization, but paralyze it for a long time.

At the same time we must realize that capital is limited in Latin America, particularly in the Andean group, and that not one of its members, except possibly Venezuela, has a level of internal saving which permits much investment abroad. As a result we are forced to resort to other sources of capital, much of it from the United States. This means providing an economic and political climate which will attract investment from abroad. Public policy with respect to nationalization and government ownership and control of basic industries will be an important aspect of any such effort.

Bolivian experience is instructive in this regard. Although I was and am fully persuaded of the immense political benefits for the Bolivian

194

people resulting from the nationalization of the large tin mines, I never believed in its economic benefits. Lamentably, twenty years of experience has seen our most pessimistic predictions surpassed in reality. The government corporation controlling the tin mines, once our largest source of foreign exchange, now requires great financial assistance to survive. Fiscal inefficiency, petty political interference, government and union intimidation of technicians, a huge bureaucracy, political favoritism, and nepotism have meant that the great efforts to infuse more capital have barely managed to overcome the negative effects of these sources of disorder and irresponsibility. If we Bolivians continue on this mistaken road, our economic progress and liberation will be postponed indefinitely.

The nationalization of the railroads was undertaken as a result of the losses they had suffered, partly because of competition from air and highway transport, and partly because of the private owners' lack of interest in modernizing services through new investments. Up to now, the results of nationalization of the railroads have also been negative; services have not improved, nor has the country benefited from increased revenues. Our experience in the expropriation of the foreign oil companies has been similar. The termination of the contracts with Standard Oil and the nationalization of petroleum resources in 1937 did not solve for twenty years the problem of meeting our domestic fuel needs. In the mid-fifties we reversed our policy, and private investment radically transformed our prospects. Unfortunately, without learning from our own experience, we have once again committed the same error of nationalization, abandoning negotiations which could have obtained greater benefits for our people. It is always difficult to distinguish between those who are opposing private development of petroleum resources in good faith and those who are doing so in order to embarrass the United States for political reasons which are not in the interests of the people. The fact is that the nationalization of petroleum in 1969 has tended up to now, and promises in the future, to damage rather than promote our national interests.

In so far as Bolivia is concerned, historical experience demonstrates that it is impossible to develop the country without the participation of private capital. But where are we to find the capital that the country so urgently requires? What we need is risk capital, particularly for investment in permanent industrial activities. Speculative capital, which profits from transitory situations, tends to be damaging in that it seeks to take away far more than it leaves. But even capital from socialist countries seeks profits, profits which are usually in proportion to risks. Whenever such investment achieves results which produce high profits, the public believes it has been cheated. Attacks are made on the negotiators, pressure is exerted on behalf of radical measures, and finally the episode is converted by opportunistic political groups into an electoral or revolutionary platform. The government is forced to repudiate contracts and laws to which it had subscribed, and the result is government control through nationalization or simple confiscation. Foreign capital loses confidence, and then pressure is exerted to reduce or terminate government-to-government programs of economic assistance. The only solution to this problem is the establishment of stable, legal norms governing the treatment of foreign capital. Most important is the continuity of the system so that the investor knows in advance the conditions to which he will be subject. Naturally, if we operate in a totally socialist world, these considerations are not relevant. But, with the exception of Cuba, socialism in the Americas is still only a dream. We must face the realities of the system under which we will have to live for many years.

While it is prudent for Latin Americans to adapt themselves to international realities, they also have every right to participate in defining the world's future. What will be Latin America's role? Will we simply be a passive entity, part of the spoils of victory? Or will we participate in the ultimate decisions with respect to slavery or liberation? The truth is that the decisions that the United States makes about its policies toward us will play a dominant role in the answer to these questions. Although the population of Latin America is larger than the United States, its main role in world affairs has been scarcely equivalent to that of Belgium. That doesn't make sense, and it ought to be changed in the interests of all the Americas. In the current struggle of the great powers, involving gigantic masses of humanity, will the fifty states of the North American colossus be sufficient to swing the balance as they were in the two world wars? I don't think so. The solution lies in strengthening the inhabitants of the Americas from Alaska to Cape Horn. That is easy to say and hard to do. But this could be the goal of U.S. policy toward Latin America and could justify the economic efforts which will be required to attain it.

I do not think the United States has yet reached this conclusion. During all the years I worked to improve understanding of Bolivian problems in the United States, I never perceived any profound conception of U.S. objectives in Latin America. On the contrary, it is frequently frustrating to observe the seasonal variations which arise from domestic political currents. Latin America is the "backyard" of the United States. As such, it can be a place to dump garbage or a frontier for community expansion and progress. Although this analogy may be useful in impressing North Americans with the proximity of their neighbors to the south, it conspires against what ought to be the concept of societies which inhabit that backyard. We are not gypsies who temporarily have occupied these regions. We are a people with full rights to fulfill our destiny along with the other peoples of the earth.

Does the United States have a clearly defined policy toward our continent? Although it apparently does have a positive policy toward Europe, and possibly toward Asia as well, it has no positive objectives with respect to Latin America. From the Monroe Doctrine of 1823 to the Caracas resolution of 1954, the persistent theme has been opposition to extracontinental influences without any formulation of a corresponding, constructive goal.

The Eisenhower administration's policy of economic assistance to Bolivia, in spite of reservations about the revolution, was an effort to understand and help solve our problems. This policy was applied to other countries as well, although limited by available resources. But it was never entirely clear what the purpose of the policy was. To reciprocate cooperation received during World War II? Or to achieve more important purposes, namely, to strengthen Latin American potential for participation in the international arena?

President Kennedy attempted to provide the content of a constructive program in the Alliance for Progress, the major objectives of which were enumerated in his address to Latin American ambassadors in March 1961. Unfortunately, these grandiose ideas were gradually abandoned. It seems doubtful that they were ever really incorporated into national policy. The program tended to fall apart, a not uncommon result when human affairs are subject to political passions and hegemonic interests.

The report of Nelson Rockefeller many years later had two great virtues: first, he tolerated criticism of the inter-American system even though that criticism was designed to destroy the system; second, he proposed that Congress and the executive branch jointly draw up and approve a resolution outlining the fundamentals of long-term policy toward Latin America.[1] The coolness with which leading circles of the United States received this report shows once again that the United States is not convinced of the need to strengthen the entire continent by strengthening member nations. If the demonstrations against leading Americans in Latin America, such as against Nixon in Caracas in 1958 and Rockefeller more recently, have dampened U.S. enthusiasm for Latin American development, then one must recognize that Communist tactics in this respect have been successful.

Of the nations of the hemisphere, Bolivia is among those that have suffered least from exploitation by U.S. capitalism. Americans did not own the large tin mines, and the marketing and most of the smelting of Bolivian minerals was in British hands. The British also were the contractors for Bolivian railroads. Payments to U.S. bankers for the loans contracted

1. Nelson A. Rockefeller, *The Rockefeller Report on the Americas: The Official Report of a United States Presidential Mission for the Western Hemisphere* (New York: Quadrangle Books, 1969).

in the twenties were halted after a few years, so those bankers lost rather than gained huge sums. The same can be said for investments related to oil. Standard Oil sold scarcely a barrel from Bolivian wells and salvaged only a small percentage of its original investments when compensation for the nationalized properties was paid. Gulf Oil exported minimal quantities, revenues from which did not even cover capital invested at the time these contracts were abrogated. The United States, moreover, is the only country which has demonstrated throughout the years a sincere concern for Bolivia's landlocked situation. When we showed them that the freeze on tin purchases would ruin Bolivia, the United States hastened to our aid. Consequently, morbid anti-Americanism, in so far as it relates exclusively to Bolivian interests, and which is skillfully fomented by certain Bolivians for political purposes, has no historical justification. As to the policy of feigning rapprochement with the adversaries of the United States so as to obtain advantages, I believe far more is to be lost than to be gained by such a policy.

One of the most interesting facets of the character of many U.S. citizens, which contradicts the stereotype image of materialism, is their impassioned commitment to causes they consider just and to which they are prepared to sacrifice time, serenity, and money. The Bolivian revolution was able to arouse such sentiments in many Americans. Their involvement and preoccupation provided powerful assistance to many of my efforts. Since I have not hesitated to criticize U.S. policy, it is only fitting that I express my eternal gratitude to those humane and admirable men.

Index of Personal Names

200 Index

PITT LATIN AMERICAN SERIES

Cole Blasier, Editor